FROM THE BROADCAST BOOTH

FROM THE
BROADCAST BOOTH
MY LIFE IN HOCKEY BROADCASTING

BRIAN McFARLANE

Fenn Publishing Company Ltd.

A Fenn Publishing Book / First Published 2009

Copyright © 2009 by Brian McFarlane

Library and Archives Canada Cataloguing in Publication

McFarlane, Brian, 1931-
      From the broadcast booth : my life in hockey broadcasting / Brian McFarlane.

Includes index.
ISBN 978-1-55168-327-0

    1. McFarlane, Brian, 1931-. 2. Sportscasters—Canada—Biography.
3. National Hockey League—History. 4. Hockey—Canada—History. I. Title.

GV742.42.M34A3 2009   070.4'49796962092   C2009-902087-4

ONTARIO ARTS COUNCIL
CONSEIL DES ARTS DE L'ONTARIO

The publisher gratefully acknowledges the support of the Canada Council for the Arts and the Ontario Arts Council for its publishing program. We acknowledge the support of the Government of Ontario through the Ontario Media Development Corporation's Ontario Book Initiative.

We acknowledge the financial support of the Government of Canada through the Book Publishing Industry Development Program (BPIDP) for our publishing activities.

Fenn Publishing Limited
Six Adelaide Street East, Tenth Floor
Toronto, Ontario
Canada M5C 1H6

www.hbfenn.com

Printed and bound in Canada

09 10 11 12 13 5 4 3 2 1

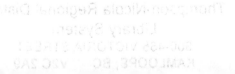

DEDICATION

Of the countless number of NHL stars I have met in more than fifty years in broadcasting and journalism, I would like to single out one individual for this dedication.

The man I refer to has all the attributes any man could wish for: leadership, wisdom, athleticism, sportsmanship, dignity and character.

He is the most admired man I know, possibly the most admired man in Canadian sports history. A superb performer on the ice, he has been a superb ambassador for hockey for as long as I've known him.

He has taken his many triumphs and honours in stride, with modesty and grace. He has battled adversity with strength and dignity, with faith and without complaint.

He is a genuine Canadian hero. He stands out from the crowd.

I have never heard anyone—not a soul—say anything negative about him. And I see no flaws in him. What a testament to his character, his integrity.

Had he sought political office, he could have been mayor of his city, premier of his province, possibly the prime minister of his nation.

Many of us wish he had accepted the role of Governor General of Canada when it was offered him. He declined for personal reasons, and while we understood, we were sad.

He is, of course, the former captain of the Montreal Canadiens, a legend, an icon, a Hockey Hall of Famer.

He is Jean Béliveau.

To you, sir, this book is dedicated.

—Brian McFarlane

TABLE OF CONTENTS

INTRODUCTION

Oh boy, this is going to be fun. Jordan Fenn, my publisher, has asked me to write about many of hockey's greats, the men and women I've met over a lengthy career in broadcasting and journalism.

And it has been a lengthy career—more than fifty years as a pro. There aren't too many of us still around who saw the Leafs win their last Stanley Cup in 1967. Bill Hewitt and I were in the broadcast booth (they called it the gondola back then) that night at Maple Leaf Gardens.

The Leafs, with a cadre of old codgers (most of them over thirty) defeated the Canadiens in six games with Johnny Bower and Terry Sawchuk performing heroics in goal.

That was an eternity ago.

My wife and I crashed the post-game party at owner Stafford Smythe's house and sipped from the Stanley Cup. We were uninvited and knew we might not be welcome, but we went anyway. In those days, Leaf owners Harold Ballard and Stafford Smythe treated team broadcasters like the beat reporters they tolerated but often secretly despised. Ballard in particular treated us like lepers.

In Vancouver one day, Leaf general manager Jim Gregory saw Dave Hodge and me waiting outside the hotel, about to hail a cab to the airport.

"Hop on our bus," he suggested. "We're leaving for the airport." We boarded and got seated. Moments later, Ballard climbed aboard.

"What the fuck are you two doing on our bus?" he roared. "Get off and take a taxi."

If we weren't allowed on Leaf team buses or charter flights, then a Stanley Cup victory celebration was the last thing we'd be invited to. But the party was fun and nobody ordered us off the premises. I remember the hooting and hollering, the beads of sweat dripping from Eddie Shack's generous nose as he danced the night away. And third-string goalie Gary Smith arriving with a Dolly Parton clone on his arm. She had an amazing chest that turned male heads like a referee's whistle. Smith got more attention that night than he ever did as a player, although I do recall his audacity as a rookie. In his NHL debut, he skated up the ice with the puck in an effort to score a goal against Montreal, forcing the NHL to change its rules to prohibit goalies from crossing the centre red line. As he made the rounds at Smythe's home, Smith showed off his prize like a tuna fisherman who'd just landed a record catch.

Sadly, that would be the last meaningful victory celebration, the last great season, for the Leafs. Within a few months, the Stanley Cup would be wrenched from their hands, never to be seen again.

Over the summer, many of the veteran players drifted off to the six new expansion teams. Smith, who'd played a mere two games for the Leafs that season, went to the California Golden Seals where, in 1970–71 he lost a record 48 games. I doubt that Dolly Parton went with him.

There were questionable trades and unproductive drafts that followed. Some teenage stars, like Craig Simpson, were delighted not to be drafted by the Leafs. Others, who'd grown up idolizing the Leafs, were quickly disillusioned once they donned the blue and white.

More than forty years would pass and the '67 triumph, a distant memory to most, would never be repeated.

Looking back, I often wonder how I survived all those years in the gondola. If my comments were the least bit critical of the Leafs, I would infuriate Ballard or manager-coach Punch Imlach, or even Dodo Imlach, Punch's wife. Not to mention some of the viewers. They could often be caustic.

I was coming down from the gondola one night to handle a post-game interview when a loud-mouthed fan bellowed at me, "McFarlane, you're the reason I come to the games. I can't stand listening to you at home." Even though his insult hurt, I gave him a friendly wave. It was a funny line.

Chicago played the Leafs one night, and I received two letters of complaint. One fan wrote, "All you talked about was Bobby Hull and you didn't mention Dave Keon—not even once." The second writer watched the same game and complained, "You went on and on about Dave Keon and you completely ignored the Golden Jet."

One night in Atlanta, there was a brawl-filled game between the Flames and the Leafs. This was thirty years ago. Dave Hodge and I did something very revolutionary and controversial. During an intermission, we raised the question, "Is fighting really necessary? Why all these ridiculous punch-ups?"

I posed the question to our rookie commentator Gary Dornhoefer, a former Broad Street Bully in Philadelphia, and he stammered out a response without really committing himself. He knew he was walking on eggshells. The newspaper columnists made a big deal about our comments the following day. "Hodge and McFarlane challenge the tradition of fighting in the NHL." The move was said to be gutsy of us, but as easily it could have been a career-ender back then, depending on whom we pissed off.

Believe me, I never intended to anger anyone. Not the players, the referees, the ushers or even the stick boy. And it would be stupid to deliberately irritate the owners. My job was to explain what was happening on the ice. Today's analysts and commentators are one hundred per cent more critical than I ever was. If Don Cherry had worked in the '60s, Harold Ballard might have nipped him in the bud.

And I was never anti-Leaf. As a kid, I wore a Leaf jersey until I wore holes in it. My first hockey hero was Toronto captain Syl Apps. As a broadcaster of Leaf games, I simply tried to describe situations and events accurately. Unfortunately, the Leafs iced some dreadful teams in the 1970s and '80s. Even so, despite my pointing out Leaf errors or miscues, I was still called a "homer" by many—and a traitor by some.

In Montreal, Dick Irvin had a similar problem. He was said to be a "real homer." Dick would say to me, "Guy Lafleur gets three goals in a game and Robinson gets two. The Habs win 6–0 and some fans write and complain, 'All you did was talk about Lafleur and the Habs.' Should I have ignored Lafleur's hat trick? Not mentioned Robinson's fine play?"

Dick and I both learned early on: as a colour man, you couldn't win.

In the late '70s, it became easier to call Leaf games. Ballard finally had a solid club, with Palmateer in goal, Salming and the enigmatic Ian Turnbull on defence, Sittler, McDonald, Errol Thompson and colourful Tiger Williams up front, and a great young coach in Roger Neilson.

Then, to our consternation, in 1979 Ballard hired Punch Imlach for a second term after he was fired in Buffalo. It was quite possibly the most disastrous move he ever made, for Imlach ripped the heart out of the club and left it in shambles. Imlach's feuds with his players became daily fodder for the newspapers. One day a reporter discovered several Leafs tossing darts at Imlach's photo in a bar near the Gardens. When Punch traded heart-and-souler Lanny McDonald to Colorado, the Leafs ripped their dressing room apart and many cried openly. One night at the Toronto airport, after the team returned from a road game, Imlach's car failed to start. He had no booster cables. But some of his players did, and they drove right by him, ignoring his plight. Dave Hutchinson told me, "One of the guys laughed and trailed his cables out the door as he drove past Punch."

Imlach suffered from heart disease during the 1980–81 season and was hospitalized for bypass surgery. When he returned to the Gardens, his name had been erased from his parking spot north of the building. It was Ballard's way of saying, "So long, Punch. It's been good to know you." Ballard always was gutless when it came to firing people face to face.

In the decade of the '80s, no Leaf player finished among the top ten NHL scorers. No Leaf won a major trophy. It didn't surprise the broadcasters. None of Ballard's teams came close to winning the Stanley Cup and four of his clubs missed the playoffs. In 1977, the Hockey Hall of Fame inducted Ballard as a builder. Was that some kind of joke?

I once heard that Ballard wanted me fired for suggesting the Leafs couldn't move the puck out of their own zone against the Philadelphia Flyers. After that particular game, he blasted me in front of about forty people. "You and your pro-Philadelphia bullshit," he roared. "Any more of that crap and you'll never get back in this building again."

After one of his rants, I understand that my bosses at *Hockey Night in Canada* mollified him by buying a new organ for the Gardens. The final straw for Ballard was the time I defended Darryl Sittler in his ongoing dispute with Punch Imlach. Ballard was always ambivalent about Sittler. He'd call him "my captain" and "like a son to me" one day and curse him as "ungrateful" and "a cancer on the team" the next.

Sittler, who had once ripped the C off his jersey—an NHL first— was under great mental stress and on the verge of a breakdown. He failed to show up for a game in Minnesota one night, on his doctor's advice. During an intermission segment, I defended him by saying he had the right to stay home sick just like anybody else. I suggested that Imlach should treat Sittler the same way Fred Shero treated Bobby Clarke in Philadelphia and exploit his leadership qualities.

I knew my comments might be incendiary. But they were on tape—not live—and my bosses could have excised my words had they wished to do so. I had asked them beforehand to edit anything I said if they believed it would rile Ballard and Imlach. But they chose not to. Perhaps they were happy to push me in front of the train, with Ballard at the throttle.

Ballard immediately ordered me off the broadcasts, and that would have ended my career in an instant. But the late Dick Beddoes and my colleague Dave Hodge pleaded with Ballard on my behalf, and he grudgingly allowed me back on the telecast. But not in the gondola.

"He can do intermission stuff and post-game reports," he conceded. "But I don't want him up there with Hewitt."

Hockey Night in Canada filled out my schedule with assignments in Winnipeg and Montreal for the next eight years.

In retrospect, perhaps it was foolish of me to defend Sittler, although I know he appreciated my support. Looking back, I realize that these volatile issues with players flare up and subside. How quickly they are forgotten. Imlach and Sittler were mortal enemies, and in time they both would be gone. Sittler waived his no-trade clause and was shipped off to Philadelphia. His career spun downward and ended in Detroit.

When Ballard had me fired one time, I had to chase him around Maple Leaf Gardens to confront him, and caught him sneaking from the coffee shop and taking a shortcut across centre ice in order to avoid me. He was red-faced and embarrassed when he found me waiting for him by the Leaf bench.

You may wonder how I got involved in this business in the first place. It began early for me. I did my first radio broadcast when I was twelve years old. It was during World War II—in 1943. I lived in Ottawa then, and won a city-wide essay contest. There was no monetary prize, but I was asked to record the essay at the CBC studios, then located in the Château Laurier hotel.

In addition to Canada, my essay—about a day in the life of a kid growing up in Ottawa—was heard in Great Britain and Australia. I still have a tape of that recording.

I did my most recent, and possibly my last, TV appearance during the 2008 NHL Awards show on the CBC. I was part of the ceremony that brought Gordie Howe to the stage to accept the first-ever NHL Lifetime Achievement Award. The CBC paid me $300 for a gig I would gladly have done for nothing.

In between those two broadcasts, I've worked for two of the top radio stations in Canada—CFRA in Ottawa and CFRB in Toronto. I've worked on some of the top networks in the United States—CBS, NBC and ESPN. And I was with *Hockey Night in Canada* for twenty-five years, from 1965 through 1990. I've met and interviewed hundreds of hockey personalities, many of them the finest players, coaches, builders and broadcasters in the history of the game. There was also one owner who sat on the stool next to me, reeking of liquor, insisting beforehand, "Don't ask me any shit that's going to make me look bad."

Some of the powerful owners—Ballard and Smythe, Bruce and Jim Norris, Bruce McNall, Peter Pocklington, and others—are no longer around, either deceased, retired or bankrupt. Many of the great companies they controlled are no longer in existence, either.

Some of them were boorish and arrogant, full of themselves. Others were admirable, wise and courteous, passionate about the game and its future.

I can tell you, it's been fun. And I can tell you this. Hockey players and hockey people are, for the most part, the most accommodating people, the best people in any of the major sports.

THE NAME-DROPPER

Let me begin by dropping some names.

I hope to make you old crocks, all you NHL wannabes, really envious when I tell you I skated with Cyclone Taylor (when he was ninety) on national television and I played against Wayne Gretzky when he was twelve. For more than twenty years I played with the NHL Oldtimers (the only amateur on the team), and in many of those games I discovered how futile it was to try to outsmart Gordie Howe and Ted Lindsay, Rocket Richard and his brother Henri, John Ferguson and Elmer Lach.

One night, I played on a line with Bobby Hull in an exhibition game in Belleville, Ontario. The Golden Jet was there to put on a show, and—can you believe it?—the opposing team double-teamed him and tried hard to keep him off the score sheet. They kept him from wowing the crowd.

On another occasion, on a rinky-dink rink in the Catskills one afternoon, Mario Lemieux set me up for a goal I'll long remember. Norm Ullman, Andy Bathgate, Bob Baun, Dick Duff, Ron Ellis, Paul Henderson, Frank Mahovlich and even Eddie Shack were among my teammates on the NHL Oldtimers. Shack delivered one of the hardest checks I ever received—and that was in the warm-up before a game.

I got in his way and he flattened me. Was it deliberate? Who knows?

How did I get to play with a bunch of NHL Oldtimers? That's a good question. The team needed an extra body one night, and I was invited to come along—don't ask how or why. I was an amateur—a lowly ex–college player. But I stayed around for the next two decades. And I learned so much from these canny old guys. Control the puck—don't panic and give it up. Keep your head up. Play with confidence, even against thirty-year-olds or good junior teams. Make good passes, take accurate shots. Play your position. Shorten your stick an inch or two. Make sure your skates fit properly. Force the opposing team to make mistakes.

Some of these things I'd learned in junior hockey. But not all of them. In junior A, I once shadowed Jean Béliveau (not very well) in a playoff series. The same year, I scored a goal on Glenn Hall, the goalie for the Windsor Spitfires, and I played against future Hall of Famers Pierre Pilote and Alex Delvecchio.

Some of the Oldtimers—Johnny Bower, Red Kelly, Bob Goldham, Wally Stanowski, Goose McCormack, Ivan Irwin, Jackie Hamilton, Sid Smith, Harry Watson, Cal Gardner and Pete Conacher—became close personal friends. As did players on opposing teams, like Ted Lindsay and Jean Béliveau. I place a high value on those friendships.

Prior to a fundraising game at the Montreal Forum one afternoon, my equipment went missing—Air Canada had lost my gear. Who came to my aid? Henri Richard. He took me the Montreal dressing room and handed me his skates—an extra pair—and made sure I was outfitted. He smiled when I skated out an hour later, wearing Maple Leaf blue and white. That was so thoughtful of Richard.

You may be thinking, "What a name-dropper. Why is he bragging about all his pals with famous hockey names?" I'll tell you why. When you're closing in on eighty, you can say what you like. You're entitled. When I worked next to Gordon Sinclair at CFRB he was outspoken, loud and controversial. I admired his style, his crusty attitude. Now I'm following his lead.

I even played for the Flying Fathers during one of their tours of the Maritimes. And I'm not even Catholic. "Doesn't matter, come with us," Father Les Costello said. "You've got three kids, so you're a father. If you score three goals we'll make you a bishop." I scored three in Moncton and became Bishop McFarlane.

What a great fellow Les Costello was. A former Leaf, he chose to forgo an NHL career in favour of the priesthood. He became more popular, more influential as a priest than he ever would have been as an NHLer.

I loved Father Les and those wonderful priests. The Flying Fathers toured Europe one season and took a side trip to the Vatican. I asked Father McKee about their visit on a radio interview for the CBC.

"Well, we had a little trouble controlling Father Les," he told me. "First, he wanted to sit in the Holy Father's special chair and the Swiss guards came running over. 'No, no, no,' they hollered. 'You can't sit there.'

"Then when the Holy Father arrived, Father Les presented him with a hockey stick. I'm sure there'd never been a hockey stick in the Vatican before. When the Holy Father looked at it rather quizzically, Father Les said, 'If you don't know how to use it, you can always stir spaghetti with it.'"

Father Les confirmed the story to me. "I'll tell you this," he chortled, "I probably set the Catholic Church in Canada back about two hundred years on that visit. And because of me, you can rest assured there'll never be a Canadian pope."

I worked my first network telecasts in 1960 in the U.S., for CBS. Some people believe that CBS was the first U.S. broadcaster to cover hockey. Not true. Back in 1940, a station in New York City produced the first telecast of a hockey game when it covered a game between the New York Rangers and the visiting Montreal Canadiens at Madison Square Garden.

The camera work was laughable—there was only one camera—and an announcer named Skip Walz, who preferred to be called Bill Allen, described the on-ice action. There were approximately three hundred TV sets in all of Manhattan at the time, and most—if not all—had tiny, seven-inch screens. I have no idea how they filled the intermissions.

I feel very fortunate and proud that I became the first Canadian hired to cover hockey on TV for CBS. I was told I'd been hired on the strength of my hockey career at St. Lawrence University in upstate New York, and the fact I'd gained some valuable experience as a sportscaster on WRGB-TV in Schenectady, New York.

Fred Cusick, the play-by-play man and the voice of the Boston Bruins, was asked to recommend a colour commentator—one who could skate. He told CBS, "There's a young fellow in Toronto you should consider. He was an All-American at St. Lawrence University. I think we'd make a pretty good team."

At that time, I was a sports announcer at CFRB radio in Toronto and I was thrilled to get the call from CBS. Earlier that very week, I'd failed an audition for the host's job with *Hockey Night in Canada*, having been told, "You're too young for our show. We're going with Ward Cornell." I was then about twenty-eight, Ward was in his forties.

I was extremely disappointed because I thought I was ready for prime time and I'd heard that Cornell was a football man. He'd watch American college football on TV right up until it was time to introduce the Leaf game on *Hockey Night in Canada*. He often had to be dragged away from the TV and into the studio, especially if Ohio State had the ball on Michigan's five-yard line. But he did a decent job on hockey for many years, commuting from London, Ontario. When Dave Hodge replaced him as host on our telecasts, *Hockey Night* finally got a hockey man.

But the CBS job more than made up for my disappointment in losing out to Ward. It paid $200 per game, which seemed like a lot of money to me because, a year earlier, I'd been living with my wife and six-month-old son in an unfurnished apartment in Toronto, eating off a card table. I knew what it felt like to be broke and depressed.

But the CBS remuneration didn't impress an agent I met at the time. "What turnip truck did you fall off?" he asked me. "Surely you could have negotiated for much more than that."

"Hey," I said, "I'm just happy they wanted me."

The CBS assignment required a fitness level I hadn't anticipated. I would work in the booth with Cusick, chipping in with colour commentary until each period was almost over. Then I'd dash down the back stairwell in the Boston Garden or the Chicago Stadium—a different arena each weekend—and throw on my skates at rinkside. I'd hop over the boards and onto the ice, where a player would be waiting to be interviewed by me. I'd repeat the trek after the second period, and at game's end I'd hustle down the stairwell one last time in order to interview one of the stars of the game.

"You know all the players on the six teams, don't you?" a producer asked me before my first game.

"Oh, sure," I answered. "Most of them, anyway."

Truth was, I hardly knew any of them. I had interviewed several during my regular duties as a sportscaster with CFRB in Toronto, but they were mostly Toronto players or visiting team coaches. And I'd been away at an American university for four years and worked as a sportscaster on a TV station in Schenectady for two years after that. It was hard to follow the NHL from a distance back then.

But in Toronto, with a press pass to Maple Leaf Gardens, I worked hard at getting to know them. It would have helped if they'd had their names on their jerseys as they do now.

My first interview in my first game for CBS was to be Gordie Howe, the NHL's premier player, and I had prepared four or five questions to ask the big fellow. But when I jumped on the ice, I found myself face to face with Red Kelly of the Red Wings.

"But I thought . . ."

"Gordie can't make it," Red explained. "He got hurt late in the first period. They asked me to take his place."

I was totally unprepared to interview Red Kelly. But I stumbled my way through it. And he was very helpful, giving a flustered rookie thoughtful responses to my questions.

When Red's playing and coaching career ended, my wife, Joan, and I became fast friends with Andra and Red.

That was the beginning. Four or five years later, I joined *Hockey Night in Canada* and stayed around in one role or another for the next quarter of a century.

In 1990, I was shown the door. Reluctantly, I stepped through it. There was no fuss, no farewell lunch or party. No gold watch. No letter of thanks. No invitations to come back from time to time and see a Leaf game from the alumni box. It was over.

Was I hurt? Of course I was. But I got over it quickly. I decided to look ahead, not back. There were books to write, a hockey museum to run, Peter Puck to promote, my Oldtimer mates to meet at monthly luncheons and for thrice-a-week games on the rink.

I could plant a garden, paint with oils, build a log cabin, and spend winters in Florida—close to a hockey rink. I could golf and fish and attend my grandkids' hockey games.

I said that I was never invited back. Not quite true. There was one invitation to return to the Gardens that I shall never forget. In November 1995, Bill Torrey, a teammate of mine at St. Lawrence, and I were inducted into the Hockey Hall of Fame.

We walked the red carpet to centre ice together and faced off the puck. I remember the comforting waves of applause that rippled down from the crowd—comforting, because I was worried I might be serenaded with catcalls and boos.

Afterward, I joined Bob Cole and Harry Neale in the gondola and kibitzed with them throughout the game. I even threw on my old powder-blue *Hockey Night in Canada* jacket for the occasion. I'm sure my good friend Mark Askin, a senior producer, came up with the idea, and for that, I will be forever grateful.

Now, while my mind is still active and my memory strong, let me share with you many of the stories I've collected over the years, some of them culled from my vast collection of audiotapes. The tapes will go to the Hockey Hall of Fame someday soon. There, researchers, young kids interested in hockey's rich history, will hear the voices and yarns of Cyclone Taylor, Newsy Lalonde, Derek Sanderson and Gordie Howe, the humour of Dennis Hull and the strong opinions of Ted Lindsay, Carl Brewer and Phil Esposito. They may chuckle when they hear my late friend Gus Bodnar talk about setting two splendid records—the fastest goal by a rookie (fifteen seconds) and the three fastest assists (in twenty-one seconds, pushing Bill Mosienko to the fastest hat trick in history, in 1952).

These tapes, these stories, are my contribution to the game I've always loved. But I must caution you. Some of the tales ahead, or a portion of them, I may have told before in other books. Not many, but some. One book in particular, *Team Canada: Where are They Now*, contained some fascinating accounts of the Summit Series of 1972. But the publisher went bankrupt just as the book went to market. As a result, distribution and sales were spotty. Most readers never have seen the book. So I ask your permission to edit the interviews I did years ago and deliver a chapter about Team Canada that I hope will interest and please you.

Oh, yes, putting these pages together is going to be fun.

Like a player's life, a hockey broadcaster's career flies by. One season melds into another. One of my first long chats was with Stan Mikita of the Blackhawks. He was just out of junior and concerned about his future in the NHL. He admitted to me that the adjustment to pro hockey was difficult. He said he wanted to cut down his penalty minutes. He was very candid. Soon he was a league-leading scorer, a superstar, playing on a Stanley Cup–winning team. Then, almost overnight, he was winning the Art Ross (scoring champion), Hart (most valuable player) and Lady Byng (most gentlemanly player) trophies in back-to-back seasons—all the while being named to the

NHL's first All-Star Team. In no time, he was an elder statesman with the Hawks. And just as suddenly, *poof!*—he was gone, retired, and swept into the Hockey Hall of Fame.

"Wow!" I thought. "How fast was that?" I saw him join the league and saw him leave the league twenty years later. Only Gordie Howe and Johnny Bower seemed able to slow things down—and stretch their careers to the limit. And more recently, Chris Chelios. I saw Sittler and Salming come and go, as well as Lafleur and Robinson, Hull and Dionne. Then Orr, Gretzky, Lemieux, Messier, Patrick Roy, Ray Bourque. Why, I was still around long after my nemesis, Harold Ballard, had mismanaged a once-great Leaf franchise for twenty-five turbulent years.

How lucky can a hockey commentator be? To witness and chronicle the game's greatest decades. The birth and demise of the WHA, Team Canada in '72, Canada Cups, expansion to thirty teams, the invasion of skilled Europeans and Americans, Darryl Sittler's ten-point night, Gretzky's incredible season of 92 goals and 212 points, the astonishing growth of women's hockey, Bobby Orr Night at Boston Garden, the Stanley Cup being hoisted by Carolina, Tampa Bay and Anaheim. Two team owners (Harold Ballard and Bruce McNall) sent to jail. Alan Eagleson sentenced as well, crashing to the earth like Humpty Dumpty. Mario Lemieux saving the Penguins, then giving way to two young superstars, Sidney Crosby and Evgeni Malkin, zooming to the top of the scoring ladder.

It's been fun, all right. As King Clancy once told me, "If you don't have fun, what's the sense of playing?"

I still have fun playing the game. In Florida, I play three times a week with a group aged sixty and over. No kids allowed, except for goaltenders. And visiting relatives from the north-sons and grandsons. We call ourselves the Snowbirds. I'm the oldest, at seventy-seven. My legs and wrists are weak, diabetes is causing my vision to fade, and I hate falling down because it hurts—and it's difficult to get back up. I grumble at teammates who can't take a pass or give one. Then I think, "Well, they were never as fortunate as I." They never played with or against real players—Ullman, the Big M, Le Gros Bill, Wayne or Mario.

Former NHLers Steve Jensen and Don Awrey join us from time to time, and we welcome them, impressed by their skills. We usually have two netminders, sometimes three.

Last winter, Bob Murdoch, a ten-year veteran of the NHL and a former coach of the Blackhawks, showed up and proved he still has plenty of talent. Thankfully, he played down to our level and made it fun for all of us. Even better, he provided me with a couple of good stories for this book over post-game beers at the Time Out restaurant.

There are dozens of fascinating stories to be told. Perhaps I'll begin with the Snowbirds.

So tighten your skates, throw on your helmet and let's hit the ice!

HOCKEY IN FLORIDA

It's Friday morning in April 2009, and we've just finished a brisk hockey game at the Skatium, a tidy little rink with good ice in Fort Myers, Florida.

The ice is reserved for the Snowbirds Hockey Club. We're a mix of Canadians and Americans, with a couple of Europeans thrown in for good measure. You must be over sixty to play—and a few of us are closing in on eighty. Hockey takes priority over golf and tennis for most of us. Some of us keep active in other ways. One old bachelor—I nicknamed him Ronnie Romance a couple of years ago—is intent on bringing pleasure to several love-starved matrons in Fort Myers whenever possible. We say he starts each day with a bowlful of Viagra. He says the wonder drug is pumping too much blood into his privates and not enough into his feet. "My feet are always cold," he complains.

I scored a nice goal today—top shelf—and that always makes me feel good. I love to hear a goalie mutter "Shit" when I put one by him. But the goals don't come like they used to. However, like golfers who try to shoot their age, I aimed this year to match my age with points. That means seventy-seven this season, and I passed the mark in late March. I'm at ninety at the time of this writing, so I've upped the target to a hundred. It provides a little incentive.

A newcomer joined us this week: former NHL defenceman Bob Murdoch. He joins Don Awrey and Steve Jensen on a short list of former NHLers. Murdoch goes back to the early 1970s, when he played for the Habs, Kings and Flames. I remember him as a solid stay-at-home defenceman. He also played on Canada's National Team with men like Ken Dryden, and he played and coached in Germany for a spell.

Over beer and grilled cheese sandwiches at the Time Out tavern—with a dozen of us at the table—I ask Bob to tell us a story or two.

He laughs. "I remember my first year in the NHL, with Montreal. The most significant thing that happened to me was taking a penalty in Boston. While I was in the box, Phil Esposito scored his seventy-fifth goal—a record at the time. Esposito was an amazing scorer. It didn't matter how hard he shot the puck, as long as he shot it on the net. And he always got himself in good position to score.

"But here's a story few people have ever heard. I was traded to Los Angeles, and Jack Kent Cooke was the owner there. When I was traded, I'd had a couple of concussions, so I was wearing a helmet—makes sense, eh? But Jack Kent Cooke didn't like helmets. I didn't know that. But I had a good year with the Kings and played in the 1975 All-Star Game.

"Our coach in L.A. was Bob Pulford and our manager was Jake Milford. At the time, Jack Kent Cooke had moved to Las Vegas because he was going through a divorce and if he'd stayed in California he'd have to give his wife 50 per cent of everything."

"We were invited to his home in California," I interject. "We featured him on Hockey Night in Canada. His wife Jean was a lovely woman. He wound up paying her millions in the divorce proceedings."

"Well, when I was there," Bob continues, "he was in Las Vegas and he would listen to the Kings' games on the radio. Bob Miller did the play-by-play.

"One day, Cooke called Jake Milford and told him bluntly, 'Murdoch wears a helmet and I don't want him playing tonight.'

"Milford was amazed. 'But Mr. Cooke, Bob is our top defence-man.'

"'I don't care. He's not playing.'

"Well, Milford ran to Pulford and told him what Cooke had said. 'We've got to play Murdoch,' Pulford told him. 'Here's what we'll do. We'll tell Bob Miller not to mention Murdoch's name during the radio broadcast. Not once. Mr. Cooke will never know he suited up.'

"And that's what happened.

"Trouble is, I had a career game that night. And Miller kept referring to me as 'the L.A. defenceman.'

"He'd say, 'The L.A. defenceman has the puck, up to Kannegiesser, back to the L.A. defenceman. He shoots, shit, he scored!'

"I don't know if he actually said 'shit,' but he probably thought it. I scored two goals that night and Miller described them both without ever mentioning my name. But Cooke must have read the papers the following day, because Milford and Pulford took a lot of flak from the owner for playing me."

The boys around the table laugh. They seldom get to hear stories from a former NHLer.

"I recall when Subaru sponsored some of the Kings' games," I say, "and Cooke wanted his announcers, like Miller, to say, 'Dionne speeds up the ice like a Subaru.' None of them could bring themselves to do it."

"Owners can have their quirks," Bob says. "When I coached Chicago after my playing career, team owner Bill Wirtz was often drunk. He came into our dressing room inebriated and I was upset about it. He knew I was mad. We had a practice and afterward Pully [then Chicago's general manager] pulled me into his office.

"'Who are your three best players?' he asked me.

"'That's easy,' I replied. 'Denis Savard, Rick Vaive and Steve Larmer.'

"He said, 'Why aren't you playing them together?'

"'You know why,' I told him. 'Savard is a passer, but when he passes to Vaive, Vaive won't pass it back. They're not even speaking to each other. I can't play them together.'

"Pully says, 'Well, do me a favour and play them together tonight.'

"I shrugged and said, 'All right, I'll try it, but it's not going to work.'

"So I started them together against Buffalo that night, and we're down 3–0 at the end of the second period. Savard, Vaive and Larmer are each minus 3.

"So I break them up, and we eventually won the game 6–5. I was pumped. We had a great third-period comeback.

"After the game, Pully calls me into his office. 'What in Christ were you thinking, breaking up that line?'

"I said, 'Bob, they were terrible together. And we won the game. What's the problem?'

"Later, I learned what the problem was. During the previous game, Bill Wirtz had been sitting in his private box with his buddies, having a few drinks, when one of his pals said, 'Bill, why isn't that rookie coach playing Savard with Vaive and Larmer? That's pretty dumb.'

"Bill Wirtz says, 'You're right. But don't worry. I own the goddamn team. I'll make sure Murdoch puts them together for the next game.'

"So when I start them together for the Buffalo game, Wirtz turns to his pals and says, 'See? I told you I'd get the coach to play them together.' And they have a few more drinks.

"But when I broke the line up in the third period, his pals jumped all over him. 'Bill, we thought you had clout over the lineup. What the hell's going on?'

"I was told they gave him quite a ribbing.

"Of course, all the details of this incident didn't come out until the end of the season—after Wirtz fired me.

"And Pully said to me before I left, 'You know, Bob, Bill Wirtz never forgave you for showing him up that night.'"

Bob and his brother Doug get up to go. Did I mention they grew up in Larder Lake in Northern Ontario, just around the corner from my uncle Graham?

"One more story," I plead. "What happened the night you got locked in the coaches' room?"

Bob tells the group. "We made the playoffs that season, but we're down to St. Louis by three games to two. And now we fall behind by two goals in what could be our final game.

"I was upset and I threw a little tantrum in the dressing room between periods. I knocked over some buckets and shouted and screamed.

"I stormed out of the room with my assistants, Darryl Sutter and Wayne Thomas, and walked across the corridor in the old St. Louis Checkerdome. We had our coaches' room set up nearby. There was a big metal door on the room, and I slammed the door behind us. I was still ranting and raving when I noticed Darryl Sutter trying to pull the door open. And it would barely budge. It was stuck.

"But I noticed a little crack in the door, so I shouted out to whoever was on the other side, 'We're stuck in here. Get us out. But don't let my players leave their dressing room.'

"Meanwhile, we have the TV feeds in the room and we can see these damn cameras converging on the door. People are pulling on the door and we can hear the TV announcers saying, 'There seems to be a bit of a problem down there.'

"And I'm yelling through the crack, 'Don't let the players leave the room!'

"Then we hear a bullhorn. 'Stand back in there. Get in the shower room. We're coming in.'

"On the TV screen, we can see this big forklift approaching so we run for the shower room. And *bang!* The metal door came flying into the room along with a lot of plaster. There was dust everywhere.

"We came storming out of that room, brushing dust from our hair and our clothes. Everybody with a TV set is watching and I was really upset. The cameras were on us as we ran for the team bench.

Everybody was waiting for us to appear—the fans, the players, and the game officials.

"I remember how flustered I was and how Denis Savard, a great, great hockey player, tried to calm me down.

"'Hey, coach, don't worry. We've got everything under control. Don't worry, coach.' And he patted me on the leg.

"Denis Savard was a great pro. I loved the guy."

TED LINDSAY WAS A FIREBRAND

Let's move on to another story that begins in Florida. But first, let me introduce my publisher, Jordan Fenn. Jordan loves hockey, so I throw a question at him: "Before we move on, Jordan, I want you to name the most successful U.S.–based team in the NHL. Would it be the Boston Bruins of the Orr–Esposito era? The Chicago Blackhawks featuring the Bobby Hull–Stan Mikita tandem? Or the Detroit Red Wings, propelled by the old Production Line of Howe, Lindsay and Abel, whose excellence has been matched by the current group of winning Wings?"

"That's a long question," he replies, "but I'm going to say the Detroit Red Wings."

"You've got it. The answer is the Red Wings. The Wings topped the 100-point plateau for the ninth consecutive time in the 2008–09 season—an NHL record. The Wings have won more Stanley Cups than any American club."

"Do you have a favourite Red Wing?" Jordan asks.

"You bet," I say. "He's Ted Lindsay, now eighty-four years old. Do you know they think so highly of Ted in Detroit that management keeps a locker for him in the team dressing room? And recently, a handsome statue of 'Old Scarface' was unveiled in the Joe Louis Arena."

"Then I assume you've been writing about him."

"True enough. He even stopped by my place in Florida to make sure I got the facts straight."

It's late March of 2009 and Ted Lindsay and his wife, Joanne, are in Naples, Florida, on vacation. Next week they will celebrate twenty years of marriage, and we congratulate them.

My wife, Joan, and I look forward to these annual get-togethers. We go to dinner, and in the restaurant Ted hands me a gift—a beautiful book with a large number seven, the hockey numeral he made famous, on the cover. Inside the front cover he has written: *To Brian. A long-time friend and hockey historian. Remembering the great years with NBC with Scotty and crew. Ted Lindsay 7.*

Instantly, my eyes grow moist. I am so honoured to receive such a gift. I read the inscription again. Approaching his mid-eighties, Ted's penmanship is clearly legible, unlike many of today's young players whose autographs are hastily scrawled and indecipherable.

The inscription refers to the three seasons we worked together on the NBC hockey telecasts in the early 1970s, three of the most enjoyable years of our careers. Scotty Connal was our boss back then—a great leader. Tim Ryan, a Toronto native younger than the rest of us, was the third man in the broadcast booth. Another good man.

Joanne has some photos to show us. "This is the new statue of Ted they unveiled at the Joe Louis Arena. Right in the concourse level. Look how beautiful it is. Imagine honouring someone with a life-size statue—it's actually larger than life—while he's still living."

It is indeed a splendid statue. It is so . . . so Ted Lindsay. If Joanne had told me the statue sprang to life, skated off its pedestal and slammed into some innocent fan wearing a Leaf jersey in the concourse, I wouldn't have been surprised.

Then she unfolds a tissue and hands me a ring. I can tell immediately it's a Stanley Cup ring. Gorgeous!

"The Ilitch family," Joanne explains, "discovered that Ted and several other players from his era never received Stanley Cup rings. So Marian Ilitch had several created and delivered to these aging former Wings. I'm sure they were as thrilled to receive one as Ted was."

In the book, the Red Wing owner has written a preface, a tribute to Ted. It reads:

Tonight we honor Ted Lindsay by installing a larger-than-life statue of him in the concourse level at Joe Louis Arena. Ted established his hockey career at Olympia Stadium but he is no stranger around The Joe. He rarely misses a Red Wing game and he actively participates in Red Wings alumni activities to support the community. The Hall of Famer is always willing to share his expertise with those around him.

Ted joined the Red Wings when he was only 19 years old and wore the Winged Wheel for 14 of his 17-season playing career. He is one of the best left wingers of all time and was a fearless competitor, earning him the nickname "Terrible Ted." Some reporters called him "Scarface." Off the ice, Ted is anything but "terrible." A kind soul, he created the Ted Lindsay Foundation to battle autism and consistently assists with community activities to help charitable causes.

Hockey fans everywhere will remember Ted's position on The Production Line with Gordie Howe and Sid Abel. Long before we became owners of the team, we were avid Red Wings fans and we remember vividly the success of that line. It was unbeatable! During the 1949–50 season, when the Red Wings won their fourth Stanley Cup, Lindsay took the scoring crown and the trio finished 1–2–3 in NHL scoring.

Seven: A Salute to Ted Lindsay tells the story of Ted's outstanding hockey career as a Red Wings player, coach and general manager. It certainly rekindles fond memories of the days we attended Red Wings games at Olympia Stadium. We

are so thankful that way back in 1950 Ted started the
tradition of skating the Stanley Cup around the arena. It is
the fans that make the sport of hockey so special. Ted
clearly understood that more than fifty years ago when he
spontaneously seized the Cup from an on-ice table and skated
with it around the boards to share it with the fans. Ted also
understood the players' needs and fought tirelessly for the
establishment of a players' association and fair play. Hockey
today is a better sport because of Ted Lindsay's action and
humanitarian spirit. We congratulate him on a successful
career and thank him for being our friend.

"So you still keep busy with the Detroit alumni?" I ask Ted.

He laughs. "I sure do. Shawn Burr is our leader and he does a great job. And I'm in and out of the Red Wings' dressing room a lot. I like to get to know the current players. They even gave me my own locker in there. It's in a corner, out of the way, but it's got my name on it."

How cool is that? I think. The Rocket, Béliveau, Bobby Hull, Bobby Orr—none of *them* has a locker in their old team's dressing room.

"Earlier this season," Ted continues, "Red Wing coach Mike Babcock invited me to sit in on a team meeting before a game. There was video of the opposing team and all the players on it. Each Red Wing player had a notebook and had a chance to speak up about their opponents individually, noting any little quirks or habits they might have. It showed me how far coaching has come from the old days. I was very impressed."

"And how is Gordie coping after the death of Colleen?" I ask.

"I give Gordie tremendous credit. Colleen looked after most of Gordie's business for all those years, and when she got terminally ill he devoted himself to her care. There was nursing care 'round the clock. He refused to put her in a home. He was always there for her."

I'm pleased to hear Ted speak glowingly of Gordie. At one time their relationship was strained. But time smoothes out old differences—to some degree.

One year ago, after a coffee shop meeting with Ted, I wrote some words about Ted for this book. I encouraged him to write his memoirs, but he declined. He doesn't think many people would be interested. I tell him a multitude of fans—and not just seniors, either—would enjoy reading his autobiography.

My hockey-playing pal Bob Posch, an excellent stand-up comedian and musician, joined us for coffee that morning. He's from Michigan, is a Detroit fan, and Ted Lindsay has always been his favourite Red Wing. Bob asks Ted about his relationship with Gordie Howe.

"Gordie and I had a falling out a long time ago. I can be civil to him at social functions, but we don't speak other than that. There was one little incident that bothered me. Sid Abel, Gordie and I—the old Production Line—were asked to sign posters of the three of us. Sid is not a wealthy man and we discussed what fee we'd settle for. Nobody's going to pay three old codgers seventy-five bucks per autograph. We thought ten bucks apiece would be fair. So we signed a lot of posters and Sid made out pretty well. A thousand posters at ten bucks is $10,000. When it came time to sign another thousand posters, Gordie copped out. He wanted a lot more money than that. So the signing stopped and Sid Abel, the guy who set Gordie up for a lot of his goals, lost out on a lot of money—money he could have used."

"I don't blame you for being ticked," says Posch. "And Abel, too. How about some of your favourite players in the game?"

Ted doesn't give it more than a second's thought.

"I am a great fan of Jean Béliveau. He is the classiest hockey player I have ever met—a real gentleman. And the same goes for Steve Yzerman. They held a night for Steve in Detroit and he was tremendous. He thanked every person who had helped him along the way. He is a marvel. On that night, Jimmy Devellano spoke and you'd think it was *his* night."

I ask Ted to tell Posch about a long-ago fight he had with Wild Bill Ezinicki of the Bruins, a vicious battle that occurred sometime during the early '50s.

Ted grins and says, "Well, in the case of Bill Ezinicki, it started in junior hockey when I came down from Kirkland Lake and played at St. Mike's. Ezzie had already played a couple of years at Oshawa, and everybody thought that you had to watch him because he was the tough guy in the league. Well, he was tough and he was rough. But I figured nobody was going to run me out of hockey and he bleeds the same as I do. We had a couple of confrontations, and then Oshawa beat us out for the Ontario championship. At that time it was the end of the Second World War and Charlie Conacher was the coach of Oshawa. He picked up four of us from St. Mike's—Dave Bauer, who later became Father David Bauer, goaltender Johnny Marois, Gus Mortson and myself. I ended up playing on a line for Oshawa with Ezzie when we won the Memorial Cup.

"I turned pro with Detroit the next season, while Ezzie spent some time with Pittsburgh and then got called up to Toronto. Later, he was traded to Boston. We started our feud when he came up to the Leafs and it carried on when he went to Boston.

"One night, we met in Detroit and the whistle had stopped play. The faceoff was right at the blue line in front of the Boston bench. I remember Ezzie took his stick and he hit me just below the hairline and the blood began to flow. The place was packed and I began thinking, 'Geez, if I let him get away with this, the fans will think I'm scared of him.' So I took my stick and I whacked him on the head and *he* starts bleeding. Then he drops his stick and his gloves and I had no place to go and hide. Not that I would have, anyway. But he was a tough guy and he was strong. We had a nifty fight and I must say I did all right. In fact, I gave him a pretty good beating. George Gravel was the referee and big George Hayes was the lineman and they said, 'You're both done for the night!' So I was pleased with myself. I got this one cut where he hit me with his stick. But I cut him for twenty-some stitches and I knocked a couple of his teeth out. So I turn away and I'm heading up the boards past the Red Wing bench to the exit that leads to our dressing room. Then I hear Gordie Howe shout a warning, 'Look out, Ted! Here he comes!' Ezzie had broken away from the linesman. I don't know what he was thinking, but when he charged me, I turned quickly and swung from the ice and I hit him. Oh, did I hit him. Well, he fell down on the seat of his pants and his head flopped back and hit the ice. As you know, we didn't wear helmets in those days, so when he went down, I straddled him just like a saddle on a horse. Now I'm pulling him up by his jersey and I'm punching him and I hear Gordie say, 'Ted, he's out, he's out cold.' I said, 'I don't give a damn, I'm gonna kill him!'

"Anyway, they pulled me off and I went into the dressing room. I showered and calmed down, and by the time I came out Ezzie was still in the first-aid room getting stitched up. Then I made a big mistake: I opened the door and I said, 'Ezz, you all right?' and he snarls back, 'I'll get you, you son of a bitch.'

"But he never did."

"The Boston fans couldn't have been happy with you," said Posch.

"The Boston Garden was filled with loudmouth fans. Mostly they got on Gordie because Gordie was big and he had some of his best nights against the Bruins. There was a long, narrow corridor from the dressing room to the ice, and the fans would line up on each side. Gordie and I were always the last ones out of the room, and we held our sticks in close with about eight inches of butt end sticking out. If someone took a swing at us, those butt ends would make them think twice. They learned to jump back."

Bob Posch was taking this in, still mulling over Lindsay's fight with Ezinicki. He said, "I guess you never spoke to him again after that time you knocked his teeth out?"

"Oh, I did," Ted said. "Bill got to be a good golf pro—a great driver, but not so good around the greens. He was in a tournament at Oakland Hills one year, and my house was on the eighteenth tee.

So I went to see him play. I sought him out and I walked the course with him."

"You did?" Posch was incredulous.

"Sure. Old hockey players forget about all the past battles they've been in when they retire. I don't think that battle we had ever came up for discussion."

Posch had more questions. "How about a word on Alan Eagleson?"

I chuckled, thinking back to 1974, when Ted and I worked for NBC. I recall him telling me then that he hated all lawyers, and Eagleson in particular. He told me Eagleson was the biggest detriment to hockey he could think of.

Ted says, "Alan Eagleson served nine months in prison and he should have served nineteen years. He stole from the players and it took a journalist—Russ Conway from the *Lawrence Eagle-Tribune*, based in a suburb of Boston—to dig into his dealings, along with some of us who went after Eagleson.

"Well, it was finally proven, Eagleson is a convicted felon and that will stay with him for the rest of his life. He can BS his way around with his big mouth, but he will always be the thief who stole money—lots of money—from hockey players, from the guys who trusted him.

"Now, Bobby Orr could have been the guy to fix him. When Orr finished hockey, he was bankrupt—Eagleson had taken all his money. If Orr had sued Eagleson then, he would have won his case and Eagleson would have been exposed. But Bobby, for whatever reason, chose not to do it. He doesn't like confrontations."

Ted tells Posch more about his junior hockey days. "Brian and I and our wives were out with John 'Goose' McCormack the other night for dinner. Goose was a pro with Montreal, Toronto and Chicago. When I was a junior at St. Mike's, Goose was my teammate. We would have beaten Oshawa out for the Eastern championship if only we'd had Goose at centre. But Goose was injured and we lost out to Oshawa because of it. That was when Oshawa coach Charlie Conacher picked up Ezzie and me from St. Mike's to play in the Memorial Cup finals against the Western champs, the Trail Smoke Eaters.

"They came east billed as the greatest junior team ever to represent the west. In the first game at Maple Leaf Gardens, we beat them 15–0. They were stunned. And they realized they weren't nearly as good as they thought they were. So Trail picked up a couple of my St. Mike's teammates for the second game, and we beat them 9–2. They took two more St. Mike's players for the rest of the series. But it didn't help. We walloped them twice more by 15–4 and 11–4. Those were the most lopsided scores in Memorial Cup history. Can you believe it? There were eight St. Mike's guys on the ice the rest of the way: four with Oshawa and four more with Trail."

Bob says, "When I watched Detroit, I always liked Alex Delvecchio. I liked his style."

Ted grins, thinking of Delvecchio. "When Alex joined the Red Wings, Gordie and I would sit on the bench and watch this kid. He was amazing, the things he could do with the puck. He was so smooth out there. Remember, he didn't start skating until he was twelve years old. And in the NHL he seldom got his skates sharpened. Alex would go all season on the sharpening he got in training camp. He played with Gordie and me on the Production Line. And he played more games with one team than any other player in history. Scored over 450 goals in twenty-four seasons. Won three Stanley Cups and three Lady Byngs. And he's a Hall of Famer, of course. Those are wonderful stats."

"And he went on to coach and manage, too," I interject.

Posch is back with another question. "What about Carl Brewer?"

"Carl Brewer was a good player—not a great player. He was about 60 per cent of what Red Kelly was. But what I really admired Carl for was stepping up for the players. I was in the Boston courtroom when Eagleson was convicted. Paid my own way to be there. Carl asked the judge if he could say a few words. And he said, 'Thank you, your honour. Thank you for having a court situation that takes care of people like Eagleson. If this case had been tried in Canada, it would never have happened.'"

I ask Ted if he'd like to lace them up with a group of Oldtimers, including Posch, who play a couple of times a week in Fort Myers.

"No. I had my fun. I had lots of fun in hockey. Now I've got a steel brace in my back and some metal pins in there. And I limp because I let a tendon in my heel go unattended."

"It's just as well," I tell him. "If you played with us, you'd take a run at the first guy who tried to take the puck away from you."

Ted chuckles. "Yeah. You've seen me do that. So I'll take a pass. No, hockey is over for me, and people ask me if I miss it. Well, I do. But what I really miss is downhill skiing. I'd love to get back on the hills again. And I envy my old friend and business partner Marty Pavelich. He's out in Big Sky, Montana, skiing every day. What a life that must be."

Our coffee cups are empty but the questions never stop. Posch says, "Here's another name from the past, Ted: Milt Schmidt. What do you think of Milt?"

"Milt Schmidt is the greatest competitor I have ever played hockey against, bar none. He was a tremendous team player and a great skater. Now, they talk about great skaters today, but they never saw Milt Schmidt skate in his prime. Schmidt would come down on the right, and if he didn't make it, he would come down the left side, and if he didn't make it, he would come right over top of you—that is the type of competitor he was."

I say, "Milt passed his ninety-first birthday not long ago. I have two Milt Schmidt stories for you, Bob. When he was a seventeen-year-old kid living in Kitchener, Milt was invited to the Boston Bruins' training camp. He was so naive he wrote to the Bruins stating he would get an extra summer job to pay for his bus fare and travel expenses to camp. The club wrote back saying all his expenses would be covered.

"Then Milt performed so well in camp that the Bruins offered him a contract. Manager Art Ross threw a contract in front of him for $3,000 and said, 'Sign here.'

"But Milt wasn't intimidated and asked Ross to sweeten the pot. 'How about giving me an extra $500?' he said.

"Ross glowered at him. 'Five hundred?' he bellowed. 'I'd have to go down the hall and ask the owner, Mr. Adams, for permission to give you that kind of money.'

"'Would you do that for me, Mr. Ross?' Milt asked politely.

"Ross got up from his desk. 'Wait here, kid. I'll be right back.'

"Five minutes later, Ross returned. He shook his head and said, 'I argued for you, kid, but you're out of luck. Mr. Adams was adamant. He says to tell you it's three thousand—take it or leave it.'

"Milt shrugged and signed the contract.

"But on his way out of the Boston Garden he thought he'd stop in to see Mr. Adams. He wanted to ask him why he wouldn't cough up the extra five hundred.

"He knocked on Mr. Adams's door. A secretary answered.

"'Hello. I'm Milt Schmidt and I just signed with the Bruins. Could I speak with Mr. Adams, please?'

"The secretary said, 'Oh, he's not in this week.'

"After Milt told me the story, he laughed and said, 'The Bruins lied to me from day one and they were still lying to me fifty years later.'"

Bob and Ted chuckled over my Schmidt story.

"What's the second story?" Bob asks.

"Milt roomed with a rookie on the Bruins one season. When it was time to leave for the arena one afternoon, the rookie was fast asleep. So Milt went over to his bed, wet his finger and stuck it in the kid's ear. When the kid woke up, Milt was pulling up his pants and zippering his fly. The kid didn't know what to think."

Then Bob asked Ted, "Johnny Bucyk? Bucyk was in Detroit before he went to Boston. Do you think it was a big mistake to let him go?"

"It was a major mistake. I was team captain in Detroit at the time. Bucyk's only problem when he first came up was his checking. Jack Adams used to say, 'Where did John learn how to check?'"

"An opposing player would skate in behind the net and John would try to time his bodycheck to stop the guy in his tracks. Well, he'd turn his ass to the guy and nail him. Pretty soon the guys would get to know John, and they would take two quick strides and John would miss. His rear end would hit the boards and he'd fall down. By the time he got up, the other player would be at the blue line. That ticked Adams off, so he traded him. I guess he figured Bucyk would never learn how to check. Bucyk goes to Boston and he plays for twenty-one years. He was one of the best left wingers in the game for fifteen of those years. He scored 545 career goals. Yeah, I'd say it was a major mistake letting him get away from Detroit."

I can't help but interject. "The amazing thing with Bucyk was the time the Boston fans honoured him on Johnny Bucyk Night at the Boston Garden during the 1967–68 season. The fans gave him all kinds of gifts, including a new car, a new boat and motor. I guess they figured he was getting close to retirement because his goal production had slipped to eighteen the season before and they wanted to send him off on a high. Well, what a surprise! The guy played another ten years in the league. Scored another 319 goals, won two Stanley Cups and two Lady Byngs. At thirty-five, he became the oldest player to score over fifty goals in a season. The damn boat and motor were worn out by the time he finally retired at age forty-three."

"Ted, what do you have to say about Terry Sawchuk?"

"Sawchuk? I can say this. For the first five years he played in the league, he was the best there ever was. There will never be a better goaltender. He weighed 205 pounds and he was so fast and so quick. We won the Stanley Cup in 1952. We beat Toronto and Montreal in eight straight games and neither team scored a goal at the Olympia. And Sawchuk was the main reason for the four shutouts."

"Ted, you say you were banished from Detroit to Chicago after you tried to form a players' association back in 1957. What was your first reaction to news of that deal?"

"Well, I did get involved in the formation of the players' association, and that upset a lot of team owners. That was certainly the reason I was traded. I was dealt following my best year with the Red Wings. I would do the same thing again as far as the association was concerned because it was sorely needed. The thing is, the players were not interested in running hockey. We did it because we simply needed a voice. The owners and managers had full control back then. It was a dictatorship back in the six-team league. It was a case of them saying 'Jump' and you saying, 'Sure—how many times?' I had wind of the deal before it happened. I could have stuck it out in Detroit, I suppose, but I knew Jack Adams was praying for me to have a bad season and then he was gonna hang me out to dry. We hadn't spoken to each other in three years. That wasn't a problem for me because I didn't play hockey to please Jack Adams, I played hockey because I loved the game. I must admit, though, after going to Chicago, I still felt like a Red Wing. I spent three years in Chicago and unfortunately enjoyed only one good year there. My first year in Chicago was Bobby Hull's rookie season in the NHL and my second year was Stan Mikita's first. I quit after the third year because I felt I was simply existing—I wasn't living. After the trade, I moved my family over to Chicago and we had a nanny. But I was on the road so much I barely saw them. For the next two years I left my family in Detroit. Eric Nesterenko, Glen Skov and I got an apartment on the Near North Side on the lakeshore, and after my third year I decided I'd better quit and go back to living again."

"Glenn Hall was your goalie then?"

"Glenn and I were traded to Chicago. He was traded because he was a Ted Lindsay fan. And Jack Adams didn't want anything to do with Ted Lindsay. Adams even told Hall not to talk to me, and Hall, to his credit, told Adams he'd talk to anyone he wanted to. The beautiful thing about the Hall deal is that Adams spent the next fifteen years looking for a goalie. For fourteen of those years, Hall was the best goalie in the NHL."

"Ted, you told me once that Adams could have traded Sawchuk for Montreal's Doug Harvey and the Red Wings might have won a couple more Stanley Cups."

"I think more than a couple. When we won in '55 he traded nine players away from our championship team. The five Stanley Cups that Montreal won after that could easily have been ours. We only had one weakness on our team, and that was defence. Bob Goldham was getting older, so if we could have gotten Harvey for Sawchuk, who had not yet established himself—or even Tom Johnson, another Montreal defenceman—we would have won those five Stanley Cups. I figure if we'd traded for Harvey, we might have won seven Cups."

"Harvey was that good?"

"There will never be a better defenceman than Doug Harvey. I have always said that the only thing Bobby Orr did better than Doug was skate. Doug was a master at controlling games and power plays. The games were as fast or as slow as Doug wanted them to be."

It's my turn to toss a question at Ted. "Ted, I have another memory from 1974, when you were critical of Derek Sanderson on our NBC games. But I'll say this for Derek. He told me later he'd never say anything against you because he respected you so much. That was after you lashed out at him on our telecast one day."

"It didn't bother me that Derek jumped to the WHA, or that he squandered all of his money. I think it was mainly the drugs. I don't think he was worth all the money he got. People said he was the highest-paid athlete in the world. If some foolish owner pays him a couple of million, that's fine. But the drugs, that's what I was objecting to."

As recently as 2007, after the Anaheim Ducks captured the Stanley Cup, Lindsay was still voicing his opinions. At a golf tournament in London, Ontario, I called him up to the microphone to say a few words and he jumped all over Chris Pronger of the Ducks.

"During the playoffs, all I heard was, 'Chris Pronger: Future Hall of Famer,' 'Chris Pronger—what a great player.' Pronger this and Pronger that. I say if Chris Pronger played in my era he'd be lucky to get out of his hometown."

Ah, Ted. We enjoy your annual visits to us here in Naples, Florida. We treasure your friendship. Remember the last time you were here? Six of us arranged to go to dinner: you and Joanne, Johnny Bower and his wife, Nancy, and the McFarlanes. You said you'd pick us up at our condo in Pelican Bay. Well, just as you arrived, my neighbour from Halifax, Chuck Williams, walked outside. I said, "Chuck, come over here. I want you to meet a couple of friends of mine: Ted Lindsay and Johnny Bower."

Now, Chuck is a cool guy, a former head of Hewlett-Packard in Canada. Not easily fazed. But he almost jumped out of his skin when he saw you and Johnny.

"My God," he said. "Two of my biggest hockey heroes, standing right outside my door. I can't believe it. I'm overwhelmed. Don't run off. I've got to get some paper. Got to get your autographs." And he did.

What an enjoyable evening that was. And there were others like it. I can't remember all the stories you and Johnny told. But I recall some of them.

I remember you told us about your remarkable comeback with Detroit at the age of thirty-nine—four years after you'd retired from hockey as the third-ranked scorer in NHL history.

"My old linemate, Sid Abel, saw me playing with some Oldtimers and asked me to consider playing again—with the Red Wings. Chicago owned my NHL rights but I relished the idea of winding down my career in Detroit.

"So Abel bought my rights from Chicago, and there I was on the opening night of the 1964–65 season wearing number 15 for the Red Wings.

"They gave me a standing ovation when I skated to left wing. I know my appearance irked NHL president Clarence Campbell, who called my return to hockey 'a black day for the league.'

"During that era, most players dropped out of hockey in their mid-thirties. I had toiled for thirteen years with Detroit, helping them to seven consecutive league regular-season titles and four Stanley Cups."

Lindsay's comeback in 1964 was truly remarkable. Playing on a line with twenty-three-year-old Bruce MacGregor and twenty-one-year-old Pit Martin, he tallied fourteen goals and fourteen assists at a time when twenty-goal seasons were reserved for only the most prolific scorers.

His leadership was a major factor in Detroit's rush to the head of the NHL standings after pre-season polls indicated they were destined for sixth place. The Red Wings won twenty-five of their last thirty-nine games to capture first place.

By then, Clarence Campbell had issued a public apology to the fiery winger. "Lindsay has done what I thought to be next to impossible. His comeback is one of the most amazing feats in professional sport."

Lindsay's comeback ended in the Stanley Cup semifinals, when Chicago—his former team—ousted the Wings in game seven.

Lindsay tells us what happened next. "I was intrigued with the idea of playing again in 1965–66. But a ploy by Maple Leaf general manager Punch Imlach pushed me back into retirement.

"Imlach claimed me in the waiver draft, even though he knew damn well I'd never play for Toronto. He was just trying to screw me. So I walked away for good."

He did as a player, but he returned as Detroit's general manager and interim coach in the late 1970s.

Lindsay works out vigorously every day. A back operation several years ago left him with two metal rods and a dozen titanium screws in his back.

Today, forty years after he tossed his NHL skates aside, Lindsay's popularity with Detroit fans rivals that of Gordie Howe and, yes, even Steve Yzerman.

"Ted," I say to him, "I never did thank you properly for writing an introduction for a book I wrote about the Red Wings. It went like this:

It's been forty years since I played my last game in the NHL. All of my seventeen years in the league were spent in the Original Six era. Every day I meet fans who witnessed games between those teams—Toronto, Montreal, Detroit, Chicago, Boston and New York—and most of them still insist that those rivalries were the fiercest, most thrilling they ever saw.

Those of us who played in that era will agree that today's players are bigger, faster, and stronger. They are better equipped and better coached. And they have sticks that shoot bullets. And yet, we are quick to argue that none of today's stars is tougher or more talented than big Gordie Howe or Milt Schmidt, more dynamic than my archrival Rocket Richard, more rugged than Tim Horton, more spectacular than the era's goalies—Plante, Sawchuk, Bower and Hall, to mention a few.

And today's NHL, with the constant movement of players from team to team, can't boast of line combinations that performed dazzling feats year after year. The Original Six produced Montreal's Punch Line (Richard, Lach and Blake), the Production Line I played on in Detroit (with Howe and Abel), Chicago's Million-Dollar Line (Hull, Hay and Balfour) and Boston's Kraut Line (Schmidt, Bauer and Dumart).

In my era, teams faced each other fourteen times a season and rivalries were often bitter, acrimonious. There was no fraternization, no players' association (although I tried to start one and was banished to Chicago for it), no cozying up with rival players at golf tournaments or hockey schools.

Original Six teams were often forced to travel between cities on the same train, and even though the teams occupied separate Pullmans, how we'd bristle when we passed opposing players headed for the dining car. Just the sight of Rocket Richard ambling down the aisle was enough to bring a scowl to my face and spoil my appetite for a week. It's a wonder we didn't go at each other with knives and forks, plucked from a dining car table.

In those days, we'd talk about pride and loyalty to our team and to our city, and our passion for the game. Few players thought the grass was greener elsewhere. My teammate Alex Delvecchio was a Red Wing for twenty-four years. Milt Schmidt and his Kraut Line mates were loyal Bruins for as long as they played. Béliveau and the Richards—Maurice and Henri—wore the Habs logo with great pride throughout their careers. It was unthinkable that they would play anywhere but in Montreal. Kids in English Canada idolized Apps, Kennedy, Armstrong, Bower and Keon because they wore the Maple Leaf year after year.

Some memories of those good old days of Original Six hockey will never fade. I guarantee it.

I get the last question. "Ted, should they take fighting out of hockey?"

"No," he fires back. "And if they are worried about some guy hitting his head on the glass in a fight, then they should bring back the chicken wire."

Chicken wire? Now there's a thought.

TALES FROM THE OLDTIMERS' DRESSING ROOM

I ask Jordan Fenn if he liked the chapter on Lindsay and he says, "I did. The man is a hockey icon. It's hard to believe the Red Wings still have a locker for him in their dressing room. And a statue of him in the arena. It's obvious they love the old guy in Detroit."

"They do. And when you stand next to him, you'll be amazed at how small he looks. I'd guess he weighs about 150 pounds. And this is a guy who never backed down, who took on the meanest, toughest players in the game. Even today, he rates among the best left wingers in NHL history."

"Do you have some more stories about players from Ted's era?"

"Sure, lots of them. Let me show you some."

I met some wonderful men in my years with the NHL Oldtimers. Consider Bob Hassard, a Toronto forward who played in the early '50s. He enjoyed a five-year career despite scoring only nine goals in 126 games. He was on the Leaf bench when Bill Barilko scored the Cup-winning goal against Montreal in 1951. A few months later, he scored the first Leaf goal ever seen on television. Bob was a popular member of the NHL Oldtimers for many seasons. Hassard tells me about a former teammate, Bob Solinger.

"Solly loved kids but he had none of his own. He came to the game a little late one day. He rushed into the dressing room, threw off his clothes and announced proudly, 'Good news, guys, the wife is pregnant.' I said to Bobby, 'That's great news, Solly. How far along is she?'

"He laughed and looked at his watch. Then he winked and said, 'Oh, about twenty minutes.'"

I ask Hassard to tell me about Max Bentley, one of the best playmaking centres of his era.

"Max was something special. He knew the crowd loved to see him jump the boards and get into the game. He often timed his entrances into the game perfectly, waiting for the most dramatic moment to leap over the boards. He'd slap the top of the dasher board with one hand and leap gracefully onto the ice. One time, just as Max made his leap, I unintentionally threw open the gate where he was about to place his hand. Well, his hand hit nothing but air and he sprawled out on the ice, an awkward bundle of Maple Leaf blue.

"On game days, we all waited for Max to show up at the Gardens. He was a hypochondriac, always moaning about some injury or another. If he entered the Leaf dressing room whistling, coach Hap Day would say, 'Oh, no.' But if Max came in groaning about one of his many ailments, Hap's face would light up. He knew Max would play the game of his life that night."

Sid Smith, a former Leaf captain, recalled the time Leaf goalie Harry Lumley sent a gullible rookie around to a number of hardware stores with a bucket. He ordered the kid to return with a "bucket of muckets." "At each store, a clerk would say to the kid, 'Muckets? What the hell are muckets?'"

"Sounds like the same rookie they had in Los Angeles one year," someone says. "The kid had a bad toothache and the trainer sent him all across town to see a dentist—Dr. Pull."

I relate a story from Red Wings' trainer Lefty Wilson: "This rookie came to me one morning with a case of the crabs. 'What'll I do, Lefty, what'll I do?' he moaned.

"'What you gotta do,' I told the kid, 'is take this ice pack and leave it on your groin all night. Then come see me tomorrow.'" The rookie reported in the morning, his groin all but frozen. "The crabs were still there," recalled Lefty, "although some of them were in their overcoats. Finally, we got rid of them in a more traditional way.

"This was the same rookie," Lefty said, "who came to me one day. 'Where's our next game, Lefty?'

"I told him it was in Washington.

"He says, 'Oh, good. I've always wanted to see the Pacific Ocean.'

"That rookie didn't stay with us too long."

Among my notes, I have an entry dated November 20, 1984. Oldtimers' practice at Doublerinks in Toronto. Ron Hurst, a former Leaf, went into the john and threw up, much to the delight of the rest of us. I suggested to Aggie Kukulowicz (an Air Canada rep and former Ranger) that he bring some Air Canada barf bags to our next workout.

Ronnie said, "I'll go along with that. Nothing worse than trying to dig last night's chili beans out of your skate laces on Sunday morning."

Bob Hassard belched loudly. Someone said, "What was that?"

Gary Collins said, "I thought someone turned on *Wild Kingdom*."

Goose McCormack, who played with the Habs, Leafs and Hawks, a good Catholic and a straight arrow out of Saskatoon and St. Mike's, talks about the time he was sent to the minors by Conn Smythe for getting married in mid-season.

"Hell, I didn't know anything about it," says John. "All I know is Fleming Mackell picked me up one morning to go to practice. He says, 'Hi, John, how are you this morning? Come on. We're going to the rink to pick up your skates. You're going to Pittsburgh.'

"I said to Mackell, 'I'm really not planning on going anywhere. We've got dinner plans for tonight.'

"Mackell laughs and says, 'Well, you'll have to cancel them. You're going back to the minors.'"

"How come Mackell gave you the news?" I ask.

"Well, I didn't have a phone. He was told to give me the message. And the message was that Conn Smythe disapproved of mid-season marriages. But things turned out all right for me. Before I left for Pittsburgh, the Leaf players had a wonderful going-away party for me. Then it wasn't long before I was traded and found myself playing with Rocket Richard and the Montreal Canadiens."

"Being sent down is almost as bad as hearing you've been traded," says Gus Bodnar. "One night, all of the Leafs are goin' to the Old Mill. The Leafs always went there as a team on Monday nights. And suddenly we hear about this big trade on the car radio. Suddenly we're all gone—to Chicago. A bunch of us: defencemen Bob Goldham and Ernie Dickens, and a whole forward line—Gaye Stewart, Bud Poile and me. We're gone. Conn Smythe wanted Max Bentley and gave up all of us to get him.

"So we decided to have a hell of a party—a last hurrah. The Old Mill was jumping that night. Everybody was talking about the big trade. One of the biggest in history. And I remember some guy made some smartass remark behind Harry Watson. Harry seldom gets mad, but he grabbed that poor fucker and threw him across the room. And the restaurant had one wall all enclosed in glass with some beautiful stuffed birds in there. And Harry threw this pecker right through the glass. Those birds flew. They were stuffed, but they flew that night. Their feathers were all over the Old Mill."

Wally Stanowski slaps his knee and bursts out laughing.

"That's right, those birds did fly out of there," he says. "I was there that night. The guy Harry threw into the glass showcase came upstairs covered in feathers. Pieces of glass sticking out of his hair. What a night!"

I say to Danny Lewicki, who is sitting next to me, "Tell me about the time Squib Walker, the old Leaf scout, signed you to your first contract."

Lewicki says, "I was just sixteen and he came to my house to offer me a C-form. I didn't even know what a C-form was. Found out later it was a form that tied you to a pro club for life. Imagine that—for life!

"So he sits at our kitchen table, pulls out his wallet and starts putting money on the table. He put some ones and twos down, and then a five and a ten. He threw a twenty down and I gulped. I'd never seen a $20 bill. Geez, I couldn't wait to sign that form. But my mother was from the old country, and she was in the kitchen watching this scene. She hardly spoke a word of English. And when she saw I was going to grab a pen and sign, she stepped in and belted old Squib with her broom. All she knew was this guy was going to take her son away. She chased him right out of the house, belting him a few more times and telling him, 'You no taka my son away. You getta out. You sonnabeeth. Getta out!' I had to meet him later and sign with the Leafs."

"Aw, he was a mealy-mouthed so and so," says Wally. "Had a little Hitler moustache. He signed me, too. He'd throw those little bills on the table—fives and tens—until he got to a hundred. He signed a lot of guys that way."

"Then, when he signed you, he'd sell you some insurance," laughed Goose. "The year I played for Tulsa I was gettin' $2,000 and Walker sold me $1,000 worth of insurance. We could hardly pay the premiums."

"He sold everybody insurance policies," said Wally. "He'd force it on you. Actually, he made more as an insurance guy than he did as a scout—ha, ha, ha. Oh, we were clever little suckers, weren't we? Ha, ha, ha."

Gus said, "I'll never forget the day he put the bills in front of me. First, green ones, dollar bills, then a couple of twos. And some fives. Then a twenty. My eyes got wider all the time. He'd look at me as if to say, 'Is that enough?' Well, I was so stunned. I guess I didn't give him an answer, so he put down a brown one. I said, 'What's that, another one?' It had zeros on it. And he said, 'No, Gus, it's a hundred.' Fuck me, a $100 bill! Well, I wasn't going to lose that, so I grabbed the pen out of his hand and signed. Then he says, 'Well, now, if you're going to be a big NHL star, you'll need insurance.' So he reaches out and starts taking some of the money back. I wanted to grab him by the wrist. Geez, he must be turning over in his grave now hearing us talk about him like this."

I say to Bodnar, "Gus, you still hold the NHL record for the fastest goal scored by a rookie in his first NHL game—in 15 seconds. Can you recall the events leading up to that big moment for you?"

"I'll never forget it," Gus says. "It was October 30, 1943—my first game with the Leafs. I remember the team we played: the New York Rangers. I was certainly a nervous young boy coming into Maple Leaf Gardens from Thunder Bay—Fort William, they called it in those days. I remember not eating my steak, which was the pre-game meal, because I was so nervous. My landlady said, 'Son, all you can do is your very best.'

"So the puck was dropped, and that was about all I can remember after that. I scored, and we went back and faced off again. I couldn't tell you anything about that goal except I think it was against Lorne Anderson in the Ranger net."

"It couldn't have been Anderson," I point out. "He didn't join the Rangers until the '50s."

"Then it was Ken McAuley. It was against Anderson I set a record for the three fastest assists. That was in '52, when I was with Chicago. Three assists in twenty-one seconds."

"Who was on your line in your first game?"

"[Sweeney] Schriner and [Lorne] Carr. We started the game, and that was surprising because it was very unusual for a rookie to have a starting assignment. It was a great thrill in my life, getting the fastest first goal and playing with those two old pros who'd come over from the New York Americans. They were a couple of smoothies."

"But you can't recall much about the goal itself?"

"Not much. After I got the draw, my only thought was to get it in the Ranger net. I just circled around, then walked in between the

Ranger defence and put it in the net. That was it. I'm surprised it took me fifteen seconds."

"You must have thought that this NHL hockey is easy."

"I guess maybe I did. But I remember a good lesson that I learned at training camp in St. Catharines that year, a lesson taught by a veteran—Bucko MacDonald. Here I was, an 18-year-old rookie coming up from the juniors. In those days my hair was wavy and long and I was in great shape. So here's this smart rookie with the Leafs, out there dipsy-doodling around the ice, wondering how long this has been going on, and how come these guys don't look any better than I do. Then I looked down for the puck in a scrimmage and Bucko hit me. My, how he hit me. And that was the end of it. He picked me up and carried me off, put me on the bench, and said to me, 'Son, this is a good lesson for you. Keep your head up. Now here's another tip. Go and get your hair cut.' So even though my brain was still rattled, I went to the barber and got my hair cut down to the old brush cut which was popular in those days."

"Was there much reaction to your record goal?"

"No, not much. I remember the next day my landlady, Mrs. Lambert, baked me a big cake, even though we had been told not to eat too many desserts."

"Mrs. Lambert?"

"Quite a few of the Leafs boarded at Mrs. Lambert's house. She was a very strict old lady who really kept the players who boarded with her on their toes. She had a player piano in the parlour and she used to tell the boys to go in there and play the piano because they had to pump the pedals. That would keep us in shape. And if we weren't in by curfew she threatened to phone the coach and tattle on us."

"Gus, I bet you can't tell me who has come closest to breaking that record. Can you?"

"Yes, I can. It was Danny Gare in Buffalo. He scored in eighteen seconds. It's funny. I was coaching in Oshawa and somebody called me at home and said, 'Gus, your record has finally been broken.' I said, 'Well, records are made to be broken. Who broke it?' He said, 'Danny Gare. He scored after eighteen seconds.' So I said, 'Well, smartass, he was three seconds too slow. He didn't quite do it.' And I hung up.

"And he'll never get a second chance at it, either."

"You've got that right."

There is more chatter about "dumb rookies," and someone tells a story about Montreal rookie Michel Plasse—a goalie.

"Plasse was initiated twice. He dared them to do it a second time. This was after they caught him in New York and dyed his hair with shoe polish—bright red. They shaved him and he dared them to do it again two months later. Of course they did. Who could refuse a dare like that?"

"There was another kid in New York, what was his name . . . Larry Somebody. The Rangers put a little hot stuff in his inner jock. When he was out on the ice he felt this burning sensation, and his teammates told him he'd probably caught one of those social diseases. That scared the hell out of him, so he went to the team doctor and the doc prescribed dextrose tablets the size of elephant nuts. He was told to take sixteen of those pills every day. Then what the Rangers would do every morning is put more of the hot liniment in his inner jock again and he'd say, 'Geez, guys, it's still burning like hell.' They'd say, 'Keep takin' those pills, rookie, and get lots of sleep.' Well, he couldn't sleep, he was so wired on dextrose and so worried about having a social disease."

We get to talking about penalty shots and I tell the boys about the strangest one I ever saw. One night, Bobby Rousseau of the Canadiens took a penalty shot—from just inside the blue line—and scored! Why he shot from so far out has always baffled me.

Jackie Hamilton, who played in the NHL as a seventeen-year-old during the Second World War—making him the second-youngest NHL player ever—played at about 150 pounds and is now about a hundred pounds over that weight. "Hell," he scoffs, "I took two consecutive penalty shots one night and scored on both of them. Don't believe me? I'll show you the clipping. I'll bring it next week."

"How did that happen?" I ask.

"In my day, in the '40s," he says, "for a brief time there were two types of penalty shots in the NHL—a major and a minor. I was tripped up or pulled down and was given a major penalty shot, which meant I could skate in at will and try to score. Just like today. And I did. But the opposing team's coach squawked and insisted the referee had made the wrong call. The ref skated over to me and said, 'Jack, the guy's right. I should have made you shoot the puck from behind the line painted on the ice. You'll have to try it again.'

"So I said, 'Sure. No problem.'

"I took my place behind the line—I believe it was twenty-eight feet out from the goal—and scored on my second attempt. There it was: two penalty shots after one infraction. They only counted one, but it got me in the hockey trivia books."

A week later, Jackie showed us the newspaper clipping of his feat to prove to us it really happened.

Many of the old-timers mentioned above are gone now. Max Bentley, a two-time NHL scoring leader, winner of the Hart Trophy and a Hall of Fame inductee in 1966, died in 1984. Sid Smith, former Leaf captain, two-time winner of the Lady Byng Trophy, three-time Stanley Cup champion and leader of the world champion Whitby Dunlops when they defeated the Soviets in 1959, passed away in 2004. He went into hospital for a routine knee operation and contracted a virus that proved to be fatal. Detroit trainer Ross "Lefty" Wilson, who was an emergency goaltender in the era when teams carried only one netminder and who played three NHL games for three different teams, died in 1983. Aggie Kukulowicz, who served as translator for Al Eagleson and Team Canada in 1972, died in 2008.

Kukulowicz once told me he was recruited out of Winnipeg by the Quebec Aces to replace Jean Béliveau. "First, I'd never seen a urinal until I saw them in the Quebec dressing room. Can you imagine? My teammates tried to get me to wash my feet in them.

"My coach in Quebec was Phil Watson, and he had a fiery temper. One night I scored a hat trick, and team sponsors showered me with gifts. Before our next game, a new bicycle was wheeled in, and then a new suit of clothes was handed to me. After that, it was a new watch.

"In the game that night, I had a bad first period, and when I came back to the room, Watson was livid. He threw my new watch across the room, he ripped up my suit and he trampled the spokes in my bicycle. All my new gifts were ruined."

Harry Watson died of cancer in 2002. He was inducted into the Hockey Hall of Fame in 1994 after the Oldtimers lobbied hard on his behalf. Harry was mild-mannered but tough when he had to be. He told me once, "I pinned Rocket Richard to the fence at Maple Leaf Gardens one night and the Rocket said, 'I want no part of you, Har-ree.'"

Gus Bodnar, a Calder Trophy winner in 1944, set up Bill Mosienko for a record three goals in twenty-one seconds against the New York Rangers and rookie goalie Lorne Anderson at Madison Square Garden in 1952. Gus and I were fellow diabetics. He died in Oshawa in 2005.

Jackie Hamilton died in 1998.

Those of us who are still around, a shrinking number but one that includes a spry Wally Stanowski, age ninety, sure miss you guys.

MY HOCKEY LETTERS

Jordan and I discuss the next chapter. I tell him, "Jordan, I'd like to include a number of hockey letters in this book, letters to hockey men I've encountered in my career."

"Letters? You mean real letters?"

"Real enough. It's just that I never sent them. A few I couldn't send if I wanted to—some of the recipients are deceased."

Jordan frowns. "I'm not so sure . . ."

"Tell you what, Jordan. You read a few of them through and see if you don't agree that my readers will find them interesting, that they deserve a chapter or two in this book."

"I can do that. I'll keep an open mind."

When I was a boy, with a three-cent stamp, an envelope and a sheet of paper you could send a letter anywhere. In school, teachers emphasized penmanship. In the course of a year, we all wrote a lot of letters. And we looked forward to replies. Some of us saved the stamps and placed them carefully in a book. Servicemen overseas counted on letters from home—from parents, friends and, most important, love letters from wives and sweethearts. Mail boosted their morale.

Today, why write a letter? We keep in touch through emails and cell phones. It's instant communication. In time, these modern-day messages will be erased or deleted. But letters, carefully structured, with real signatures, can be saved for a hundred years, can be handed down to the next generation, can open a window to our lives and times as we see them.

In this chapter, I would like to try to revive the lost art of letter-writing with messages to a select group of people in the hockey world—past and present.

Let's begin with a letter to one of my favourites.

TO WALTER GRETZKY

Dear Walter,

What a rare gem you are, Walter. I really hope you understand and appreciate that thousands of people across our great nation think of you as a truly remarkable person. You are, without any doubt, Canada's Hockey Dad.

Thank God you survived a near-death experience—a brain aneurysm in 1991—and made a miraculous recovery, even though your memory loss sadly prevents you from recalling many of your famous son's fabulous achievements.

A couple of years ago, at a sports banquet in Clarington, Ontario, I was called upon to introduce you as the guest speaker, and you wowed the audience with your presentation. This was old hat to you, but before I turned the microphone over to you, I thought the audience would be interested in hearing about some of Wayne's astounding accomplishments in hockey.

In minor hockey, Wayne scored a thousand goals before he was thirteen years old. In junior hockey with Sault Ste. Marie, he scored 70 goals and 182 points in his only season there.

Then I threw out a hard-to-answer trivia question, Walter. Before he played in the Soo, what other Junior A club did Wayne play for? Hardly anybody in the room knew the answer: the Peterborough Petes. Three games, three assists.

As a rookie in the NHL in 1979–80 he scored 51 goals and 137 points, but the NHL denied him the Calder Trophy because he'd played in the WHA for a season. Peter Stastny, at twenty-five a veteran of European hockey, won the Calder with 109 points that season. The decision upset a lot of Canadian fans and I, like them, thought it was unfair, that Wayne was robbed. I can only imagine how upset you and Phyllis must have been.

Wayne holds almost every NHL scoring record. He tallied 894 career goals and 1,963 assists for 2,857 points.

I love the next Gretzky fact I tossed out that night: if your son had never scored a single goal in the NHL, he'd still be the all-time scoring leader based on his assists alone. And another little-known fact: how many know that your son Brent, Wayne's kid brother, scored a single goal (in 1993–94) plus three assists for the Tampa Bay Lightning in a thirteen-game NHL career?

Isn't that fantastic, Walter? Between them, Wayne and Brent have collected more points, counting playoffs, than any other brother combination, including the Sutter brothers—all six of them.

Wayne holds sixty-one NHL scoring records—forty for regular season play, fifteen for playoffs and six for the All-Star Game.

He captured nine Hart Trophies as most valuable player; ten Art Ross Trophies as scoring champ; five Lady Byng Trophies as most gentlemanly player; and two Conn Smythe Trophies as the playoff MVP. He holds the single-season records for goals (92) and points (215). Is there anyone on the hockey horizon capable of surpassing those totals? I don't think so.

Wayne had fourteen 100-point seasons, and in four of those seasons he topped 200. Of the five times he scored more than 60 goals in a season, there were two 80-goal campaigns.

When he retired in 1999, his number 99 was retired by the entire league—a hockey first.

Walter, we talked that night in Clarington about the first time I encountered Wayne. It was on the ice in either Hamilton or Stoney Creek—I've forgotten which.

I was a walk-on with the NHL Oldtimers back then—they needed an extra player one night, and I stayed around for the next twenty years—and we were playing a media team for charity.

Suddenly, the doors flew open and this little tow-headed kid skated out, legs churning—a little bundle of energy. I skated straight to our bench and said to our coach, "That's the Gretzky kid. He holds all kinds of records. They say he's going to be a huge star in the NHL someday."

The coach, Art Smith—Sid's brother—gave me an odd look. "Oh yeah? He's just a peewee. How can anybody say that?"

Anyway, Wayne played a few shifts in the game that night and skated around Andy Bathgate, a former Hart Trophy winner, to score a couple of goals. To this day, I don't know if Andy eased up to let him get by, but I prefer to think not. I like to think that even then Wayne could dazzle everyone, even ex-pros.

I told you about meeting you and Phyllis that night, and Wayne's coach, Ron St. Amand, after the game, and your eyebrows shot up. "How would you remember that? Even the coach's name?"

I said, "I don't know, Walter. Generally, I have a lousy memory for names. But somehow I knew instinctively that that night, that game, that kid, that coach and those parents should be remembered."

I also recall following Wayne's exploits at the fifteenth annual Quebec Pee Wee Tournament that year, when he ran into his first major setback in hockey.

Walter, you must remember a young player named Grove Sutton? Most fans won't, but you certainly will. Almost thirty-five years ago, playing before thousands of fans who came to ogle Wayne Gretzky tournament, Sutton became an overnight hero.

It was 1974 and the tiny tornado from Brantford was the biggest story at the tournament. Everyone was aware he'd scored 378 goals in minor hockey in one season alone. More than ten thousand fans turned out to see him play in his first tournament game. Brantford humiliated a nervous group of youngsters from Richardson, Texas, by a score of 25–0 in that game. The Texans were novices to hockey. They'd never seen slapshots before and seldom played before more than a handful of people. Their goalie was so frightened he couldn't perform, and a teammate who'd never donned goal pads before had to take his place in the net.

During the game, Gretzky scored seven goals and added four assists for eleven points, breaking Guy Lafleur's single-game tournament record by one. He followed up with two goals and three assists in Brantford's 9–1 victory over Beaconsfield, Quebec. Game three was against Verdun, Quebec, led by a flashy little centreman named Denis Savard who would go on to a Hall of Fame career in the NHL. Fan interest was so high that Gretzky had to battle his way through the crowds to the dressing room. Brantford won again, 7–3, with Wayne notching three goals.

His next test—in the tournament semifinals—was against a team from Oshawa, Ontario, a solid club that had often spelled trouble for the Brantford boys in the past. Wayne played both defence and forward and managed a goal and three assists. But Oshawa's Sutton, a heads-up player, outshone Wayne with five goals in the 9–4 Oshawa victory. Sutton wasn't just a one-game wonder—he collected seventeen goals in the tournament, four more than Wayne. In the championship game, Sutton led his team to the peewee title with a victory over Peterborough.

When the semifinal game was over, Wayne sat in the dressing room and cried. He was devastated.

Walter, few could have foreseen at the time that your son would grow up to become hockey's greatest scorer. Just as no one could have predicted that Grove Sutton would soon fade from the hockey scene.

I interviewed Wayne on *Hockey Night in Canada* one night when he was a teenager—outside the Leaf dressing room. Just then, Leaf enforcer Tiger Williams, looking ferocious, came out of the Leaf room and stood nearby. He wore a white robe and his face was puffed up from a number of recent fights. He gave Wayne the once-over as if to say, "Who's this skinny kid McFarlane's talking to?"

And Wayne remembers thinking, "Don't tell me I'm going to have to play against guys like that when I get older."

Back then, Walter, most scouts didn't think your son would ever make it to the NHL. Too small, too skinny. A choppy skater. Not much of a shot. How wrong they all were.

During the season-long lockout of 2004–05, I heard Wayne on the CBC. The host asked him about the famous photo of him standing next to Gordie Howe. Everyone has seen it. There's Howe with a hockey stick wrapped around Wayne's slender neck.

Wayne recalled the moment: "My dad told me I was invited to some kind of a banquet. I said, 'I don't want to go to any banquet.' He said, 'All right. But Gordie Howe's going to be there.' I said, 'Gordie Howe? I'll go, I'll go.' Gordie was my idol. At the banquet I sat next to Gordie and I was thrilled. Then a guy took some photos of us together. I laughed when Gordie held a hockey stick across my throat. I was wearing a brand new suit my folks had bought for me. And I remember thinking that sometimes the people you look up to are never quite as nice when you meet them in person. But Gordie wasn't like that. On the way home I told my dad, 'Gordie Howe's ten times greater that I imagined he'd be.'

"That's when I decided I'd like to wear number nine. But I ended up with 99 in junior hockey because in the Soo some other kid had already been given number nine. It wouldn't have been fair for me to get it. I was just a rookie."

Walter, I know that Wayne always tells young players that an assist is just as important as a goal. I always thought that was good advice. It's commendable that he passes that message along to young players.

When someone asked him about pressure, he said, "Pressure? There was never much pressure when I was on the ice. The pressure came before and after games. On the ice, I was always at home, most comfortable. But I always regretted I couldn't play hockey in my hometown, close to my family. There was pressure back then—a little too much pressure. I had two good seasons playing junior in Toronto, living with another family, but I often wished I could be playing in Brantford.

"My love for hockey was such that even when I was in Edmonton, I'd go out and play road hockey—ball hockey. Kevin Lowe and I did that all the time, outside our apartment. We'd be out there when it was thirty, forty degrees below. Playing for hours."

There was one touching moment Wayne recalled.

"I visited a hospital and one kid there was all wired up—fighting a terminal disease of some kind. A really good kid. And I visited him after a game in which I'd been badly cut around the eye. There was blood in the eye socket and it looked pretty bad, I guess. The kid looked up from his hospital bed and his eyes got wide. 'Wayne, are you all right?' he said in alarm.

"I assured him I was fine but his concern for me was so sincere, so touching. I was dating Janet then and she started to cry. She had to leave the room. And I was all teary-eyed myself. Here's a kid fighting for his life and he's more concerned about my welfare than his own. I'll never forget that day."

You taught him well, Walter, out there on that famous backyard rink.

In a recent *Globe and Mail* article, Roy McGregor, an outstanding writer and a hockey enthusiast, lamented the dearth of backyard rinks in Canada, like the ones you and I played on as kids, and the one you meticulously built each year in your back yard for the Gretzky kids to skate on.

Do complete strangers still knock on your door and ask to peek in your basement, hoping to see all those trophies? Do they ask you to show them where the backyard rink once stood? When they leave, do they pluck clumps of grass from your front lawn as a souvenir? I'll bet they do, Walter.

A few years ago, Roy McGregor and I skated on a frozen lake in Quebec—during an NHL seminar of some kind. With sticks and gloves we joined in a free-for-all game of shinny. But not for long. The pace was fast and we were old. And when we hit deep ruts in the ice, we nearly took some nasty tumbles. So we retired to the bar.

Roy and I agreed on one thing. Those ruts wouldn't have bothered us when we were kids. You laughingly told Roy about how you, as a boy, would "skate on the Nith River for miles—until you hit the rapids." Smart thinking, Walter. Those rapids will turn even the best skaters into swimmers pretty darn quick.

"Now you can't even keep ice on a backyard rink," you told McGregor. "Winters are warmer now. And the river rarely freezes over."

You taught your boys the skills, and both you and Phyllis taught them manners and how to behave—you taught them respect. Heck, for the first five years of his NHL career Wayne was still calling me Mr. McFarlane.

Some observers think Sidney Crosby or some other young hotshot will equal or surpass many of your son's records.

Wayne has proven that anything is possible in hockey. I'm sure that most hockey men, when Wayne started out, never believed he'd surpass his idol, Gordie Howe. They never thought he'd collect more points than much bigger men—fellows like Jean Béliveau and Phil Esposito.

I'll bet you smile when you think of those sixty-one NHL records, Walter. That is simply mind-boggling, a fabulous achievement. I'm sure you wish Sidney and the others all kinds of success. I know you hope they'll taste champagne from the Cup more than once. But for Sid the Kid to shatter many of your boy's marks is a stretch—a really long stretch.

I hope we're both around long enough to see how it all turns out.

Oh, by the way, Walter, I play hockey in Florida with a bunch of old-timers and we were talking NHL trades the other day. A guy named Jimmy asked me, "Brian, who was the star player the Montreal Canadiens traded to Los Angeles who became a big wheel with the Kings?"

I drew a blank.

"Yeah," he continued, "he was the Habs' leading scorer, their captain. Can't think of his name."

I said, "Jimmy, I don't have a clue who you're talking about. Steve Shutt and Larry Robinson were ex-Canadiens who wound up in L.A. It wasn't one of them?"

"No, no, bigger than those two. Much bigger."

"Jimmy, you're not thinking of Gretzky, are you?"

"That's it!" he shouted. "It was Gretzky."

I laughed. "Jimmy, Gretzky played for Edmonton, not Montreal."

"Oh," he said, taken aback. "Guess I had the wrong team."

"Yes, you did, my friend."

"By the way," Jimmy asked. "What's Gretzky's first name?"

TO BOBBY ORR

Dear Bobby,

First, I want to thank you for being part of our foursome in a long-ago golf tournament north of Toronto. The guys were thrilled to be in your company and you treated us all like you'd known us for a lifetime. You were limping a bit that day, and when we finished the round somebody drove you off in a golf cart. I recall the rest of us gathered together off the eighteenth green and talked about you.

"Wasn't he great company?" someone said.

"That was the greatest day I've ever had on the golf course," said another. "All because of Bobby. He kept telling me, 'Come on, bud, we need a solid drive from you' and 'Great putt, pal.' Things like that. I'll never forget it."

Bobby, I asked you for a favour that day. I told you I had a small hockey museum in Niagara Falls and I needed an autographed photo of you to put on display. You said, "No problem. Leave it with me." A week later, you shipped me a dozen photos—including the famous one of you scoring the Stanley Cup–winning goal in 1970—a really large photo. All of them autographed. Was I thrilled? You bet I was. Cost you a bundle in postage to mail them to me. I'm sure I sent you a note of thanks. But I thank you again, all these years later.

I knew of your generous nature from my friend Russ Conway, the Hall of Fame journalist from the *Lawrence Eagle-Tribune*. Russ was nominated for a Pulitzer Prize for his expose of Alan Eagleson. His research and articles helped in the conviction of the former executive director of the NHLPA for fraud. A lot of Canadian journalists are still embarrassed that Russ beat them all to the story.

Russ told me a story about you once. Here's what he said.

This happened when Bobby was at the peak of his game, the greatest player in hockey. I was on my way to a Bruins morning skate, and it was one of those days when everything was going wrong in my life. You know how it is—the car wouldn't start, I slipped on a patch of ice and I found some letters I forgot to mail—a dozen little things that really aggravated me. So when I get to the Boston Garden and pass Bobby Orr, he slaps me on the shoulder and says, "Russ, how's everything with you?"

I say, "Everything's horse bleep" or something similar, because I'm having a lousy day.

Bobby laughs and says, "I've got a cure for that. Meet me after practice."

So now I'm curious, and of course I meet him after practice.

He takes me into the Bruins' dressing room, where I wait while he showers and gets dressed. Then he talks to the trainer, who loads him up with a lot of pucks and sticks and team souvenirs and we go to the parking lot. He throws all this stuff in the trunk of his car, tells me to hop in and we drive off. He doesn't say a word as we drive away.

Now he pulls off the highway and drives into the parking lot of a major hospital. "Get out," he says. Then he turns and wags a finger at me. "Not a word of this trip gets in your newspaper. A deal?"

"Sure, Bobby. If you say so. It's a deal."

In the hospital, he says hello to everyone he meets. Then he makes his way to the children's ward. Obviously, he knows the way because he doesn't need to ask directions. He goes from room to room, from bed to bed. Keep in mind these are sick kids—cancer patients and others with major health problems. But they all know Bobby Orr, and how their faces light up when he kibitzes with them and hands out his hockey souvenirs—photos for all, a stick here and a puck there. I get a big lump in my throat watching all this.

Finally, he says his goodbyes and I turn to go.

"Not so fast," says Bobby. "We've got two more floors to cover."

It's another hour before we're out of there. And the lump in my throat has doubled in size by the time we reach the parking lot.

He starts the Caddy and we drive away, neither of us talking, both of us moved by the experience. Finally, he turns to me and grins. He says, "Well, Russ, how's your day now?"

Bobby, it's a shame the kids playing hockey today didn't get to see you perform. When my grandsons ask me, "Who was Bobby Orr?" I try to take them back to the late '60s and early '70s. They can hardly believe there were only six teams when you arrived in the NHL as an eighteen-year-old. I tell them Bobby Orr was the most exciting player in hockey, one of the best I ever saw. Even as a junior, he was phenomenal. He played for the Oshawa Generals as a fourteen-year-old and was better than most even then.

Bobby, before you arrived in the NHL, hockey people—and I was one of them—thought it impossible for a defenceman to win the Art Ross Trophy, awarded annually to the highest scorer in the game. You changed that thought in a hurry. In your rookie season, you won the Calder Trophy, and by your third season you set a goal-scoring record for defencemen with 21. In 1969–70, you stunned us all by finishing on top of the scoring race with 120 points. That was 21 more points than your teammate Phil Esposito, one of the greatest scorers in history. No defenceman had ever come close to that kind of production. It was unthinkable.

Then, five years later, you won the Art Ross Trophy for a second time, with 135 points. In between, you finished second in scoring three times and third once (all four times behind Esposito).

What made your mind-boggling accomplishments even more remarkable was that you played for most of your career on wonky knees, knees that had required numerous operations. I've had three knee operations; you must have had a dozen—all before arthroscopic surgery made the outcome of such procedures so much more successful.

And while your scoring titles have been well publicized and never duplicated, one of your most amazing records has hardly been talked about at all. It's your career plus-minus rating of plus-597. To the uninitiated, it means you were on the ice for 1,188 even-strength goals and on for only 591 goals against. In your all-too-brief career you won three Hart Trophies, two Art Ross Trophies, two Conn Smythe Trophies and eight consecutive Norris Trophies as best defenceman. You won the Lou Marsh Trophy as Canadian athlete of the year and *Sports Illustrated*'s annual award to the athlete of the year. The honours go on and on.

In 1976, you were named the most valuable player of the Canada Cup tournament—your only appearance in the international spotlight. No wonder both Harry Sinden and Don Cherry—who seldom agree on anything—call you "the greatest player in hockey history."

Speaking of Don, I asked him about you when I was writing a book about the Bruins. He said, "Bobby was supernatural. Terry O'Reilly came up with a good idea one day. He said they should pass Bobby around from team to team. That would keep things even.

"One time, we're on the ice in L.A., getting the jet lag out. Bobby comes out and snags a puck behind the net, flicks it in the air and sends it rocketing two hundred feet down the ice into the upper corner of the empty net. I gape and say to one of my guys, 'Ever seen anything like that before?' He says, 'Never. I don't believe it, either.'"

Bobby, in Florida I have a hockey-playing friend, Norm Bradley, who started a cable TV business in Parry Sound when you were just a kid. He told me he hired a young lad who lived nearby for a summer job. That was you, Bobby. You had to be in your early teens at the time.

Of course, the name meant nothing to Norm and he understood when Doug, your father, came around and said, "Norm, my boy is too young to work for you. I'm going to send you my older son in place of Bobby."

Norm told me, "So I didn't have Bobby on my staff for more than a day or two. But then I played hockey on the local rink one day and I recognized Bobby. How could I not? He was head and shoulders better than the other kids on the ice. Now, I was a good player back then—good enough to earn a tryout with the Canadiens one year. And here was this baby-faced kid gliding around that ice and we couldn't get the puck away from him. What a standout he was even then. But I never dreamed he'd become one of the greatest of all time."

Bobby, if you don't remember Norm, you'll be pleased to know he built that cable company into a hugely successful business.

Don Cherry is right. There are so many Bobby Orr stories and it would take volumes to tell them all.

As for me, it was a privilege to work with you on *Hockey Night in Canada* when you were a guest analyst on our show from time to time. I know you never felt comfortable in our world of television, but we all felt thrilled to have you with us.

And it was an added thrill for me to be in the broadcast booth at the Boston Garden on Bobby Orr Night. It was January 7, 1979. The game was a meaningless exhibition contest against the Soviets, which really ticked Cherry off, and I have little recollection of the game itself. But the opening ceremonies—wow! They will stay with me forever. The ovation you received that night from the Boston fans was simply incredible. It seemed to go on forever.

I remember the pin-striped suit you wore that night. During the ceremony, Johnny Bucyk handed you your number 4 jersey. You pulled it on, and the arena exploded in cheers. Then, a large banner with your number on it and the years you served the Bruins—1966 to 1976—was raised to the rafters. Some speeches were curtailed because of the lengthy ovation, which lasted about eleven minutes. I remember wondering what the visiting Soviet players were thinking when the ovation went on and on. A few of them may have played against you in the Canada Cup series. The others could only gawk and marvel at the well-deserved adulation you received that night. Such a night would never have happened for one of them, in Moscow or anywhere else. Their eyes were popping while ours were filling with tears.

That was the year you were named the greatest athlete in Boston sports history, ahead of legends like Ted Williams, Bill Russell and Bob Cousy. Another poll listed you at number 31 on the list of greatest athletes of the twentieth century. That's pretty heady stuff, Bobby. For a crew-cut kid from Parry Sound to reach such heights—unbelievable!

The next time you brought tears to our eyes was in Chicago, on the day you announced your retirement from hockey. Shame on the Bruins for letting you go to the Blackhawks. You should have remained a Bruin forever. If Eagleson convinced you to sign with his old pal Bill Wirtz, then shame on him, too. Is it true he never told

High above the crowd, the Hewitts (Foster and Bill) and I broadcast hundreds of games from the famous gondola at Maple Leaf Gardens. (*Author's collection*)

Talking hockey with fans at the Canadian National Exhibition in Toronto in the sixties— when sideburns were in vogue. (*Author's collection*)

Appearing on stage at the London Fair with the late Bob Goldham on my right and Montreal's Gilles Tremblay on my left. Producer Bob Gordon is in the foreground. (*Author's collection*)

In 1961, at CFCF-TV in Montreal. Dick Irvin and I with host Jimmy Tapp, weather girl Marg Anthony and newscaster Art Leonard. (*CFCF-TV*)

Hockey helped provide me with a solid education at St. Lawrence University in Canton, New York. Accepting a scholarship to St. Lawrence was the single best decision I ever made. (*St. Lawrence University*)

For decades, Maple Leaf Gardens in Toronto was one of the world's most famous arenas. A sex scandal resulting in a suicide soiled its reputation before it closed. It remains deserted, its future uncertain.

With goalie Dennis Riggin on a CBS telecast in 1960. This photo is the only memento I have of my first network hockey assignment. (*CBS photo*)

My friend Bill Galloway of the National Film Archives was a world-famous authority on vintage hockey film and photos. (*NBC photo*)

With NBC in the '70s. I teamed up with Peter Puck to explain hockey fundamentals and the game's rich history to countless fans. (*NBC* photo)

During a brief stint in public relations at Maple Leaf Gardens, I called the shots as Leaf fan Tiny Tim tried to hit the open net. He missed. (*Author's collection*)

At CFCF-TV in Montreal fitness guru Bonnie Pruden appears to be unconcerned about the effect of her exercise program on two volunteer sportscasters—Irvin and me. (*CFCF-TV*)

With NBC, our telecast hockey team captained by Ted Lindsay, faced challenges by media teams prior to our weekly NHL game productions. (NBC photo)

On Hockey Night in Canada, Don Cherry and I got along well from the beginning. Whenever we worked together, he would call his mother in Kingston after the show. "How'd it go tonight, Mom?" (*Author's collection*)

Phil Esposito was always a colourful and outspoken guest when he appeared on our NBC telecasts. (*NBC photo*)

you that Boston was willing to give you part ownership in the team—as much as 18 1/2 per cent if you'd stay? Is it true he convinced you that the Bruins no longer wanted you? That was so wrong, so unethical, and so preposterous. We'd all like to know the facts—the real story behind that deal.

In Chicago, on November 8, 1978, we at *Hockey Night in Canada* were there with our cameras for the press conference at which you called it a career. Your knees were shot and you'd struggled through a few games with the Hawks over two seasons. Everyone in the packed room was crying. It was a very emotional parting. Others have retired—Gordie, Guy Lafleur, Ron Ellis, Ted Lindsay—only to come back months later. With you, we all knew it was final. You would not play again. And we were all choked up.

One year later, you were ushered into the Hockey Hall of Fame. No waiting period for you, nor should there have been. At age thirty, you became the youngest member of that elite group.

Bobby, you left such an indelible mark on the game.

I asked Hall of Famer Milt Schmidt, now ninety-one years old, to talk about you one day in Kitchener.

Well, Bobby was the type of person who never wanted any publicity. A lot of the writers thought he was uncooperative or shy, but it wasn't that. He wanted his teammates to get the attention. He'd say, "Milt, I don't want to talk to them. Tell them to talk to so-and-so." He was swamped with requests for his time.

Here's the kind of guy he was. When I managed the Bruins, we were playing up in Montreal one night late in the season. Tommy Williams was with us at the time, and Tommy had a bonus coming if he could score one more goal. But he wasn't getting many chances, and now it's the second-last game of the season. The way Tommy was keeping himself in condition, it looked to me like he was never going to get that goal. Now Orr scores a goal against the Canadiens and the PA announcer says, "Boston goal by Orr." Bobby skates over and tells the timekeeper and the scorer and the referee that he didn't score the goal, Tommy Williams scored it. Well, who's going to argue with Orr? So they announce the change and Tommy gets credit for his bonus goal. What bothered me was that Tommy Williams was sitting on the bench when that goal was scored.

After the game, I was a little upset. I felt a guy like Williams had to earn his bonus. So I went up to Orr and I said, "For Chrissakes, Bobby, if you're going to do something like that, would you please wait until your teammate is on the ice?" He just laughed. "Williams got his bonus. Yeah, I gave it to him." But that's the type of person Bobby Orr was and still is.

I can see you squirming, Bobby, and saying, "Come on, Milt, no need to tell stories like that."

Bobby, not too many people know about your friendship with Ray Lussier, the photographer who snapped that famous photo of you flying through the air a split second after you scored the Stanley Cup–winning goal in overtime against St. Louis. It was on May 10, 1970, forty seconds into overtime.

Most fans have never heard the story behind that photo—how Lussier, working for the *Boston Record-American*, was stationed at one end of Boston Garden. He figured the Bruins would go for a quick overtime score, but they'd be attacking Blues goalie Glenn Hall at the other end of the arena. So Lussier scrambled around the rink, gambling that he could find a location next to the St. Louis goal. He lucked out. He found an empty stool near a hole cut in the Plexiglas. Someone told him the photographer occupying the stool had gone for a beer because the heat in the building was excessive.

Lussier thrust his camera lens into the hole, and forty seconds into overtime he snapped a series of shots as you took Derek Sanderson's pass and drilled the puck past Hall.

Just then, the other photographer came rushing back, shouting, "Hey, you're in my seat!"

Lussier laughed and said, "It's all yours, pal. Game's over." He hurried off to his newspaper.

His editor looked at his photos and whooped. "That one! Blow it up big for the front page. That's one of the greatest sports photos I've ever seen." Thanks to you (and Lussier), the NHL named it the greatest moment in Stanley Cup history.

Lussier died young—at fifty-nine. But not before you invited him to a reunion of the Stanley Cup winners you organized in 1990. And not before he realized that millions of hockey fans had marvelled at his shot—his best-ever photo—of you winning the Cup.

Garnet "Ace" Bailey, a popular teammate, was at the reunion. Years later, you and your Bruin mates would mourn his loss when the plane he was on—a flight from Boston to Los Angeles—crashed into one of the World Trade Center towers in New York on September 11, 2001.

Milt Schmidt told me you did an amazing job of bringing former teammates and coaches back to Boston to relive your team's glory days.

I saw you play junior in Oshawa, Bobby. What were you, fourteen years old? A homesick, shy, 125-pounder being tested by bigger, stronger, meaner juniors, all of them intent on a pro career. How your mom, Arva, must have worried about you initially. It must have been an agonizing decision to let you go.

You wore number 2 during your four years with the Generals and, in late November 2008, the Oshawa club finally retired your number. You were teary-eyed and told the crowd, "To be honoured in this fashion is something I'll never forget."

Wren Blair, then eighty-three, the man who discovered you, was there, beaming with pride. And Don Cherry quipped, "Sure, Bobby was a good player. But remember, he had a great coach."

The jersey retirement should have happened many years ago—long before the Generals retired Eric Lindros's number. Thank goodness Colleen Corner, the Gens' office manager for over forty years, wagged her finger at you and told you, "Bobby, you better get back here and get this thing done—or else!" After two decades of pleading with you, Colleen's persistence finally paid off.

"Bobby is a very humble man," she told the *Toronto Star*. "He doesn't care for a lot of pomp and attention."

Bobby, I wish you success in your role as a player agent and I commend you for the avid interest you take in helping others, especially the children who touch your heart. I'll wager you are still saying to journalists like Conway, as you rush off to do good works, "Not a word of this gets in the paper—a deal?"

TO DON CHERRY

Hello Don,

I just want to tell you how much fun it was working with you on *Hockey Night in Canada* back in the '80s. I have so many fond memories of the telecasts we did together and the road trips we took.

Remember when I took you on a tour of the Montreal Museum of Fine Arts, and all you cared to look at were the paintings of sailing ships?

Then I took you to a used bookstore in Lower Town and you bought two big shopping bags full of books—all about sailing ships. Then you grumbled as we made our way back to the Mount Royal Hotel: "McFarlane, you're as bad as Larry Hillman. He used to take me shopping and I'd come away with everything in the store. He never bought nothing."

Grapes, I remember the time you stood up for me after a game in Montreal. This was in our favourite Irish pub. Some guy horned in on a nice conversation we were having and you bristled when he said something critical about my TV work.

"What did you say?" you shouted. I thought you were going to grab the guy by the throat and choke him. "Get the fuck out of here. You say one more word and . . ."

Geez, Grapes, the guy disappeared like Jimmy Hoffa.

How about the time we were taping an opening to a Habs telecast in the studio at the Forum? Neither one of us liked the crew there very much. Most of the Radio-Canada guys—*most*, not all—were lazy and disinterested. And they were all heavy smokers, even the makeup girl. And there were always guys walking in and out of the studio, opening and closing doors, and I know it made you furious.

We were nicely into our opening that night when the door squeaked open and a CBC guy walked in eating an ice cream cone.

"Stop the tape!" you shouted, your face beet red. You pointed at him. "Will you get the fuck out of here and stay out!" He scuttled out that door like a mouse with forty cats in pursuit. And when the door hit his backside, the ice cream popped out of his cone and splashed all over the floor. *Voilà!*

We weren't too popular with that crew, were we? You'd leave the studio and they'd say some things about you in French. And when the game started, they'd flee the premises—probably to smoke—until the first intermission.

Remember how I really pissed them off one day, Grapes? After the makeup girl—well, she was hardly a girl—puffed smoke in my face while she powdered my brow, I'd had enough. I put up a big sign on the wall: "Defense de fumer!"

After that, I was even less popular than you, Mr. Cherry.

I want to thank you for the endless number of fascinating stories you'd tell me. When I asked you to tell me about Bobby Orr, you said, "I know this will really surprise you, but at first I couldn't stand Bobby Orr. That's right. He stood for everything I was against. I was a big defenceman, and when I'd watch him on TV, I would say to myself,

'This guy isn't a defenceman. He doesn't stay back. This guy is all over the place.' I was playing for the Rochester Americans then, and we had a practice one morning at the Boston Garden, right after the Bruins' practice. So I walk in early, and I saw Orr practising and my mouth fell open. I was mesmerized—a good word, eh?—by the things Bobby was doing. I had never seen anything like it and he was just jerkin' around. Nobody ever skated like him or handled the puck like him. Little did I know then that four or five years later I'd be coaching him.

"And the type of guy he is, he's not a hot dog. When he'd score a goal, he'd put his head down. It was almost as if he would be saying under his breath, 'Sorry, guys. I really didn't mean to embarrass you like that.'"

Grapes, I could always count on a good chuckle, if not a belly laugh, when you reminisced about your coaching career with the lowly Colorado Rockies.

"I had a guy out there named Turner. He flew in and I met him at the airport and took him home, and my wife, Rose, made him some sandwiches. Well, he wolfed down those sandwiches and my dog Blue sat there at his feet looking up at him. The guy didn't offer Blue so much as a bite. Not a crust! Blue finally shakes her head and I could almost hear her sayin', 'Who's this bleepin' bleep? Get rid of him.'

"Anyway, I wasn't too happy with Turner because he ignored Blue. But he thought I was a great guy because I went all the way out to the airport to pick him up. What I didn't tell him was I didn't go out there to get him. I went to the airport to pick up my goldfish. That's right: my goldfish. I flew them in from Boston for my aquarium. Turner just happened to be comin' in at the same time. He told everybody that I was a great coach. Well, he got that part right."

Grapes, early in your TV career, you and Brian Williams covered the World Junior Championships from Piestany, Czechoslovakia. The two of you watched on a monitor from a CBC studio in Toronto. Canada was leading the Russian team when suddenly the Russian coach sent all of his players over the boards. They jumped the

Canadian kids—twenty against six.

Naturally, the Canadians leaped into the battle, and one of the longest fights featuring the most players in hockey history erupted. The goalies were throwing punches. Even the trainers got involved.

You became irate when Williams was critical of the Canadian kids, suggesting they shouldn't act like hoodlums. It became almost as testy in the studio as it was on the ice. When Williams called it a "black mark for junior hockey," you went nose-to-nose with him during a commercial break. You told him, "Brian, you say 'black mark' one more time and I'm going to grab you—right on TV."

I was told that Brian moved slightly away from you.

During the break, to lighten the mood, someone suggested that you put your hands around Williams's neck. It would be the first thing the viewers would see when you came back on camera. But you refused.

"I can't do that," you told the director. "If I do, I might never let go."

Then there was the time you called time out in a game—and wound up signing autographs. It was December 2, 1979, and you were itching for a win when you brought your Rockies into Boston Garden for the first time since Harry Sinden sent you packing. You'd heard that two Boston players, Gilles Gilbert and John Wensink, had bad-mouthed you to the press.

"I can understand Gilbert criticizing me," you snorted. "Did he tell you how I tried to start him five times last season and he came up with five different excuses why he couldn't play? It's got to be a joke.

"As for Wensink, [for him] to say I played favourites really disappoints me. He should thank the Lord that I *did* play favourites or he'd have been batting his brains out in the minors."

You couldn't have been expecting a win that December night. The Rockies had won just five of their twenty-two starts while the Bruins were on top of their division.

I'll say this: those Boston fans were quick to show you how

much you were missed. They gave you a standing ovation when you took your place behind the visiting team's bench. As usual, the Rockies got off to a sluggish start and fell behind 2–0. Then someone said, "Come on, guys, let's dig in and win this for Grapes." And they did, squeezing out a 5–3 victory with the last shot hitting the empty Boston net.

The most talked-about moment in the game came in the third period, when you called a time out. The Rockies gathered at the bench, but you ignored them. You discussed no strategy, offered no words of encouragement. To their amazement, and to the delight of everyone in the building, you turned your back on them and started signing autographs. We'd never seen *that* before, Grapes.

"It was just somethin' that happened," you told me later. "I didn't plan it. I wasn't tryin' to twist the knife in or nothin'. I was just tryin' to give my defencemen a rest. Then people started askin' me for my autograph, so I signed some things. You can bet my bosses in Colorado weren't too happy about that."

But we thought it was hilarious, Grapes. Typical Cherry.

One of your big supporters that night was D. Leo Monahan, a longtime Boston hockey writer. The following day, he wrote, "Grapes couldn't have written a better script. The man may showboat a bit, but he's a gem among his drab, colourless, cliché-speaking brethren. Hail, Don Cherry, hail."

That may have been the year you grabbed one of your players by the throat and created a few headlines. You admitted you were about to throttle Mike McEwen for not doing what you told him to do. You asked your team captain, René Robert, what he thought about your actions and he said, "When you had him by the throat, Don, you should have squeezed a little harder." I guess you weren't surprised when McEwen told reporters, "Cherry is the pits as a coach."

Journalist and broadcaster Al Strachan, who helped you write a great little book, told me once of an extended trip he took with you years ago to jolly old England.

Travelling anywhere with Don is an experience! Back then, he still lived his life like he was a hockey player. He had a hockey schedule. That meant he took a nap in the afternoon. And from his years in the minor leagues, when he had to abide by a curfew—in bed by eleven o'clock—he didn't let eating meals cut into our drinking time. So we'd knock down a few pints until eleven o'clock and then order a clubhouse sandwich to take up to our room. In England, all the pubs close at eleven o'clock anyway.

So we toured around over there, and Don was most concerned that someone might recognize him—and that he might not be properly attired. I said, "Don, don't worry about it. You can wear whatever you want. Dress casually. Nobody over here will recognize you." So after two days of wearing those high collars and those ties and suits, he finally relaxed.

One afternoon, he decided he wouldn't wear a fancy tie, and sure enough, somebody recognized him. He came over to me and said, "Just met some people from Canada."

I said, "Oh, yeah?"

He said, "Do you know the first thing they asked me? 'Where is your tie?'"

Don thinks the three greatest people in the world, in order, are Lord Nelson, Winston Churchill and Margaret Thatcher. He is particularly enamoured of Nelson. We went to St. Paul's Cathedral to see Nelson's tomb. Don looked at that building and he was tremendously impressed. He thought it was fantastic. We went down to Portsmouth to see the refurbished Nelson's flagship *Victory* and Don actually got to stand on the deck where Nelson had fallen. And we went over to the Maritime Museum on the South Shore and he got to see the actual uniform that Nelson was wearing when he was killed by a French sniper. To him, that was tremendous. He has been reading about Nelson for most of his life. He got to see that uniform, that ship, that deck. It was one of the crowning moments of his life!

Finally, we went to see the Crown jewels. The guards protecting them are all former British army people. Following behind us, and chattering loudly, were a bunch of German tourists. Don looked up at one of the guards, nodded toward the Germans and said, "They're probably talking about how close they came to having all this!"

Don, you faced many problems during your coaching career in the NHL. One night before a game at Maple Leaf Gardens, you told me you had a goaltending choice to make. It was February 7, 1976, a night neither one of us will ever forget. Your Bruins were facing the Leafs that night and you had to decide on your starter. Would it be Dave Reece, the rookie who'd won seven of fourteen starts, or veteran Gerry Cheevers, who had just jumped back to the Bruins from the Cleveland Crusaders of the World Hockey Association? You asked Cheevers, "Are you ready to go?" Cheevers said, honestly, "Not really. I haven't played lately and I'm not in top shape."

"Then I'll go with Reece," you decided.

Poor Reece was in for the shock of his life. The University of Vermont grad would emerge from the game shell-shocked, with Leaf captain Darryl Sittler accounting for most of his suffering. Sittler scored six goals and added four assists for ten points. It was the greatest individual scoring performance in a single game in NHL history. It happened over thirty years ago, and no player has matched that mark. The Leafs won the game 11–4. Poor Reece. His confidence shattered, the rookie goalie never played another game in the NHL.

Grapes, here's a story you might prefer to forget. It's about the confrontation you had with Boston Bruins player Steve Kasper a few years ago. It took place in the stands in Edmonton one morning and the late Don Wittman, a wonderful man and my broadcasting colleague on *Hockey Night in Canada*, was there. He described what happened when I talked with him the following day.

I was assigned to the L.A.–Edmonton series that year. In the second game, played in Los Angeles, the Kings' Steve Kasper struck his head on the ice and suffered a concussion. Before the third game back in Edmonton, Kasper took part in the morning skate, but didn't dress for the game that night. Cherry goes on the air on "Coach's Corner" and says, "I don't understand this. Steve Kasper took the morning skate and yet he isn't dressing because he was knocked out in the game in L.A. That was three days ago."

Well, Don continues on with his usual rant, and that was that. The next morning, come time for the morning skate, I'm standing by the boards when Kasper walks in and makes a beeline for me.

He says, "Where the hell is that asshole Cherry?" I told him that Don was around somewhere—I'd just seen him.

Kasper says, "That sonofabitch, I almost jumped out of bed at the hotel last night. I was watching the telecast and I heard him ranting and raving about me not playing. He virtually called me a coward. He said that I was yellow and chickenshit and wouldn't play. What does he know? He doesn't know my medical history. I have had eleven concussions. For Christ's sake, the doctors wouldn't let me play."

My, but he was upset. I said to Kasper, "Let's try and find him." So we walk around and we couldn't find him. He goes into the dressing room and he comes out and asks whether I had seen him yet.

I said, "Yes, he is sitting up in the stands." He bolts up into the stands and comes up behind Cherry and says, "Cherry, you son of a bitch," and the two of them started to cuss, yelling and screaming at each other. "You rotten bastard, you

asshole" echoes through the arena. Kings coach Tom Webster
is standing there, and all his players are on the ice and the
practice comes to a halt. It absolutely stops while Kasper and
Cherry yell and scream at each other. This went on for about
five minutes. I thought they'd be wrestling or punching each
other any second. It was really funny.

Grapes, I'm sure if you met Kasper today you'd both laugh about that
spat and talk about it over a couple of pops.

Having a profile as high as yours isn't always easy, Grapes. Hell,
you couldn't even walk down the hall to the men's room at Maple Leaf
Gardens without being followed by a crowd of autograph seekers. I'm
sure some of them asked for your signature while you were unzipped.

I was standing in there one night having a pee when Michael
Caine, the famous movie actor, sidled up to the urinal next to me.
Nobody bothered him, and I certainly wasn't about to strike up a
conversation with him under the circumstances. It was no time to
offer a friendly handshake or ask for an autograph.

It would have been a different story with you, Grapes. Even while
you were at the urinal, people would be tugging at your sleeve.

I recall a game on New Year's Eve. You came in to our pre-game
meeting at Maple Leaf Gardens and took off your overcoat to reveal
an incredible tuxedo jacket. You called the material "crushed swirly
velvet." You took quite a kidding from the boys that night. Rick
Briggs-Jude said, "Grapes, did the shoes come with it?" and "Do you
do magic tricks as well?"

You said, "Listen. You gotta wear patent leather shoes with a
jacket like this. This thing cost me 575 bucks."

But you wouldn't walk down the hall wearing it.

"Are you kiddin'? In front of the fans? No way. If I gotta take a
leak, I'll put my overcoat on."

Grapes, remember the summer weekend when *Hockey Night in
Canada* invited all of the on-air personalities, producers and directors

and brass to a seminar at a posh resort in Quebec, north of Montreal?

When we arrived we were told all the VIPs would be staying at the ritzy resort while the "talent" would be quartered in a dumpy motel a mile down the road. Some of us were ticked off about that. I, for one, voiced my displeasure.

There was a dinner at the resort that night, and you were the guest speaker. Just as you got up to speak, a waiter toured the room taking drink orders.

"Scotch and soda, please." "Another beer, waiter." "Yes, sir."

You became very annoyed. The waiter moved back and forth in front of you, distracting you. Finally, you erupted: "Will somebody get this guy the fuck out of here?!"

It turned out to be the biggest laugh you got that night.

When are you going to quit, Grapes? You've had this "Coach's Corner" gig for a long time. It's been a huge success. It's made you one of the most famous men in Canadian history. What are you, seventy-seven—almost my age? Perhaps it's time to put all your incredible suits and ties in a Don Cherry Museum—in Kingston, maybe—and take life easy for a while. Surely you're beginning to feel overdosed on hockey.

I know you've come knocking at the door of my log home in the country from time to time, and each time I wasn't there. Too bad. I'd have loved to have shared a couple of pops with you and talked about the good old days.

TO BRUCE McNALL

Dear Bruce,

What in the world were you thinking?

For a guy with no background in hockey, a guy who never played a game in his life, you were skating recklessly on the thinnest of ice. Did you think you'd never fall through?

Well, you did. Your fat little body took a plunge that shocked the hockey world. No one was more shocked than one of your best friends, Wayne Gretzky.

There you were. King of the world one day, a convict the next.

You were a much bigger con man than your Canadian counterparts Alan Eagleson and Harold Ballard. They too wound up wearing striped shirts—and we're not talking referees.

It's inconceivable that you could have fooled so many of us, and for so long. It took a full decade for investigators to catch on, to find out what a naughty boy you'd been.

You were so impressive in our world of hockey that you were anointed as chairman of the NHL's Board of Governors, for heaven's sake. These governors are not saps, Bruce. Well, most of them are not. The rest hide it pretty well. They are hard-nosed businessmen. They claim, when they're sober, that they can spot phonies and scam artists the moment they walk in the door. How come they didn't spot you? Or one or two others, like John Spano, who took control of the Islanders with loans he obtained illegally, and Boots Del Biaggio, former part owner of the Nashville Predators who falsified his worth?

When I say "king of the world," I mean it. When you were sailing along at your peak as owner of the L.A. Kings, you were the man most responsible for bringing a basketball guy, Gary Bettman, into the commissioner's office. You were the man who astonished us by bringing Wayne Gretzky to California in what was the hockey coup of the century. You even convinced the Walt Disney organization to create a team with a goofy name—the Mighty Ducks—and buy into the NHL. And you persuaded Blockbuster Video founder Wayne Huizenga to bring NHL hockey to Florida. We thought you were headed for the Hockey Hall of Fame someday as a builder.

You had wealth beyond belief. You owned a full or part interest in three hundred racehorses—or so you claimed. You possessed a priceless antique coin collection and two film companies. You had homes or vacation retreats in Los Angeles, Palm Springs, Hawaii, Utah and the fashionable Trump Tower in New York. Your cars included a Rolls-Royce, a Bentley, a Range Rover and an Aston Martin. You purchased a Boeing 727 jet and had it refitted to accommodate two dozen hockey players and your friends. You allowed me on that plane for a few minutes, just to look around, and it was fabulous. If that 727 didn't get you in the air fast enough, you also owned a Jet Star cruiser and a helicopter.

You and Wayne purchased one of the rarest sports cards in existence: a turn-of-the-century Honus Wagner baseball card. Years later, when you fell like Humpty Dumpty, Wayne generously paid you $225,000 for your half of the card.

Let's make it clear here and now: Wayne played no role whatsoever in the financial machinations that ultimately led to your downfall and sent you to a prison cell. When you needed bank loans, you brought the bankers to one of your homes, where you proudly showed them thousands of sports cards laid out on a black velvet backdrop. You had the *cojones* to tell them the cards were as priceless as your famous coin collection. You showed them rare baseball uniforms once worn by famous players. The bankers didn't know you'd acquired the memorabilia on consignment and it would someday be reclaimed. They thought it was yours. They had no idea you'd purchased the cards for pennies apiece. That was clever of you, Bruce. Oh, how you charmed them. They were so impressed with you and your riches they granted you all the loans you needed. Millions of dollars' worth. They wanted to be your friends as well as your bankers. And why not? You were being hailed everywhere as the most glamorous sports owner on earth. Financial know-it-alls claimed you had a net worth of $133 million.

Everyone chuckled over rumours you'd done some smuggling early in your career. Spiriting rare coins out of European countries was easy—you simply put them in your pocket with your other coins.

Sometimes you'd pull a rare coin from your pocket and flip it in the air to impress your pals. I wonder if you did that with the Athena, history's most coveted coin, for which you paid $420,000, outbidding Aristotle Onassis. You sold it within days to a California movie mogul for a $50,000 profit.

Buying and selling rare coins made you wealthy so you bought a minority interest in the L.A. Kings. By 1988 you owned the club and impulsively paid Peter Pocklington $15 million for the best player on the planet, Wayne Gretzky.

There were other players involved in the deal, but they were unimportant. Gretzky fans in Edmonton never forgave you or Pocklington. They wanted to lynch both of you.

That was on August 9, 1988, the day before my birthday.

But I'll say this. Gretzky in a Kings uniform made a huge impact on hockey in the U.S.

Gretzky couldn't believe the salary you offered him—$3 million. "That's way too much," he told you. "But I'll take $2 million."

"I'll get you more," you promised Wayne, dangling the prospect of letting him be your partner in the horses, rare coins and memorabilia.

I was there for *Hockey Night in Canada* when Gretzky made his Los Angeles debut. It was a memorable night. I was able to chat with Roy Orbison, who sang the national anthem (I love his music) and died a few weeks later. There were movie celebs everywhere. I even bumped into a guy on a camera crew who introduced himself.

"My name is Viktor Nachayev," he said.

"I know that name," I replied, shaking his hand. "You were the first Soviet player to play in the NHL. The first Soviet to score a goal."

He grinned, pleased to be remembered. "Yes, that was in 1982. But I didn't score any more. The Kings sent me to the minors."

I'm surprised the Reagans, Ron and Nancy, weren't there. You were pals with them. As well as Goldie Hawn, Michelle Pfeiffer and so many others. I talked with Michael J. Fox in the Kings' locker room after the game, looking so diminutive among those husky hockey players.

Bruce, I remember that you had an amazing woman working for you back then named Susan Waks. She and others worked hard to make your most ambitious dreams come true. You—and she— must have known your efforts weren't always legal.

And you paid Susan well—$450,000 a year. Then you added perqs to keep her happy, like a decorating allowance of $7,000 per month. You let her use the company plane for visits to her in-laws. In 1992 she spent $165,000 of your money on a wardrobe and other necessities. She convinced you to pay off her debts—a couple of hundred thousand—and to pay her attorney husband $6,500 per month. He tooled around in a leased Porsche that cost you $1,600 a month. The Wakses loved you, Bruce. Everybody did. You were a generous guy.

I even talked to you about adding Peter Puck to your sports empire. I'm glad that proposal never went anywhere.

You were generous to a fault with another top employee, a man named Nesenblatt, especially when he threatened to spill the beans on your shenanigans. Nesenblatt helped you out of a jam with a major bank by bribing the loan officer, who was $50,000 in debt. Nesenblatt made the debt disappear. You paid Nesenblatt $500,000 a year, even after he moved to Lake Tahoe and showed up in your offices only occasionally.

You made fools of those bankers, Bruce. When they asked to examine your rare coins, and you no longer owned them, you simply had your flunkies take coins from the vault and tell the bankers they were worth a fortune—and they believed you. Are all California bankers as dumb as a goal post, Bruce?

Even *Sports Illustrated* was fooled. The magazine estimated your fortune at a couple of hundred million and marvelled that "everything McNall touches turns to gold."

You and John Candy and others bought the Toronto Argonauts and while you put up a good front—flying in the Blues Brothers for a halftime show on one occasion—the team lost millions. Much of it went to that dud Rocket Ismail. But the Argos did win the Grey Cup in 1991.

When things began to go sour, and suspicious souls began asking hard questions, you almost found the financing you desperately needed. Norm Green, the former Calgarian who owned the Minnesota North Stars, wanted to shift his team to Anaheim for the 1993–94 season. You chortled over the $25 million indemnification fee you would receive if the deal went through. At that time, Disney head Michael Eisner had just produced a movie, *The Mighty Ducks*, and you came up with a bright idea: Why not convince Eisner to bring the Disney brand to the NHL? You went after Eisner and put Green on hold. Then Eisner asked you a question that made you squirm. Eisner was a bit confused. He wanted to know just how much the NHL would pay to have Disney join the NHL.

"No, Michael," you told him. "You've got it backwards. Disney has to pay to get in—$50 million. And $25 million more comes to me."

Eisner's reply: "You've got to be kidding."

Eventually, Eisner negotiated a better deal with you and Bettman than other expansion clubs received: a $50 million entry fee, half of which went to you, the other half to the rest of the clubs.

Then you had another brilliant idea: Why not bring in a second expansion team, one in Miami, with Wayne Huizenga as owner? Norm Green felt betrayed, but so what? He wound up moving his team to Dallas.

In a way, you were betrayed too. Eisner paid you only half the territorial fee—$12.5 million. A promissory note for the remainder was attached. By then, you owed creditors far more than that. And you were shocked when Eisner told you he was going to name his team the Mighty Ducks—hockey's goofiest nickname since the Portland Rosebuds.

In 1994, in an interview with *Vanity Fair*, you bragged about smuggling coins into the U.S. Not a good idea, Bruce. Someone should have duct-taped your mouth. A class action suit by collectors followed. The FBI came nosing around. Creditors began demanding payments.

People were stunned—and that's putting it mildly—to learn you had no money to cover millions in debt. In May 1994, your house of cards came tumbling down around you. You threw in the towel and confessed that your life, your kingdom, was all a sham. Charges were filed against you—bank fraud, mail fraud and conspiracy. Seven of your former employees were also charged, including the brainy Susan Waks. You were convicted and ordered to serve five years and ten months in prison. You were fortunate that some of the lawyers guessed wrong—they said you might be sentenced to forty-five years in jail. Oh yes, you were also ordered to pay back $5 million, but where would you get that kind of money? From a Swiss bank, perhaps? During the proceedings, you were accused of stashing millions away in a Swiss bank account. You said that was hogwash.

David Begelman, your partner in the movie business, was another shady character who was involved with you, Bruce. You must have known that Judy Garland once sued him for stealing copious amounts of money from her. Knowing you had blabbed to the police, and fearful for his own future, Begelman checked into a posh hotel and blew his brains out. That never goes over well with the hotel cleaning staff.

Obviously, David wasn't happy with the life choices he'd made. He was a confessed embezzler and gained notoriety for forging actor Cliff Robertson's name on a $10,000 cheque. You picked some interesting associates, Bruce.

Your Hollywood chums did some really stupid things. Does anyone out there know the meaning of the word morality? Like them (and like all of us), you had some character defects. You desperately wanted to be liked. You were smart but greedy, enamoured with owning things. In financial matters, you were as bright as a 25-watt bulb. A GQ magazine writer said, "Bruce couldn't see his way around a financial statement without two accountants and a seeing-eye dog."

You were an oafish and clumsy womanizer. Two wives, a number of lady friends and a $5,000-a-month "trysting hideaway." You thought it was a compliment when you said to a woman, "Nice boobs, babe," and made other suggestive remarks. The F-word rolled off your tongue.

Almost overnight, you lost the Kings, although you did negotiate a sweet deal for Gretzky with the new owners. Wayne got his money from them, and when there was nothing left, he was dealt to St. Louis. You lost your homes, your cars, your love nest, and your wife. The 727 you paid $5 million for was sold for $500,000.

I'll close by bringing my readers up to date on your life today, Bruce. You served your time in seven prison sites, often in a cell smaller than the stalls that once housed your thoroughbreds. In jail, your visitors included Wayne and Janet Gretzky, Luc Robitaille, Rob Blake, Goldie Hawn and Kurt Russell. We are amazed that you were so popular, even as a felon. But then, Al Eagleson still has a number of loyal supporters too.

After serving some time in a halfway house, you came back to Hollywood and found a job with a movie company, reading scripts and consulting. You refuse to have anything to do with company financial matters. Smart man. No boss would be foolish enough to ask you to do that, anyway.

You wrote a book, *Fun While It Lasted*, that received mixed reviews. Half of your salary goes to paying off the $5 million in court-ordered restitution you owe. That may take a few years to accomplish, but we all hope you'll get it done, Bruce.

Gretzky gets the last word. "Bruce went to jail for the things he did wrong. But he did a lot of things right. He has a big heart and I've decided to stay by his side."

And finally, a postscript to this story.

My readers may wonder about the famous Honus Wagner card purchased by McNall and Gretzky. The card became valuable in the 1930s because fewer than two hundred were printed. Wagner apparently was against children smoking and refused to allow his card be circulated by a cigarette company. In 1933, the card, which eventually became known as the Gretzky T206, was valued at $50, making it the most valuable card around in those days. Gretzky and McNall purchased the T206 in 1991 for $451,000. Gretzky acquired sole ownership (as you now know) and sold it to Wal-Mart in 1995 for $500,000. A Florida man won it in a Wal-Mart promotion and auctioned it off for $640,000. In 2000, it was sold on eBay for $1.23 million. It changed hands again for $2.35 million, and the most recent owner paid $2.8 million for it.

I recall talking to Scotty Bowman once, and he told me he was an avid card collector. He said he had fifty Brett Hull rookie cards. Hang on to them, Scotty. They may be worth a million someday.

And we all know you need the money.

TO CARL BREWER

Hello Carl,

I want you to know the guys on the team all miss you and talk of you often.

Joan and I often talk of the day you came to our country place to help me celebrate a birthday. And how you charmed everybody there. Not long afterward, you came to our house in the city to return a manuscript I'd given you to read because I valued your input and opinion. I remember the date: August 25, 2001. Joan would say later that day, "It was as if Carl was tidying up loose ends. His visit was really interesting but eerie."

The three of us sat around the kitchen table and talked about serious issues—mortality and other things—not hockey. Not much hockey, at least. You told us, "I'm staying too long. You guys want to get out to your country place." And I replied, "No, this is important. It's a special time. We don't do it often enough. We're having a great discussion. Let's enjoy it. Forget a trip to the country."

So we talked some more. We talked about the time you invited me to a hush-hush meeting at the Ramada Hotel in Toronto, where many of hockey's former greats gathered to begin a battle to recoup millions of surplus dollars the league owed the players. Gordie Howe was there, and Bobby Hull and Andy Bathgate and Frank Mahovlich. I was the only media guy in the room and I had a great story for *Hockey Night in Canada*. Or at least I thought I did. But the producers chickened out, fearing repercussions from the NHL and possibly Leaf owner Harold Ballard. One of the biggest stories of my career never made it to the telecast.

Carl, you discussed your problem with sleep apnea and how you were using a special device to help get you through the night. You talked about your father and how he had died young, and how surprised you had been when so many people came to his funeral.

Then you left.

The following morning, your longtime companion Sue Foster called and tearfully said, "Brian, Carl is gone. We found him in bed this morning. There was no pulse."

It was an incredible shock.

Sue explained, "We got up in the night because Carl was restless, had trouble dozing off. He said, 'I'm not going to put that thing over my face. I'll sleep without it.'

"We had tea and returned to bed.

"I arose early and decided to let Carl sleep in. But by midmorning, when he still hadn't come downstairs, I was concerned. I went up and found him. He had passed away quietly sometime in the early morning."

Carl, you would have been amazed at the number of people who turned out for *your* funeral. The church was packed, all walks of life represented. You would have laughed at your former teammate George Armstrong. I passed him standing at the back of the church and whispered to him, "It's good to see you here, George." He whispered back, "Oh, fuck off, McFarlane." His comment caused a ripple of laughter among the other Leafs nearby.

Bruce Dowbiggin gave you a wonderful, well-written eulogy. A good choice on Sue's part, Carl.

My friend, you achieved much in your turbulent lifetime. You were a marvel on the ice and a stubborn, dedicated overachiever off the ice, with much of your boundless energy spent on a prolonged battle with the NHL moguls who claimed that $45 million in pension surpluses belonged to them, not to the players. That battle has been well documented and the successful outcome much applauded. It resulted in hundreds of former NHLers getting money they never expected to receive.

A few weeks later, Sue asked me to speak about you at one of our old-timer luncheons. I had read her book, *The Power of Two*, a fascinating story of her relationship with a man we knew and admired.

Here is what followed.

Our friend and teammate Carl Brewer would squirm in embarrassment—or perhaps he'd just laugh—if he heard someone use the word "beautiful" to describe him. But to the old-timers gathered here today, those who knew him well, Carl Brewer might well be described as a beautiful man.

Carl, your close friends also knew you as a sensitive man, an articulate man, a highly intelligent man, a compassionate man, a controversial man and—what was equally important to us—a hockey man. An immensely skilled hockey man— one of the very best on ice.

You were our friend and our teammate. Perhaps we should have told you more often how much we enjoyed you and appreciated you on and off the ice. Because all too soon you were gone. It was then too late.

You could fire a pass up to Peter Conacher on the wing and the puck would be right on the tape. You could deke your way past Ivan Irwin (not an easy thing to do), leave Goose McCormack spinning in your wake (also not an easy thing to do) and whip the puck past the opposing goalie and you made it look so easy. You could do it all, Carl.

You bonded with us because you liked us and trusted us, whereas you did not bond with everybody. When you played for the Leafs in the '60s, helping them to win three Stanley Cups, you battled opponents and often felt the sting of their anger, along with their grudging respect and envy for your considerable skills. You even cut the palms out of your gloves so that you could grip them more tightly.

Had you not insisted on marching to a different drummer, had you been more conformist, like a Horton, a Stanley, an Armstrong or a Baun, you'd be in the Hockey Hall of Fame today. But you were willing to pay the price a non-conformist—a rebel—always has to pay. You took the hits, the slings and arrows and shrugged them off. You simply didn't like the little dictators who kept popping up in your path, with their "do it my way or it's the highway" edicts.

As a result, you battled men with names like Ballard and Imlach, Ziegler and Eagleson. Especially Eagleson. You angered these men when you dared to strip the shine off their glossy exteriors, pricked their puffed-up egos and sometimes embarrassed them, often by scoffing at the ploys they used to make you toe the line.

When you'd heard enough of their dictates and seen enough pettiness, you'd simply retire from the game—something other players would never dare to do. You would blithely go your own way—back to university, perhaps, or to the national team or overseas to Finland—branded as an ungrateful shit disturber. Most players leave amateur hockey to join the pros; one year, you left the pros to become an amateur. It was unheard of in that era, but you did it. It was your choice. You still found joy in the game, whether it was coaching in Finland or playing in Muskegon, but always on your terms. And when you chose to return to the NHL with Detroit, you were better paid than Red Wing immortal Gordie Howe.

I can see you chuckling over the irony in that while Gordie fumed and sizzled.

In another comeback, at age forty-one, back with the Leafs, the players resented your presence and treated you like a leper—they even refused to pass you the damn puck. Yes, it was childish and only hurt the team. You could have taught some of those awkward young pups on the Leaf defence a few tricks—except for cutting the palms out of your hockey gloves. Because of you, that was no longer legal.

When you felt the team had reneged on a salary commitment, you took delight in antagonizing Imlach and Ballard by taking the Leaf name, which you discovered had never been trademarked, and claiming it as your own. The case went to court and the Leafs eventually won the name back—but it cost them well over $150,000.

Your feud with Eagleson, which you won by a knockout, saw the disgraced head of the players' association wind up in prison for several months. The Eagle crashed to earth with a thud; his reputation sullied forever, his resignation from the Hockey Hall of Fame quickly accepted. I'm sure you wondered, Carl, why men like Bobby Clarke and your old pal Bob Pulford just didn't get it. Blinders snugly in place and judgment dramatically impaired, these two stubbornly

insisted that Eagleson had done no wrong. They stood
tight with the man who'd just picked their pockets. It's like
catching your neighbour robbing your home and you say,
"Aw, we all make mistakes. Let's forget it and go have a beer."

You and Sue worked arduously to prove that Eagleson and
others were dead wrong when they claimed the $40 million
pension surplus belonged to the league, not the players. Oh,
it belonged to the players, all right. You and Sue proved that.
Then you made certain the players got their share of the money.

Disgraced, Eagleson went to jail, the central figure in the
biggest scandal in the entire history of the NHL.

Carl, your stubborn resolve, your determination to right a
wrong, gives you a unique niche in the game we all love. Will
it earn you a place in the Hockey Hall of Fame? No. Will it
earn you an Order of Canada? No, too late for that. But you
never expected rewards or honours.

Will you be remembered for doggedly insisting on doing
the right thing, for taking on the hockey establishment and
winning a war they said you couldn't possibly win? The
answer is an unequivocal yes.

And here, in this room, you will be remembered for being
our friend, our colleague and our teammate. Carl Brewer, you
were a complex man, a fascinating man, and a strange man
in many ways.

You were also a beautiful man.

THAT SUMMER OF 1972

I t's hard to imagine that a majority of hockey fans have only the vaguest recollection of that summer of 1972 and how a hockey series gripped a nation by the throat. Two nations, really: the Soviet Union and Canada. American fans, deprived of TV coverage of the event, never knew what they were missing.

Millions of current-day Canadian fans were too young to experience the gut-wrenching emotion produced by that series, one that lasted less than a month. On the final day, for the final game in Moscow, there were TV sets in every school classroom, in every office building and in every Canadian home. Nobody wanted to miss a word of play-by-play announcer Foster Hewitt's description of the most fascinating game in Canadian hockey history.

In the summer of 1972, it was upsetting for those of us on *Hockey Night in Canada* to learn that Eagleson and Leaf owner Harold Ballard controlled the TV rights to the series. Ted Hough, my boss at HNIC, obviously didn't view the forthcoming series to be of much importance. He put in a bid—a low one—that Ballard and Eagleson tossed in the wastebasket. CTV quickly picked up the rights, and of our *Hockey Night* crew, recruited only Foster Hewitt and Howie Meeker.

Hockey Canada hired me in a peculiar role: to act as a buffer between the government group and Al Eagleson's Team Canada group. It turned out that Eagleson didn't even know about my role, nor did he care what I did. He would run things his way, buffers be damned. It was obvious from the start that there was friction between the two camps, and that most of the Hockey Canada staff were cowed by Eagleson. As a result, Hockey Canada didn't demand much of me. I acted as master of ceremonies at a couple of luncheons and followed the series through the first four games. After the fourth game, I decided to bow out. I felt like a square peg in a round hole and was taking money I didn't feel was well earned, so I turned in my tickets to Moscow and went home. Looking back, I've often wished I'd gone along for the ride, like a lot of others did. I'd loved to have been in Moscow to see Henderson's series-winning goal.

Game eight in the series is the only game out of the hundreds I've seen that really gnawed at my emotions. Sitting alone in my living room, watching the opening ceremonies, somebody knocked on my door—a salesman, a Jehovah's Witness, I don't remember. "I haven't got time for this crap!" I shouted, slamming the door. "Don't you know there's a hockey game on?" Then the telephone rang—twice. A radio blared somewhere.

I lost it. I bolted from my chair, dashed out to my car and drove to the shopping mall about a mile away. Rushed into a bar and grabbed a seat near the TV set. Watched the entire game from there, cursing all salesmen and telephones.

Childish? You bet.

In the beginning, Team Canada head coach Harry Sinden was cool—like all of us. Calm and collected, too—like all of us. But midway through game one, he was shocked—like all of us—when the Soviets outscored and outplayed the NHL's best players in the Montreal Forum.

I sat in a rinkside seat—three rows up, next to an American women's golf pro who was watching her first hockey game ever. She appeared to be awed by the fan reaction on every play. I heard some-one tell her, "The Russians have no chance."

Even Bobby Orr, who was injured and could not play in the series, was not impressed with the Soviets. Earlier that day, I sat with Bobby high in the stands at the Forum and watched the Soviets work out. They peppered goalie Vladislav Tretiak with shots from close range and Bobby nudged me. "See that?" he said. "They fire away from too close in. Our goalies would scream at us if we did that."

Young readers may not understand why old men maintain such an interest in the Canada–Soviet series. They might ask, "Why all the fuss over games played in 1972? It wasn't for a world title or Olympic championship, was it? The Stanley Cup wasn't at stake. How come it became such a big deal?"

Well, it simply *was* a big deal. Kids today can watch such multi-talented Russian stars as Evgeny Malkin and Alex Ovechkin play in the NHL. In 1972, Russian players, then called Soviets, were thought to be second-rate—utter amateurs. NHL observers scoffed at their porous goaltenders, their ragged equipment, their hand-me-down skates. But at least they were smart enough to wear helmets—Team Canada play-ers, except for Paul Henderson, did not. And both teams wore "old-fashioned" tube skates. The Tuuk blade had not yet been invented.

Canadians smiled when they heard that the Soviets had learned much about hockey strategy from a book written by Lloyd Percival, a cigarette-puffing Canadian fitness guru. Percival had never been on any NHL team's payroll. He was thought to be a trainer and a track and field man—not a hockey man. The Russians thought he was a marvel, a genius. And perhaps he was. How would Canadians know?

Decades later, players on Team Canada spoke with me about the roller-coaster series and the emotional impact it had on them.

Dennis Hull quipped, "A DVD of the series was released last year. I'm afraid to look at it. I'm afraid the Russians will win."

HARRY SINDEN

I asked Harry Sinden, who had once played on the Whitby Dunlops, a senior team that defeated the Soviets for the 1959 World Championship, to reminisce about the horrible start and the dramatic finish to that memorable series.

I still shake my head in disbelief when I think of how we were humiliated 7–2 in the opener at the Montreal Forum, especially after we fired two shots past Tretiak in the opening minutes of play.

Probably the first high moment of the series for me was Peter Mahovlich's short-handed goal in Toronto in game two. Coming off the mauling we suffered in game one, that spectacular goal by Pete helped us to a victory at Maple Leaf Gardens. It was a goal I'll never forget in a game we urgently needed to win.

The absolute lowest moment in the series was the defeat we suffered in Vancouver. That loss was a shocker because we seemed to lose not only our poise but also our fans. And that was a real blow to everyone.

After that loss, I knew Phil Esposito was out there on the ice, giving an interview on television. But I had no idea it was such an emotional speech. I didn't get to hear it until I got back to the hotel and watched it on TV. I was moved by it, like I think most Canadians were. Phil was just dripping with sincerity—and perspiration. I think Phil's honest, straightforward appeal contributed greatly to us not losing the faith.

Fortunately, we had a week in Sweden to regroup and forget the Vancouver debacle.

Another satisfying moment for me as coach came after the first game we played in Moscow—even though we lost the match. Every player on Team Canada knew it was the best game we had played to that point. It looked like we were every bit as good as the Russians were—perhaps even a bit better—so that gave us a lift even though we lost.

With all the star players I had to work with, and there were thirty-five of them, putting lines together was like a bit of a lottery. You luck out or you don't. In the case of the Clarke–Henderson–Ellis line, I really did luck out because frankly I didn't know where to go with Bobby Clarke. He was just a kid with diabetes and he ended up centring those two. It turned out he had everything we wanted. On right wing, Ronnie Ellis was such a tremendous all-around player and Paul Henderson, on left wing, scored all those big goals. It was a line with balance that was almost magical.

Henderson and Phil Esposito were two players you could single out for five stars. Paul was the guy who scored the goal of the century, the guy who scored the most goals in the series, and to have him representing that team in admirable fashion since the end of the series to this day, has been another slice of good fortune for that wonderful group.

I loved working with John Ferguson. I wanted him to play for Team Canada and he said no, he'd prefer to stick to the coaching. He was invaluable in that role. I know the players all respected him and that helped me immensely.

As for those players who grew frustrated and decided to leave the team in Moscow, there was little anger or resentment toward those who packed up and left. A couple who left us, like [Gilbert] Perreault and [Richard] Martin, were quite young and perhaps felt, rightfully, that their chances of playing a lot in Moscow were rather slim.

The late Gary Bergman was an unsung hero who played the best eight games of his life in the series. Bill White was another one we could always count on. (Author's note: Without NHL expansion in 1967–68, White would not have played for Team Canada. He was a career minor leaguer for seven seasons in Rochester and Springfield. Only after the NHL expanded to twelve teams did he become a star with the Los Angeles Kings and Chicago Blackhawks.)

At least half of our defencemen had Hall of Fame potential: [Brad] Park, [Serge] Savard and [Guy] Lapointe were certainties even at that time. I'm sure our goaltenders, Ken Dryden and Tony Esposito, have some strong memories, both good and bad, of that series. They were two of the finest netminders in the world, but neither of them had ever played against a team like that. I really don't think that either Ken or Tony played up to the form they had consistently displayed in the NHL. I don't mean to imply that they were really off form or really bad, but facing facts, the Russians had the outstanding goaltending and we didn't.

Tretiak's superb goaltending greatly surprised me. We didn't know anything about him until we received a scouting report stating that he wasn't very good. But wasn't he fantastic against us? And only twenty years old.

The refereeing over there was atrocious. The official who was supposed to referee the final game, a Swede, suddenly bowed out. He said he was sick and we were told an East German referee was going to handle the game. John Ferguson became so furious with the change that he threatened not to play the game. When we tried to reason with Fergie, he said, "You'll have to go through me." And he was talking to us, his own people. He was so livid over the fact that they were manipulating the refereeing; Ferguson said flat out, "We're not playing." I recall saying to him, "Now, wait a minute, Johnny . . ." and he turns on me and all the officials and shouts, "What do you mean, wait a minute? If I say we're not playing, we're not playing." I'll tell you, that raised a few eyebrows. I hate to think what might have happened if one of the group had challenged him, like asking him to step outside and settle things.

I like to describe that great event like a really fine wine, one you savour and recall decades later. The taste just never goes away.

The thrills, the passion, the stunning surprises of that roller coaster ride in '72 caused our emotions to just run wild, not only among the players but among the fans who alternately supported us and critiqued us. And in the end, they roared their approval of us and loved us when we came home.

Looking back, I can recall almost everything that happened on each and every day during that time, from the shocking setback in Montreal to the riveting final seconds in Moscow. Some of the moments are clouded, but no other event in my entire life can I remember as clearly, and as fondly, as that one.

JOHN FERGUSON

There was one player on the Soviet team who really ticked me off: Boris Mikhailov. I couldn't stand him. He kicked Gary Bergman and tried to intimidate some of our guys. He skated past our bench and I let him have it. I didn't throw a punch at him, but I'd have liked to. I called him a dirty name and they gave us a bench penalty.

Paul Henderson was the ideal guy to score the winning goal for us in Moscow. Some people have mocked him for his born-again Christianity, but I look on him as a model citizen, a guy who has time for everybody and a guy who never showed a big ego. Paul has handled the hero's role really well.

When I came back from Moscow, I had a prized possession with me: a souvenir hockey stick that was signed by a lot of the players on both teams. I had it under my arm, and when Prime Minister Pierre Elliot Trudeau met us when we left the plane, Serge Savard pulled the stick away from me and said, "Look what John Ferguson brought you, Mr. Prime Minister." And much to my amazement, Trudeau accepted it. Years later, Pierre sent me a letter saying he realized it had been a prank and he would return the stick. I told him to keep it.

PAUL HENDERSON

Often you'll hear me tell people, "I'm the only guy who played pro hockey for eighteen seasons and scored just one lousy goal." It usually draws a laugh.

Still, it was a goal that people can't forget. They want to talk to me about it. Every day, someone will mention it. They want to shake my hand. Today, it happened at a hotel. Yesterday, it happened a couple of times at a golf tournament. A lady rushed over and said, "Mr. Henderson, I think your goal meant more to my husband than when our children were born." And for me to discuss the goal, well, it's become a part of my life.

How has it affected my life? Well, obviously it has. That goal in '72 has endeared me in the hearts of Canadians and given me a small niche in the psyches of Canadians. I am, and forever will be, identified with that goal, even though—and this may surprise you—it may not compare with some of the other blessings I've been granted in my life.

Obviously, the spiritual dimensions of my life have perhaps given me a different perspective on such things as game-winning goals and allowed me to understand how fortunate I am, not to be just Paul Henderson, the goal-scorer who, at twenty-eight, helped win a long-ago memorable series. I'm thankful to be blessed with other attributes, and (hopefully) I've been able to make a few other worthy contributions to my fellow Canadians, too.

So you can see that scoring "The Goal," while high on the list, is not the most important thing that ever happened to me. But I must admit it was a great feeling to be in the right place at the right time—and put that puck in the net.

As for my memories of '72? Oh boy.

I remember scoring the winning goals in game six and seven, and while everyone talks about the goal I scored to win game eight, I call the game-seven winner absolutely the best goal I ever scored in my life. It was a one-on-two situation—me against a pair of Soviet defencemen. Somehow I slipped by them both—beating two defence-men is a hockey rarity—and I scored on Tretiak.

I remember the final game, with twenty minutes to play and Team Canada trailing 5–3. And despite the deficit, everyone in the dressing room was confident and upbeat. The thought of losing didn't cross any of our minds.

In the final seconds of that game, I stood up at the bench and called Pete Mahovlich off the ice. I'd never done such a thing before. I jumped on and rushed straight for their net. I had this strange feeling that I could score the winning goal. I had a great chance, but [Yvan] Cournoyer's pass went behind me. I was tripped up and crashed into the boards behind the net. I leaped up and moved in front, just in time to see Esposito take a shot at Tretiak from inside the face-off circle. The rebound came right to my stick and I tried to slide the puck past Tretiak. Damn! He got a piece of it. But a second rebound came right to me. This time, I flipped the puck over him.

There was instant elation. Cournoyer was the first player to reach me and embrace me. Then all the players were there. And I remember thinking of my dad, who had passed away in 1968. I remember wishing he could have been there to see that goal. The final thirty-four seconds ticked away and we'd won the most gruel-ling, up-and-down series any of us had ever played in.

The Russians had a multitude of skills. In Winnipeg, they decided to go with their kid line, and we felt we'd show these young Russians kids a thing or two. Well, that line beat the snot out of us.

Playing on Team Canada was a wonderful opportunity for me. Had they picked only twenty or twenty-two players, Paul Henderson would not have been invited to camp. But when it went to thirty-five players, I really felt that I would get invited. And thank goodness that I was.

My good friend Ronnie Ellis was also invited because we had played on a line together in Toronto. In camp, there were seven lines made up of twenty-one forwards. That's a lot of talent.

So Ellis and I decided the one centreman we didn't want was Bobby Clarke. Bobby Clarke was not a household name then—and he was suspect because of his diabetes. But Bobby Clarke turned out to be one of the most dedicated great hockey players that ever played the game. He was terrific. We were the only line that played together in all eight games in that series. And the media began calling us Canada's best line.

When I came back to Canada, I was placed on a pedestal by the whole country. It was incredible. They gave me a car and golf clubs. I was at a stop light one day and a guy in the car two lanes over recognizes me. He gets out of his car and runs over and says, "Paul, I want your autograph." I said, "Hey, there's guys behind us." The light changed and guys behind start beeping their horns and he's saying to them, "Shut up, it's Paul Henderson, I'm getting his autograph." I mean, it was ridiculous.

In my early years in the NHL, I felt that I had everything that I had ever set out in life to accomplish. But deep down, there was restlessness. And I could never seem to be content. I started to ask questions like, "What is the real purpose and meaning to life?" and I could never get any really solid answers.

I realized that I had worries and fears that troubled me. Real fears, like a fear of dying young. And feelings of anger and bitterness. I realized I was furious with the man who controlled my hockey life—Leaf owner Harold Ballard. I resented the way he treated his players.

Then I asked my wife, "Do you think there is anything after all of this?" And we weren't really sure. Fortunately, we grew up going to Sunday school and church and we heard the stories from the Bible. But I'd set all that aside. I was going to be a man's man. And there were no Mike Gartners, Laurie Boschmans, Ryan Walters, Keith Browns, Pinball Clemonses or Joe Carters around—none of these Christian athletes. I didn't know a single one. In fact, I didn't even think you could be a hockey player and a Christian at that time. So I was a little negative. But I started to look into it. I got a Bible, I read it once, and for the next few months I read the Bible through several times and I tried to look at the whole spectrum. And I came to believe there was a God in Heaven who loved me very much, who didn't want me to be discontented or disturbed or restless, who wanted my life to have purpose and meaning. I had become separated from God because of things I had done earlier in my life. And believe me, professional athletes, with acclaim and money, have an opportunity to lead fast-paced, irresponsible lifestyles with seldom a thought for the consequences of their actions. I soon learned from others, and from the Bible, the penalty for breaking God's rules and commandments is not a few minutes served in the penalty box, soon to be forgotten, but it can be as severe as eternal separation from God. I realized I didn't want that.

I can tell you scoring that goal in Russia, from an athletic standpoint, was the greatest thing to ever happen to me, but when I compare it to having the Lord as my saviour and walking with him at my side, even a goal as huge as that pales to insignificance.

PHIL ESPOSITO

It was really disappointing to hear the people boo us after the loss in Vancouver. And I tried to tell the country how we felt. On TV, I told the people I couldn't believe they were booing us. I told them the Russians had a good team and we were all trying our best. That we all agreed to play because we loved Canada. That's the reason we agreed to play.

We didn't really become a team until we got to Sweden. It happened in a cafeteria when Al Eagleson, John Ferguson and Harry Sinden came in and told us that they weren't going to let the wives come to Russia. Finally, I called a team meeting and we decided, "If the wives don't come over, we're not going to play." We all agreed at that moment that we would simply come home if the wives weren't included. Imagine the furor if that had happened. Eagleson panicked and said, "Listen, we've got to get the wives over here." I remember Harold Ballard saying, "Yeah, the wives will come over with mattresses strapped to their backs."

I'll always remember that first game in Russia. I was so damn nervous. The Russians gave us these stupid flowers in the pre-game ceremonies and I squeezed my flower so hard that I broke the stem. The whole world was watching when they introduced me. I stepped on the stem and fell flat on my ass. I'll tell you, that broke some of the tension. But the ironic thing was, [Leonid] Brezhnev was premier then, and when I looked up, I made eye contact with him. There's the Soviet premier staring right back at me. Everybody in the arena was laughing at my pratfall—everybody but him. His look was as cold as the ice I was sittin' on. So I put my hand to my lips and *smack*, I blew him a kiss. And he still didn't laugh. But the guy beside him did, and Brezhnev turned and gave him a look that almost paralyzed the poor guy. I said to myself, "Holy Christ, we may not get out of here alive."

We lost that game 5–4 after blowing a 4–1 lead. But nobody got down. I was proud of the way we played and I told the guys that was it, we weren't going to lose another damn game. We had finally come together, and if we played them ten more times we wouldn't lose a single game. And we didn't. They couldn't match our emotion. It was our kind of society against theirs, and man, that series turned into a war. I hated it over there.

BOB CLARKE

I was just twenty-two years old, the last player to be named to Team Canada. I never really thought I was going to play that much. Just being invited was a thrill—a huge honour.

I think there was a lot of arrogance on our part, with everyone feeling that we were going to beat the Russians eight straight games. Many of our players weren't in very good shape at the start.

There was an incident in game seven that drew a lot of attention. I gave Valeri Kharlamov a tap on his sore ankle with my stick and he missed the final game. When journalist Dick Beddoes asked me about it, calling my shot "a wicked two-hander." I simply told him, "Dick, if I hadn't learned to lay on a two-hander once in a while, I'd never have left Flin Flon."

Team Canada '72 is right at the very top of my hockey life. I always considered winning the Stanley Cup more important, but certainly, they're close to being equal.

ROD GILBERT

In New York, Rod Gilbert is still known as "Mr. Hockey"—although Wayne Gretzky and Mark Messier may have upstaged him in the past twenty years. He recalls being in the only fight in the series.

Yeah, I played all four games in Moscow, and I remember a fight I had with this big Russian—and I never was a fighter. I've got photos of Dennis Hull and Bill White laughing their heads off because I was underneath this big guy and I was yelling, "Get this big gorilla off of me!"

But we got the win and that was very emotional, very satisfying. They were doing all this shit to us over there. They even stole our food and our beer. Can you beat that, stealing a hockey player's beer?

BRIAN GLENNIE

The downside of the series for me was all the off-ice stuff. It was watching soldiers stepping on kids' hands when we were throwing gum to them off the bus. I remember the guys getting off the bus and walking out and giving the kids a pack of gum in front of the soldiers and telling them to take off with the gum. And seeing the soldiers in the stands not knowing how to control the Canadian fans—trying to get the cowbell away from them and the Canadians kept passing it around. It's just a different way of life over there. All the political stuff that they tried to do off the ice to upset us—it became almost bigger than the games, which was unfortunate.

A funny thing happened after we got back. My wife, Barbara, had a good friend who had relatives in a place about five hundred miles outside of Moscow. Her friend received a letter from her relatives over there, and she brought it over to our house and read it to us. Basically, what the letter said was that in the great hockey confrontation between Canada and Russia, Canada had lost eight games to zero! That showed how much they controlled the media. We were at the Canadian embassy one night and somebody showed us a picture of somebody lying on a park bench. I asked one of the embassy staff who could read Russian to explain it to me. And basically, it was a picture saying, "Why would you want to live in Canada where you aren't guaranteed a home? In Canada, you have to sleep on a park bench." It was a tremendous culture shock, seeing the various ways they tried to downgrade our way of life and upgrade theirs.

ED JOHNSTON

One thing I learned in '72 that I took with me as a coach and a general manager was never, never underestimate your opponent.

That was the number one mistake we made back then.

I think our pride and determination helped us a lot, especially in that final game. It was such an emotional win. I have never seen grown men cry like our guys did. For about ten to fifteen minutes after the final game in our dressing room, it was absolutely emotional. Everybody was in there crying. I've won Stanley Cups and seen some tears of joy, but never like that. We were all overcome, all exhausted, all just overjoyed. There was such an emotional feeling in that room after it was over—it was just amazing!

When we came back, we stopped in Toronto and Montreal. There were thousands and thousands of people waiting for us when we came in. The emotion when we got off the plane was just absolutely crazy. It was bedlam in both those cities. It's something that I'll never forget for the rest of my life. Even though I've won Stanley Cups, I don't think that kissing Lord Stanley's old trophy ever had the impact on me that the winning with Team Canada did that year.

FRANK MAHOVLICH

In the thick of the final-game battle, I was on the bench sitting beside my brother Pete. Peter wasn't aware of the commotion in the stands, until I said, "Peter, look! They got the Eagle." I saw these two soldiers dragging Eagleson from the stands. They had picked up Eagleson by his two arms and he was kicking and scratching and I was pointing this out to Peter. He asked, "Where?" and I said, "Right over there, by the penalty box." Without thinking, Pete just jumped up, ran over to the penalty box, jumped over the glass and got right in front of the soldiers. He raised his stick and hollered, "Let him go!" And they did.

When Eagleson was freed, he jumped right over the bench, slid across the ice and sat down beside me on the bench. I said, "Al, you're okay now." He was white as a sheet and speechless. All some people saw on TV was the finger salute Eagleson gave. Peter didn't see what started it, when Eagleson reacted to the delayed red light following our goal. He just took off to save Eagleson. (Author's note: The goal judge, who was also a referee, shrugged afterward and said, "Switch got stuck. Light not go on.")

Despite all our difficulties over there, I love Russia. I went back in 1999 for a reunion. We had a great time and they treated us superbly.

KEN DRYDEN

If I was nervous before game one in Montreal, by the time I reached game eight in Moscow my legs and stomach were just jelly. I tried to settle myself down, but it was almost impossible. But the game has a way of settling you down.

Then, in the eighth and deciding game, something that was simmering boiled over and exploded. J.P. Parisé, always a nose-to-the-grindstone kind of player, suddenly is seen swinging his stick at the referee, stopping just before contact. Rod Gilbert in a fight—that's not Rod at all. Harry Sinden throws a chair on the ice. Pete Mahovlich rescues Eagleson.

Then, in the final seconds, Henderson's dramatic goal. He wasn't even supposed to have been on the ice in those critical seconds. Neither was Esposito perhaps, for he was at the end of a long shift. He would say later, "There was no way I was going off. It's gonna happen and I want to be part of it when it does."

I've been very fortunate to have played on six Stanley Cup–winning teams in Montreal. But nothing in hockey ever brought me so low or took me so high. And nothing meant so much.

When it comes to championships, the stakes are always so high. That's why I worried about being the most hated person in Canada if

I turned out to be the goat in game eight in Moscow. And in hockey, the goalie is most likely to be the goat. Your deeds, whether hero or goat, stay with you the rest of your life.

A FEW WORDS ABOUT VALERI KHARLAMOV

When the question is raised, "Who's the greatest Russian hockey player of all time?" the name Valeri Kharlamov surfaces again and again.

Was he as talented as more familiar Russian stars, men like Sergei Fedorov, Pavel Bure and Evgeni Malkin? I believe he was. They became NHL stars, but Kharlamov did not only because he wasn't permitted to leave his country.

Kharlamov and his wife were killed in a car accident in Moscow in 1981.

I was writing about Kharlamov in Naples, Florida, a few months back, but the story lacked a little something. I didn't know Kharlamov the way I know many NHLers. So I left the story unfinished, closed down my computer and went to the beach, where I joined some people for coffee.

Out of nowhere, an attractive woman in a broad-brimmed hat took the empty stool next to me. None of us had seen her before.

I heard her talking to a fellow sitting across the table, and even though my hearing isn't good, within minutes I heard the name Kharlamov.

I turned instantly and asked her, "Are you talking about the famous Russian hockey player?"

"Of course," she answered.

"That's amazing," I said. "I was just writing about him. How did you know him?"

"I'm from Riga in Russia," she said. "He left his wife for me. We were lovers and best friends. But after seven years he returned to his wife. He loved his son passionately."

"And your name is . . . ?" I asked.

"I am Anna Berger. I live in Boston now."

She wrote a phone number on a scrap of paper (which, within days, I lost). "Call me if I can help you with your story. Valeri was idolized in Russia. When we went to the clubs with his hockey friends, he was always surrounded by autograph seekers. He was a wonderful man. And how people mourned when he and his wife were killed at such a young age."

"He was very much admired by Canadians, too," I tell her. "Many people recall his superb play in the series of 1972. We are thrilled to see him in the Hockey Hall of Fame."

She shook hands and said goodbye. We never saw her again. And I thought, 'How fortunate was that?' If she'd chosen another stool, another table, if she begun talking to anyone but the stranger across from her, I would never had heard the name Kharlamov, never been able to put my brief conversation with her in print.

Thank you, Anna Berger. I hope you'll surprise us with another visit one day soon.

When I returned to my computer, I was able to finish the story.

Born in 1948, Kharlamov sprang to world attention with his scintillating play for the Soviet Union in that unforgettable series in September 1972. He starred with the Central Red Army team for fourteen seasons and led his nation to eight world titles and two Olympic gold medals. He was inducted into the Hockey Hall of Fame in November 2005—the first Russian forward to be so honoured.

While Canada's Paul Henderson, who is not in the Hall of Fame, has worn the hero's mantle for over three decades as a result of his series-winning goal in 1972, it might well have been Kharlamov—had he not been injured—who delivered the clincher.

Philadelphia Flyer captain Bobby Clarke made sure the Soviet ace never got the chance. Clarke chased down Kharlamov in game six and sent him crashing to the ice with a vicious slash to the ankle.

"It was just a little tap," Clarke would say.

Henderson looks back on the slash and calls it "unconscionable." Henderson must have known he was violating an unwritten code when he spoke out against Clarke. The accused was not only a teammate but also a linemate. Hockey players rarely accuse men they've bonded with of anything. But Henderson felt strongly enough about Clarke's cheap shot to rip into him.

"It was the low point in the series," Henderson told hockey writer Bruce Arthur. "For a player to go out and deliberately take an opponent out, well, where's the sportsmanship in that? Clarkie was probably the only guy on our side who would do such a thing. To me, it's the same as shooting a guy in the hallway."

He compared it to a golfer taking a club and whacking another guy in the leg.

"But that's the way Clarke was as a player. That's been his trademark. It's only my opinion, but I don't think there's any place in hockey for that."

Most of the other Team Canada members are reluctant to speak of Clarke's actions. But at the time, in Moscow, they probably breathed a sigh of relief to learn that Kharlamov would not be back.

Henderson will remain forever a Canadian hockey hero. He scored the winning goal in each of the last three games in Moscow. When he poked the puck past Vladislav Tretiak with just thirty-four seconds left on the clock in game eight, to give Team Canada an amazing come-from-behind victory, he became one of the most revered players in the history of hockey.

The date was September 28, 1972.

GUESTING ON *BASIC BLACK*

Jordan says, "You brought back a lot of memories with the Team Canada chapter. It was an unforgettable series in hockey's rich history."

"In high school, history was one of my least favourite subjects," I say. "But hockey history really excites me. This next chapter features a lot of it, beginning with some Stanley Cup history and, more recently, the birth and death of the WHA."

For almost two decades, thousands of Canadians listened each week to the CBC radio show *Basic Black*, hosted by Arthur Black. Arthur had a good, long run at it—from 1983 to 2002. During those nineteen years he interviewed hundreds of people who told him fascinating stories. Arthur was a delight to listen to, and I considered it an honour to be invited on his program from time to time. The last time we talked was in 1990. In my case, of course, the topic was always hockey. In one of my first interviews with Arthur, he asked me about the game's early days.

Arthur: Brian, hockey seems so well organized now. There's not a lot of room for surprises. I guess you can't say the same about the game's early days of Stanley Cup play.

Brian: No, Arthur, some amazing things happened in early-day Stanley Cup play. In my hockey books, I've written a lot about Stanley Cup history. Here are some stories I recollect. There was a game in 1895 when Quebec lost and the fans were so infuriated over the referee's decisions, they chased after him at the final bell. They collared him and tried to drag the man back to the arena. They wanted him to declare the game had ended in a tie. Luckily, police arrived and rescued the poor chap.

In 1899, there was a referee named Findlay who handled a Cup game in Montreal between Montreal Vics and Winnipeg. He got so fed up with the actions of the players on the ice that he took off his skates and went home. Just packed it in. In the middle of a Stanley Cup game! There was no backup referee, so there was a long delay while officials chased after Findlay in a sleigh. They persuaded him to come back, but by then the fans and the players had dispersed, probably to the nearest watering hole.

Arthur: It would be pretty tough to get them all back, I suppose.

Brian: Arthur, getting hockey players out of bars has never been easy.

Arthur: Then there was a remarkable Stanley Cup series played in Winnipeg in 1902. Can you tell me about it?

Brian: The Toronto Wellingtons journeyed west that winter to play for the Stanley Cup and the series generated so much excitement in Manitoba that some people travelled hundreds of miles to Winnipeg hoping to get tickets to witness the action on the ice. For some, it was a vain hope because the Winnipeg arena seated only about three thousand fans. A huge mob gathered outside and scalpers negotiated openly, getting ten times the cost of a $3 ticket.

Several young men found a way to get in free of charge. One would pay admission. His pals would take up a collection to buy him a ticket. He would rush upstairs and open a small window. The others would use ladders "borrowed" from the nearby Hudson's Bay Company to sneak in, even though there were a lot of policemen up there supposedly watching for trespassers.

Arthur: They were probably watching the activities on the ice and had their backs turned.

Brian: Exactly. They were watching the players warm up and thinking of the $4 in pocket money they were receiving for keeping an eye on things.

Arthur: And the game itself?

Brian: First, it was played during a blizzard. The snow fell through cracks in the arena roof and formed little lines on the ice. The Winnipeg team came out for the warm-up wearing long, gold dressing gowns over their uniforms, although nobody seems to know why. In the middle of the game, the puck was lifted high in the air and somehow became lodged in the rafters over the ice. Well, the players all gathered below and threw their sticks up trying to knock it loose. The one whose stick finally dislodged the puck earned quite an ovation.

Arthur: They didn't have any spare pucks?

Brian: None close at hand, I guess. And back then, one puck was often good for sixty minutes. Arthur, let's talk about pucks for a moment.

Pucks have always been rather standard. The pucks they used in that Winnipeg series were the same size, shape and weight as they are today. Twenty-five years earlier, sometime before 1875, they used a ball in hockey games. One night, an arena manager in Montreal who was fed up with the ball bouncing crazily all over his arena, took a knife and pared the ends off until he fashioned a flat object, which somehow became known as a puck.

In the Winnipeg series, when the puck sailed over the low boards, which were only about a foot high, a fan catching it was expected to throw it back on the ice. There was no whistle and the play moved right along. But one Winnipeg fan broke the unwritten rule by grabbing the puck and putting it in his pocket, starting a hockey tradition that has carried on to this day.

Arthur: Perhaps the pucks weren't quite as sturdy then as they are today. Didn't you tell me once that a puck split in two during a Stanley Cup game?

Brian: I did, Arthur. It was during the Toronto–Winnipeg series that a Toronto player named Chummy Hill scored a goal with half a puck. Pushed a chunk of the puck into the net, the goal judge waved his flag and the referee declared it a goal—the only goal in Stanley Cup history that was scored with half a puck.

Arthur: So the final score was three and a half to two or something like that.

Brian: Or three to two and a half. Actually, Winnipeg took the series rather easily, so that goal wasn't a key to the outcome. Incidentally, one of Toronto's top players performed despite a case of scarlet fever. And their star player—Pussy Darling—was out with an injury. What a great name for a hockey player! The Wellingtons were mauled and suffered cuts and bruises and black eyes. One came out of the game with a dislocated collarbone.

Arthur: Didn't another Toronto player miss the series for another reason?

Brian: Yes, the Wellingtons had a teenage star whose father wouldn't let him make the trip to Winnipeg. His father said he was too young and that he'd be better off concentrating on his schoolwork.

Arthur: And wasn't there another Stanley Cup series played in Winnipeg that same season?

Brian: There was, Arthur. The series against Toronto was played in January. In March, a few weeks later, the Montreal AAA team arrived to challenge for the Cup. The temperature in Winnipeg when the visitors arrived was 62 degrees Fahrenheit. Workers inside the arena mopped the ice with blankets, trying to get the water off the ice. Winnipeg won the first game 1–0 over Montreal in this slush.

Back in Montreal, over five hundred fans jammed the Montreal Amateur Athletic Association gymnasium, where they had a direct line to the Winnipeg arena and got wireless reports on the scoring. Montreal fans were so eager to get the results that ten thousand of them stood in the streets waiting and watching for the newspaper bulletin boards to provide updates. Their enthusiasm was rewarded when Montreal won the Cup two games to one. Winnipeg hasn't won it since that season.

Arthur: Wasn't one of those turn-of-the-century teams raked over the coals for showing poor sportsmanship?

Brian: You're thinking of the Montreal Vics, Arthur. During the 1902 season, the Vics lost a game to a rival team and promptly filed a protest with the league. The Vics complained that the puck used in the match, supplied by their rivals, was not a new one. In fact, moaned the Vics, it was old and had several chips on its edges. "No wonder we lost the game," griped one of the Vics. Their protest triggered an avalanche of criticism because the action was absolutely unheard of. "Small, cheap, unsportsmanlike, an absolute absurdity" were some of the words used by reporters to describe the protest.

When the Montreal players took the ice in their next game against Quebec, the fans shouted "Puck, puck, puck" every time the Vics touched the disc. The verbal abuse so rattled them that they lost the game, a fact that delighted everyone in the stands. The next day, the Vics withdrew their protest.

Arthur: You mentioned reporters. What were conditions like for reporters who had to cover these playoff games?

Brian: The reporters sat in among the fans initially. Incidentally, one Ottawa reporter accused the Wellington players of smoking cigarettes on the bench during that series. Sometime after the turn of the century, a press box was installed in Dey's Arena in Ottawa, one that held, I believe, eight reporters. So press boxes came early. But there was no press box in the Winnipeg Arena in 1902. And I'm still trying to discover when penalty boxes made their debut. In 1902, penalized players simply sat on the low boards until the referee waved them back into the game.

As for getting game results to the public, in the January 1902 series, immediately following each game, a reporter in Winnipeg would phone a man named John Ross Robertson at the Toronto *Globe* office with the result. He in turn phoned the Street Railway Company and someone there would blast three times on a big whistle if Toronto had won the game and twice if Toronto had lost. I understand folks could hear that whistle all over Toronto.

And in Winnipeg, the local paper made hockey news front-page stuff. There were long write-ups about the players and the games themselves and in some papers, reporters wrote a play-by-play commentary of incredible detail. "Green won the opening face, passed it to Smith who shot on goal. Hill returned for Toronto, but was stopped at the goalmouth. Two players fell in the corner" . . . on and on it went for a hundred paragraphs.

Arthur: I suppose there were a lot of problems with communications in those days.

Brian: Indeed there were. Rabid hockey fans thought nothing of standing out in sub-zero temperatures on windy station platforms just to get the scores. In places like Brandon and Winnipeg, if the local team had gone east to play a big game or two, fans would stand for hours waiting for a telegrapher to shout out the scores. Cyclone Taylor told me this was quite common back then.

Arthur: Didn't your father have a part-time job similar to the telegraphers?

Brian: In Northern Ontario, my father, Leslie McFarlane, who was a Sudbury sportswriter in the '20s, once told me that it was his job to report on the out-of-town scores of the Sudbury games. He would run down to the local movie theatre in town and they would stop the show while he trotted on stage and announced, "Sudbury is leading 2–0 in the Soo, folks, first period just over." Then he would run over to the hotels in town and deliver the same news. And he'd repeat this process a couple of times a night. He got $5 a week for doing that.

Arthur: Really? Big money. But what about the Stanley Cup itself, Lord Stanley's famous trophy?

Brian: Arthur, Lord Stanley never saw a Stanley Cup game. He was our governor general in 1893 and he was recalled to England before the first big game was played in 1894 and won by the Montreal AAA. The Stanley Cup has been lost, hijacked, defaced and stolen. King Clancy kept it in his living room one summer and put cigar butts out in it. Harry Smith, another Ottawa player, stuffed it in his closet one spring, and when it came time to present it to another winner the next year, they couldn't find the trophy. Smith finally recalled what he'd done with it.

Arthur, I'm sure all of your listeners are familiar with the story—or perhaps it's more legend—of the Ottawa player who drop-kicked it into the Rideau Canal one night. Luckily, the canal was frozen over. Most fans have also heard the story of the Montreal players who left the Cup on a street corner when they stopped to fix a flat tire. That was in 1924.

Arthur: Did they engrave the names of the Cup winners on the trophy back then?

Brian: Almost from the beginning, Arthur. Sometimes the players themselves would scratch their names on the Cup. Ottawa's Rat Westwick even engraved his three-month-old son's name on it. One of the team owners put his wife's name on it. It's a wonder they didn't scratch graffiti on it.

In the mid-1960s, the NHL secretly hired a Montreal silversmith, a man named Petersen, to make an exact duplicate of the Cup. For quite some time, few people knew about this change. The NHL replaced the original Cup because it was getting old and brittle. So the old Stanley Cup is now tucked safely away in the Hockey Hall of Fame and the one you see on television during the playoffs is one of more recent vintage, a facsimile.

Arthur: So the original drop-kick dent disappeared. Brian, didn't I once hear a story about Guy Lafleur borrowing the Stanley Cup?

Brian: I'm sure you did. In 1979, Guy was at a victory party in Montreal after the Canadiens won the Cup. Without telling anybody, he threw the Cup in the trunk of his car and drove to Thurso, Quebec, the home of his parents. There, he placed it on the front lawn and people came from miles around to see the trophy and have their photos taken with it. And when Guy looked out the front window later in the day, he saw his young son Martin filling the Cup with water from the garden hose. That's when he decided that he'd better take the old mug back to Montreal.

Arthur: Nobody knew it was missing at the time?

Brian: Oh yes, they knew. Around the Montreal Forum, officials couldn't figure out what had happened to the Stanley

Cup and they were really upset. Needless to say, they were quite relieved when Guy showed up with it several hours later.

Arthur: Well, Brian, I guess it's a story that's still going on. We'll have to keep watching the Stanley Cup playoffs to see if there's more lore to add to your legends.

Brian: I'm sure there will be, Arthur.

A few months later, Arthur invited me back for another session. This time he wanted me to talk about the World Hockey Association, which was born in 1972 and folded in 1979 after providing the NHL with plenty of headaches during its seven-year run. Four of the WHA clubs—Edmonton, Winnipeg, Hartford and Quebec—joined the NHL.

The WHA was the brainchild of two American promoters, Gary Davidson and Dennis Murphy, who were ridiculed when their plans were first announced. "It'll never get off the ground," was the universal appraisal of the proposed circuit. The arrogance of the NHL owners cost them dearly. They lost many of their top players, including superstar Bobby Hull. They lost millions of dollars in legal battles with the new league. It was this intruder league, the upstart WHA, that Arthur and I chatted about.

Arthur: Brian, the WHA was a league that was supposed to be in competition with the NHL, but sometimes it seemed a little closer to a fly-by-night circus than anything else. The thing I remember about the WHA was the odd location of some of the original franchises. For example, we can't forget that Miami, Florida—that hotbed of hockey—had a franchise.

Brian: That's right—the Miami Screaming Eagles. They had no rink and they never played a game in Miami. They had one player, goalie Bernie Parent, who wound up winning Stanley Cups for the Philadelphia Flyers a couple of years later.

And how about Dayton, Ohio? Another charter member team that never got off the ground. So the WHA began in 1972 with twelve teams scattered around the country, and a lot of people thought the league would never be a threat, never be successful—including NHL president Clarence Campbell.

Arthur: What did a WHA franchise cost in those days?

Brian: Only $25,000. Gary Davidson and Dennis Murphy were the men who conceived the idea of a new league. They were football and basketball people. They said, "Let's do this crazy thing and start a rival hockey league and we'll charge twenty-five grand per franchise. There are bound to be a number of people out there who'll want to get in." They were right. There were a lot of people willing to throw $25,000 into the pot in order to grab a franchise.

Arthur: Of course, it is easy to laugh at the WHA now, but it's important to remember that a fellow with the number 99 on his back came out of the WHA.

Brian: Right, Arthur. Seventeen-year-old Wayne Gretzky was signed by Nelson Skalbania for his Indianapolis club. He even let Wayne write out the contract himself, in longhand, during an airplane flight.

What a huge coup that was, signing Gretzky. At least two NHL scouts—John McLellan of the Leafs and Jack Davison of the Blackhawks—went to see Gretzky play in the WHA and they both agreed that he'd never make the NHL. He was too frail, too skinny and not nearly robust enough. They were certain he'd buckle under the grind of the NHL. They both agreed that Gretzky would never make it. By the way, Arthur, Gretzky wore jersey number 20 with Indianapolis.

Arthur: To be truthful, the old NHL was kind of a stodgy organization, and I remember the WHA was flamboyant if nothing else.

Brian: Arthur, it had to be to attract attention, and the operators had to go after some of the big-name players in the NHL like Parent, Derek Sanderson and, of course, Bobby Hull. Nobody thought Bobby would ever jump to the Winnipeg Jets.

Hull was demanding $250,000 a year from the Chicago Blackhawks and the Hawks were reluctant to give him that kind of money. Meanwhile, his agent says, "Bobby, these guys in the WHA are bugging me every day. They really want you. What are you going to do?" Hull said, "Listen, get them off my back, will you? Tell them I want a million up front and $250,000 a year. That'll shut them up." Well, it didn't. His agent phoned back the next day and said, "Bobby, I can't believe it. They're up to $750,000 already. All the other owners are chipping in and they're going to cough up your million."

So Bobby got his million, plus $250,000 a year as player-coach in Winnipeg. Only when he was about to jump leagues did Chicago wake up. The Blackhawks finally got off their butts and said, "Now, Bobby, don't be silly. We'll pay you the $250,000." Bobby laughed and said, "Sorry, guys, it's too late. I'm already committed to Winnipeg."

The WHA tried all kinds of things to attract the fans. The league used red, blue and white pucks, but the pucks chipped rather badly. When André Lacroix, who became the league's all-time-scoring leader, went to Philadelphia, he agreed to let them lock him in a bank vault for several days as a publicity stunt.

Arthur: Didn't the WHA invent the post-game shootout?

Brian: Yes, the new league invented the shootout to eliminate tie games. If the score was tied at the end of three periods, there would be a ten-minute overtime period. After that, the players would line up and take shots—penalty shots, really—at the rival goaltenders. After one game, it took eighteen shots before the outcome was decided.

Arthur: And the league was responsible for bringing Gordie Howe out of retirement.

Brian: Yes, the Howes got involved in a big way. Gordie Howe had been retired from the Red Wings for some time. At age forty-five, he was in the Hockey Hall of Fame and thought to be far too old to even consider a comeback. Detroit management had given him a job in the Red Wing office with virtually nothing to do. Gordie thought it was demeaning. That's when his old buddy Doug Harvey, who was with the Houston Aeros, said to his boss, Bill Dineen, "Hey, why don't we get old Gordie down here? We'll draft his kids Mark and Marty, too. He'll jump at a chance to play with his two sons."

So Gordie got a chance to fulfill a lifelong dream, playing hockey with his boys. Gordie told me he arrived in Houston and a fan asked him how much air was in the average hockey puck. He said they didn't know much about hockey in Houston. In time, he was named president of the Aeros—pro hockey's only playing president—and, within a few years, the game's only playing grandfather. He was still going strong at age fifty-one.

Twice, he scored a hundred or more points in the WHA. (Author's note: One of my biggest thrills in broadcasting was being invited to present the first NHL Lifetime Achievement Award to Howe at the NHL Awards show in 2008.)

John Tonelli was a rookie forward with the Aeros when Howe was there. Tonelli was sitting next to him on the bench one night when Gordie leaned over and wiped his runny nose all over the sleeve of John's jersey. Tonelli told me there was snot everywhere. But he didn't utter a peep—I mean, this was Gordie Howe.

One of Gordie's sons was involved in a fight one night, and an opposing player threw him to the ice and held him there. Gordie skated over and said, "Let him up." When the player refused, Gordie reached down, hooked two fingers in the man's nostrils and pulled him to his feet, howling like a coyote.

Arthur: Who were some of the other WHA players whose names we'll recognize?

Brian: Well, there was Dave Keon, Gerry Cheevers and Norm Ullman. Mike Gartner in Cincinnati, Frank Mahovlich in Birmingham. Marc Tardif and Réjean Houle in Quebec. And a couple of kids named Gretzky and Messier starting out in Indianapolis.

The Leafs allowed Bernie Parent, a great young goalie, to leave their organization. He fled to Miami, where he was promised a yacht, plus a lot more money than Harold Ballard was willing to pay him.

Mike Walton was a big WHA scoring star. Led the league with 117 points one season. Harry Neale coached him in Minnesota. Harry told me once he looked down the bench and was shocked to see Walton engaged in a fist fight—with one of his own teammates. Right on the bench! Harry said he'd never seen anything like it. When the referee rushed over, Harry said, "You can't give them a penalty. They're both on the same team." They were banging away at each other and when Harry got them apart, he said, "You guys get out there and play on a line." He said they played pretty well together, too.

Another time, Harry's team was practising in Winnipeg, and next to the practice rink was a swimming pool separated from the rink by huge windows. When the Fighting Saints left the ice, they looked up to see Walton on the high board in his full hockey uniform. He leaped off the board and did a big belly flop into the pool. But he nearly drowned when the weight of his equipment dragged him right to the bottom.

Arthur, you might want to take a grain of salt with that story. And another grain or two with the next one.

One night, Walton was so upset over a losing effort that he skated right off the ice in the final seconds. Instead of going to the dressing room, he dashed through the back door and into the parking lot. Then he hopped into his car and disappeared into the night. One of his teammates said later he found Walton at a nearby bar, tossing them back—still dressed in his hockey uniform. It's one of those hard-to-believe stories, but that's what I was told.

Arthur: Harry Howell, a Norris Trophy winner with the Rangers, played in the league, didn't he?

Brian: Played *and* coached. Harry was player coach for the Jersey Knights, which had been the New York Golden Blades and later became the San Diego Mariners. Harry told me his team in New Jersey was always short of cash because attendance was so poor. When the team went on a road trip right after a game, Harry would run into the box office, scoop up all the money that was in the till, throw it in a brown paper bag and then divide it up amongst the players on the trip. Sometimes Harry had enough to cover the players' meal money, sometimes he didn't.

Arthur: Didn't the new league soon become renowned for some bizarre hockey "firsts"?

Brian: Yes, Arthur. Many of them occurred during the initial season of the WHA's existence. For example, the Philadelphia Blazers called a news conference to announce the signing of Fred Creighton as coach. But Creighton changed his mind at the last minute and didn't show up. The team then announced the signing of Murray Williamson as general manager, but he quit on the day the announcement was made. Williamson's successor, Dave Creighton, showed only slightly more dedication to the position. He stayed around until the team went 1–8 before he resigned. By then, playing coach John Mackenzie had also thrown in the towel. He was replaced by Phil Watson.

The Minnesota Fighting Saints gave a tryout to Fern Tessier, just out of prison after serving an eleven-year term. Tessier didn't make the team.

Rocket Richard agreed to coach the Quebec Nordiques, but after two games, retired. He told reporters, "The pressures of coaching aren't for me."

The Los Angeles Sharks opened their first season at home on Friday the 13th against Houston. The pucks hadn't been frozen prior to the game and bounced around like rubber balls. And when the Zamboni driver flooded the ice at the intermission, black liquid oozed out from under the machine and covered a large patch of ice.

Players on the Sharks scrambled to score the first hat

trick in club history. They were told that a handsome reward awaited the scorer of the first three-goal game. When Gary Veneruzzo accomplished the feat, the club owner gave him two tickets for a trip to Hawaii.

Meanwhile, a family problem caused friction between manager and coach in Los Angeles. Manager Terry Slater of the Sharks was stunned when coach Ted McCaskill wanted to dump a player—Slater's brother. Manager Slater decided to take over as coach and McCaskill returned to the playing ranks.

Danny Lawson, who'd scored a mere ten goals with the NHL's Buffalo Sabres in the previous season, became the fledgling league's first fifty-goal scorer. The Blazers' Lawson scored number fifty against Ottawa on February 22.

Goalie Bernie Parent dropped a bombshell on the Philadelphia Blazers during a playoff series with Cleveland. Parent, on a five-year, $750,000 contract, claimed the Blazers had failed to deposit the final $100,000 in insurance on his salary. So he walked out on the team and refused to play. Without Parent, the Blazers were no match for the Cleveland Crusaders and were eliminated in four straight games.

Arthur: How long did the WHA exist?

Brian: From 1972 to 1979. It might never have existed at all if the NHL hadn't ignored it—even scoffed at it—in the beginning. NHL owners, and president Clarence Campbell, felt it would fail miserably. And when it survived, they did everything they could to squash it. When the WHA talked of placing teams on Long Island and Atlanta, where new arenas were constructed, the NHL quickly expanded into those markets.

When the Toronto Toros rented Maple Leaf Gardens for home games, Leaf owner Harold Ballard charged a whopping

$15,000 per game in rent. Then he wouldn't allow full lighting in his arena until the Toros coughed up another $3,500. After that, he forced the Toros to build their own dressing room—for another $50,000.

He even took the cushions off the players' benches and told Toro owner Johnny Bassett, "Buy your own bloody cushions." Bassett threw up his arms and moved his team to Birmingham.

In 1979, the WHA, reduced to six teams, was tottering and made peace with the NHL. Four clubs merged with the older league—the Edmonton Oilers, New England Whalers (renamed Hartford Whalers), Quebec Nordiques and Winnipeg Jets. Birmingham and Cincinnati were paid $1.5 million and told to go away. But it turned out to be more of an expansion than a merger because each club had to fork over $6 million to get in. And they had to return the players they'd lured away from NHL teams. The NHL allowed each incoming team to protect two goalies and two players. Wasn't that generous of them? NHL owners wanted to punish the upstart WHA teams, not welcome them. They wanted to keep them down. Think of how shocked they were when the Edmonton Oilers, under Glen Sather's guiding hand, soared to the top of the NHL in the '80s and won no fewer than five Stanley Cups. Many of the NHL teams may never win five Stanley Cups.

Arthur: Any final words on the WHA, Brian?

Brian: Yes, Arthur. The WHA may have been a crazy, mixed-up league, but it provided opportunity—and fair salaries—to hundreds of minor leaguers, ex-college players, NHLers who were not happy with their dictatorial managers and coaches, and perhaps most important, European players who finally were given a chance to display their abundant skills in North America. The Stastny brothers, Anders Hedberg, Ulf Nilsson, Václav Nedomanský all became household names in North America. The NHL had ignored this great talent pool for years.

A few years later, when Los Angeles Kings owner Bruce McNall went to jail for fraud and conspiracy, he wrote a book titled *It Was Fun While It Lasted*. It's a title that perfectly suits the history of the WHA.

MORE HOCKEY LETTERS

Jordan says, "You've filled a lot of pages. How much material do you have left?"

"I have more of those letters I mentioned. The one to Garry Unger will tug at your emotions. Do you know Unger scored 95 goals in his last season—in only 30 games?"

"You're kidding. I thought the NHL record was 92. Gretzky's record."

"It is—that's the NHL mark. Garry played his last season overseas—in Britain. He averaged seven points per game over there."

"Well, I wouldn't mind reading about him. We'll call this chapter 'More Hockey Letters.'"

TO GARRY UNGER

Dear Garry,

It's been a long, long time since I last talked with you. Twenty years, maybe. We don't see enough of you anymore. Although I did see you talking hockey on an Internet clip a few days ago. Everything you ever wanted to know about hockey is on the Internet.

You've aged well, Garry. You would be a good subject for a hockey series called *Where Are They Now?*

Garry, you enjoyed a long and productive career in the NHL and I can't help wondering if the Hockey Hall of Fame selection committee has you on their short list.

I would think so. You scored 413 career goals and 804 points. Surely you've wondered about it. You outscored Hall of Famers like Cam Neely (395), Ted Lindsay (379), Boom Boom Geoffrion (396), Dave Keon (396), Bobby Clarke (358) and Clark Gillies (319).

Too bad your first NHL team, the Toronto Maple Leafs, couldn't have seen your potential. They traded you to Detroit when the NHL expanded to twelve teams—after only fifteen games and before you really established yourself.

Detroit foolishly traded you to St. Louis in 1970–71—mostly because manager Ned Harkness didn't like the cut of your hair. Your shoulder-length locks irked him. Perhaps he didn't like you dating Miss America. So he sent you to the Blues, along with Wayne Connelly for Tim Ecclestone and an aging Red Berenson. What a steal for the Blues! You scored thirty goals or more in each of your eight full seasons with the Blues.

You played one season for Atlanta, and that's where you set the NHL record for most consecutive games played—914.

I was bitterly disappointed when the streak ended. And I was most surprised when you told me how it ended. Your streak began on February 24, 1968, and came to an abrupt end in St. Louis on December 21, 1979. By then you were with the visiting Flames. There was no valid reason for the streak to end that night. Shame on your coach, Al MacNeil, for arbitrarily deciding it had to come to a close.

To this day, I can't comprehend why MacNeil acted as he did during that game. He mumbled something about the streak becoming a distraction to the team. That's nonsense. You dressed for the game against the Blues. You were healthy enough, and yet you sat on the bench well into the third period.

Finally, the St. Louis fans caught on. They remembered the many splendid seasons you had enjoyed with the Blues, and when they realized you hadn't taken a single shift, they became boisterous. They hollered, "We want Unger! We want Unger!" MacNeil shrugged and turned a deaf ear to their pleas.

Then your Atlanta teammates became agitated. "Go out for me, Garry," a couple of them urged you as they came to the bench.

But you said, "No, guys, I can't do that." You stayed put, even though you were itching to keep the streak alive. Most people didn't know that the streak meant much more to people around you than it did to you. You could cope with its termination, but you worried how it would affect your sister, who suffered from a debilitating disease and could not walk. She cheered your every goal, was thrilled to see you reach milestone after milestone—200, 300, 400 goals, and all those consecutive games. She was overjoyed to know her brother was the NHL's iron man. She hoped the streak would go on forever.

MacNeil's determination to end it showed clearly in that third period. Late in the game, there was a scuffle in front of the Atlanta bench. Sticks flew high as players slammed into each other. Instinctively, you jumped up to avoid the flying lumber.

That's when you felt the strong arm of Al MacNeil on the back of your jersey. Fearing that you were going to jump over the boards, he clutched the back of your shirt and hauled you back down. How humiliating was that, Garry?

The game ended and the streak was over.

Now Doug Jarvis rules as the NHL iron man. He finished his career with 964 consecutive games. If it weren't for MacNeil, you'd be the record holder, Garry. I'm sure of it. You played the rest of the 1979–80 season and another 163 games before you retired.

Then you journeyed overseas and set some astonishing marks in a league in England and Scotland. With Dundee, in a mere 35 games, you scored 86 goals and 98 assists. The following season, with Peterborough, you clicked for 95 goals and 143 assists for 238 points in only 30 games. That's an average of three goals and seven points per game. It doesn't matter that this league was a long step down from NHL hockey. It's still hockey, with guys double-teaming you to keep you off the score sheet. And you dominated! Not a bad way to finish a career.

Garry, I'll never forget a conversation we had in a hotel lobby in Edmonton one day. You were winding down your NHL career with the Oilers and you told me the tragic story of your close friend Bob Gassoff. My tape recorder picked up your words.

Bob and I were teammates in St. Louis and he had blossomed into one of the NHL's premier defencemen. He was a fierce competitor, the toughest player I ever saw. My, how he could hit and fight. There was no more dedicated player in hockey and we became very good friends.

In 1977, our team was eliminated from the playoffs and I decided to hold a postseason barbecue at a farm I'd bought outside St. Louis. Bob and his wife, Diane, who was pregnant, were there, as well as a lot of other players and friends.

It was Memorial Day weekend and we had some motorcycles on the property and some of the boys were having fun riding them. I cautioned the boys not to ride them on the road skirting the property.

Before long, we ran out of mix for the drinks and one of the boys volunteered to drive to the local store and get some more. Bobby decided to go with them, but he didn't tell me he was going. I was a little worried about Bobby because he was not an experienced cyclist and he wore no helmet and there was no licence [plate] on his motorcycle.

I was in the kitchen helping out, unaware that he'd decided to go to the store with the others. Then came the phone call. Somebody was screaming hysterically, "Garry! Garry! There's been a big accident. Bobby's dead. Bobby's dead!"

I went into total shock. Bobby's wife was right there in the kitchen.

I was told that Bobby was speeding down the road on his bike when he pulled into the other lane and shot over a hill. He ran headfirst into a vehicle coming the other way, driven by a man named Douglas Klekamp. Bobby's bike went right over the hood and he flew through the windshield of the oncoming vehicle. One of his legs was completely severed. He was killed instantly.

Mr. Klekamp was able to walk away, relatively unhurt. But one of the boys who saw it happen ran to a field where he was violently ill.

It was the worst day of my life by far—a devastating day. I'll never get over it. I loved Bobby Gassoff.

There were lawsuits, of course. Diane said her lawyers insisted on suing me for $3 million, although she said she hated to do it. It was settled months later, with Diane receiving several thousand dollars. But no amount would ever make up for her loss.

Bobby Junior was born a few weeks later and, while he never knew his dad, he grew up to be a fine player. He skated like his dad and played like his dad. He was an excellent collegiate player at Michigan, where he played for coach Red Berenson, a former teammate of Bobby's in St. Louis. After college, Bobby Jr. served his country as an officer in the Navy Seals.

Bobby Sr. was a strong, aggressive player, a great team player. And yes, he had a bit of a temper.

Someday, if he hasn't heard about it already, Bobby Jr. will chuckle about the time his dad took on a Zamboni during a game. It happened during the 1973–74 season and the referee gave Bobby a game misconduct penalty for some reason. Bobby was so upset he flailed away at the Zamboni, which was coming on the ice. He left it with two broken headlights and numerous dents. There were stick marks all over it. There's never been anything like that in hockey. I smile every time I think about it.

After Bobby died, the Blues went into a slump. The following season, we really missed his leadership. We finished out of the playoffs for the next two years. Shortly after his death, the Blues retired Bobby's number 3—the first St. Louis player to be so honoured. Bernie Federko called Bobby "irreplaceable." And he was. Longtime fans there still talk about him.

Looking back, I feel that Bobby's sudden death played a major role in my decision to embrace God and devote much of my life to Christian beliefs. I am much like Laurie Boschman in that respect.

There was a game in Edmonton one night—the Oilers against the Winnipeg Jets, and Laurie was one of the best of the Jets. I knew it would be my role to check him in the game. Despite our beliefs, we both played the game hard— very aggressively. I was terribly worried that when Laurie and I clashed, there might be trouble. A fight, an injury, whatever. So I prayed to God for guidance, to help me get through the game without incident.

Early in the game, there was a brawl at one end. I jumped in and was flailing away when someone hit me and I went down hard. Separated my shoulder. The trainers helped me off the ice, not knowing I was murmuring, "Thank you, God. Now I won't have to worry about tangling with Laurie Boschman tonight."

I hope you are doing well, Garry, and I hope someday we'll meet again. I've always regarded you as a very classy individual.

TO BOOM BOOM GEOFFRION

Dear Boom Boom,

When the Montreal Canadiens retired your famous jersey (number 5) prior to a March 11, 2006, game in Montreal, what a shame you weren't there to be part of the ceremony. It was such an honour.

How sad we all were to learn you had passed away from stomach cancer just five hours before the ceremony. Five hours!

Had the ceremony been planned for a game earlier in the season, Boom, you probably would have been able to attend. But the organizers selected the March 11 date because the Rangers were in town, the team you played for and coached after you left the Habs. What's more, the date coincided with the sixty-ninth anniversary of Howie Morenz's jersey retirement by the Canadiens. I wonder how many fans know that the great Morenz was your father-in-law (you married his daughter Marlene). I see Howie Jr. quite often at our monthly Oldtimer luncheons in Toronto.

Bernie, how difficult it must have been for your family to attend your jersey-retirement ceremony in Montreal while you were suffering through your final hours in Atlanta. But to have them there at the Bell Centre was your unselfish final wish.

Bernie, I saw you play many times when he you were at your peak, during the 1950s and '60s. You won the Calder Trophy as rookie of the year in 1952 and captured two Art Ross Trophies as the NHL's scoring champ. And you were a tower of strength for the Habs when they tasted champagne from the Stanley Cup for five straight seasons, from 1956 to 1960—still an NHL record.

How incredibly hurt you must have been when Montreal fans booed you after you captured the scoring title in 1955. In the long history of hockey, no scoring champ has ever been booed by his hometown fans. Never. But Hab fans are more rabid than most. They resented you, and booed you, because you grabbed the scoring title away from your teammate Rocket Richard by a single point—on the final day of the season.

Oldtimers like me are well aware that Richard had been suspended for the final few games of the season—and all of the playoffs—following a stick-swinging incident in Boston. The suspension cost the Rocket what would have been his first scoring crown. But what did the Montreal fans expect you to do in those final few games—shoot wide of the net, make bad passes so that you'd earn no assists? Sit out those games?

It was terribly unfair of them to boo you. It wasn't your fault, Boom. The Rocket's fierce temper and loss of self-control cost him, and his team, dearly that season. His suspension—unduly harsh, perhaps—cost him his final chance at a scoring title. And it may have cost his team the Stanley Cup, which was won by Detroit that spring.

The Rocket was so beloved by his fans that they went on a wild rampage after his suspension. On March 17, 1955, when fans rioted during a game at the Forum and the match was awarded to Detroit, they went berserk outside the arena, destroying private property to the tune of $1 million worth of damage.

The Rocket was both a victim and a martyr. And you, Bernie, through no fault of your own, became a whipping boy, a villain, as was NHL president Clarence Campbell, who was vilified for suspending the Rocket. There has never been such an emotional ending to any NHL season as that one. You must have been seething with anger and frustration.

Over the years, people have asked me how you earned your famous nickname "Boom Boom." I tell them you earned it in junior hockey, after you displayed a slapshot that terrified goaltenders. One "Boom" was for the moment your stick struck the puck; the second "Boom" was for the sound it made when it smacked into the boards.

I tell them of the time you almost died during a practice at the Forum—how you collided with a teammate, skated a few strides and keeled over. The team doctor couldn't find a pulse and heaved you upside down until you began to breathe again. They rushed you to the hospital, where an emergency operation removed a bowel obstruction and your life was saved. We were all cheered by your speedy recovery.

I know how hopeful you were to be named Montreal's team captain after Doug Harvey was traded to New York. And how depressed you must have been when Jean Béliveau was given the honour instead. People tell me that you were angry and bitter and cursed when the votes of your teammates were counted. Still, it's difficult to argue that Big Jean was not the ideal choice.

Boom, I want to thank you all these years later for being the first guest I had on the day we opened a new TV station in Montreal, CFCF-TV. I admit we tried to get the Rocket—our first choice—but he cancelled out at the last minute. You were quick to agree to join us, and I recall how you sparkled on camera.

Later, the Canadiens' management told me they would prefer us to have players interviewed on television in order of jersey numbers. In other words, Jacques Plante (number 1) should be our first choice, then Doug Harvey (number 2), etc. etc. I countered by asking, "What if Geoffrion scores five goals in a game and it's Phil Goyette's turn to be interviewed?"

I was told, "You can find something to ask Phil Goyette about, can't you?"

It was a short-lived, ridiculous policy, but that's how much clout the NHL teams had in those days.

Bernie, I know you'll never forget the night of March 16, 1961, and neither will I. There was great excitement at the old Montreal Forum. Fans eagerly awaited your performance that night against the Toronto Maple Leafs and goaltender Cesare Maniago. You had scored a remarkable number of goals over the last ten games to pass Frank Mahovlich, who finished with forty-eight, and you were within one goal of tying Rocket Richard's elusive mark of fifty goals in a season. By this time, the fans were back on your side, cheering you on.

At the TV station, I dispatched a cameraman to the Forum with orders to film your every move. If you scored, we would have your historic goal featured on our late night sportscast. This was in an era before video cameras; 16-mm film was traditionally used.

The cameraman situated himself right in the crowd and dutifully shot several hundred feet of costly film, following your every shift, your every stride.

In the third period—do you remember?—you almost scored, ringing one off the goalpost with a blast, and the fans leaped to their feet. One of them struck my cameraman on the hand, bruising his knuckles. The cameraman stopped shooting for a few seconds to nurse the minor injury, and while he was blowing on his knuckles, you scored goal number fifty.

In shooting film, as in shooting pucks, you win some, you lose some.

But the cameraman came up with a bright idea. "Look. There's film of Geoffrion almost scoring a goal. Maybe we could use that. Maybe the viewers will think they blinked and missed it."

And by golly, Boom, that's what we did.

You had colour, Boom. And you could sing, too. I remember when the CBC had you singing with Juliette. You were never shy or nervous when the cameras were running. You were like Eddie Shack or Tiger Williams in that regard. And the fans in Atlanta absolutely loved you when you coached the Flames and starred in those Miller Lite beer commercials.

I don't know why the Habs waited so long to honour you, to retire your famous jersey. It should have happened long before they closed down the Forum, where you established yourself as one of the best right wingers of all time. It should have happened when you were in good health—and in good voice. I can see you at centre ice, blowing kisses to the crowd, tears streaming down your cheeks, savouring the moment, knowing at last how much you were loved and appreciated.

The event would have been so much sweeter had you been there to hear the crowd chant your name and give you a standing O. But I'm sure you smiled that night, from your hospital bed in Atlanta, knowing your family was en route to represent you. Knowing you, Boom, you even winked at the nurses before you closed your eyes.

And perhaps you remembered a promise you made to your wife Marlene when you were courting her.

"Someday, Marlene," you told her, "Montrealers will cheer for me like they did for your father, Howie Morenz."

On that night they did, Boom. They cheered long and hard and every bit as loud.

TO ONE-EYED FRANK MCGEE

Dear Frank,

If you could ever see these words, you'd probably laugh and say, "Why would anyone writing about hockey in 2009 be curious about me? I played the game over a hundred years ago. And my career was brief—only three or four seasons. Let me remind you, I retired from hockey at age twenty-three."

Frank, I can assure you a lot of modern-day fans are interested in your hockey exploits. Some of your feats have never been matched. You were a turn-of-the-century Wayne Gretzky. You were often described as "the finest hockey player in the world" and "the greatest stickhandler who ever carried a puck down the ice."

There were others—family members, you had five brothers and two sisters—who pleaded with you to give up the game despite your success, because you had a disability that might have ended your career at any second. You had lost your sight in one eye.

Tragedy was never far from your family. Your brother Jim, a wonderful athlete, died as a result of a horse riding accident in 1904. By then you were hockey's greatest star. And you excelled in lacrosse and football, too. In 1898 you helped Ottawa win the Canadian football championship.

You began your on-ice career as a teenager at the University of Ottawa, and it wasn't long after that that you became the youngest and most popular star of the fabled Ottawa Silver Seven, the Stanley Cup champions.

One night, early in your career, an opposing player, his stick held high, smashed into you and knocked you unconscious. You were carried off the ice, bleeding from a deep cut over your eye. Surgeons tried to save the eye but the damage was too severe. As a result of that check, you became permanently blinded in that eye. After that you became known by your famous nickname: One-Eyed Frank McGee.

"Give up the game, son," pleaded your mother. "Another high stick and you could be blind in both eyes."

And you did give it up briefly. You tried refereeing for a spell. But the lure of competition was strong and you decided to return as a player. You were just as fast on your feet and as dangerous as ever with the puck. Or so it appeared.

In the years that followed, you set some amazing records. In a 1905 Stanley Cup game against Dawson City, you scored fourteen goals—eight of them in nine minutes—marks no player has ever tied or topped. You once scored eight goals in another game and five goals in a game on seven occasions. That's incredible. In one playoff match, wearing tape to protect a broken wrist, you scored the tying and winning goals for Ottawa in a Cup-clinching game. Reporters noted that you wore tape around both wrists that night to confuse opposing players, who would certainly have tried to slash you on the broken one.

As for that fourteen-goal game against Dawson City, my friend Paul Kitchen, in his recent book about Ottawa's hockey history, revealed how that famous record came about. Apparently, Colonel Joe Boyle, the manager of the Dawson team, knowing his club was overmatched after a 9–2 opening-game loss, pleaded with you and your mates to "take it easy" on his club in the second match. He had lined up several exhibition games following the Stanley Cup matches, and he worried about poor attendance if Dawson received a thrashing. Kitchen says you had had a previous run-in with Boyle and disliked him intensely. So you pumped in fourteen goals to exact some measure of vengeance. I'll accept Kitchen's research, but that doesn't sound like something you would do, Frank. You were known for your sportsmanship and not one to hold grudges.

Frank, your stats are truly incredible. During your career, you scored 71 goals in 23 regular-season games and another 63 goals in 22 playoff matches. No player, before or since, has averaged over three goals per game.

Eyewitnesses described you as "a small [five feet, six inches] but clean player who was idolized for your stylish play and your good looks." They say your white hockey pants were always freshly laundered and creased with an iron, like a man's Sunday-best trousers. "McGee was immaculately groomed," one observer wrote, "with his blond hair always combed neatly to one side."

You were a born leader, on and off the ice. When the First World War broke out, you were anxious to serve. Despite your visual handicap, you were able to join the Canadian infantry. You quickly rose from a private to the rank of lieutenant.

On September 23, 1916, in the middle of a fierce battle in France—the Battle of the Somme—an enemy shell ended your life. This was a few months after your brother Charles lost his life in battle. There was gloom throughout Ottawa and the rest of Canada at the news of your death. One of hockey's greatest heroes was gone at age thirty-three. People everywhere mourned your loss.

I phoned your nephew, the former MP Frank McGee, one day and he invited me to play golf with him. During the round, he explained how you were able to join the military while visually impaired. "My uncle read the eye chart with one hand over his blind eye. Then he switched hands and put his other hand over his bad eye and read the chart. The official on duty obviously didn't notice.

"The McGee family was very prominent in politics back then. Frank's uncle Thomas D'Arcy McGee, was one of the Fathers of Confederation, while Frank's father, Joseph, held the top civil servant's job in the government."

Frank, you were well aware of your uncle D'Arcy's stunning assassination in 1868, the first of several family tragedies. His murder was the first political assassination in Canadian history (there have only been two). The man convicted and hanged for the murder was a Fenian sympathizer named Patrick Whalen. To this day, some think he was wrongly accused.

"One-Eyed Frank was an ardent curler and golfer," your nephew told me. He was very proud of you and proud to inherit your name. "My uncle Frank was one of the first inductees into the Hockey Hall of Fame in 1945," he reminded me.

Frank, you might have lived a full, rich life had it not been for your qualities of loyalty, fraternity and patriotism. You suffered a knee injury a short time before the Battle of the Somme and were pulled from the front lines to be treated in England. You were offered a safe posting in Le Havre, France, far from the battlefields. But you told your officers you were anxious to get back to your battalion. You wanted to rejoin your mates on the front. You were determined to serve your country.

And so you returned. And that's where you fell, never to rise. Even today, almost a century later, Canadians everywhere thank you for your ultimate sacrifice.

TO GEORGE MORRISON

Dear George,
While you only played a few seasons with the NHL Oldtimers, George, you left us enough stories to last a lifetime. You seldom

talked about your college career, but seventy goals in two seasons at Denver University is really impressive.

I remember you talking about Scotty Bowman, who was your coach in St. Louis. Here's what you said into my tape recorder after a game one night.

Remember how Scotty suffered a serious head injury while playing junior hockey, and we all heard he had a metal plate in his head? We didn't know if it was true or not, so one day I cut out a big cardboard horseshoe, with a heavy magnet attached to one end of it, and I hung it over the dressing room door. That's where Scotty always stood when he made his pre-game speech. Well, Scotty came in this night and he was ticked off about something. "You so-and-sos had better do this, you better do that," he growled. You know, giving everybody shit . . .

And while he barked at us, the guys kept looking up at this big horseshoe right over his head—pasted up there. Could have come loose at any second. They just couldn't control themselves, couldn't stop laughing. Glenn Hall put his goal mask on to hide his laughter. The Plager brothers and Carl Brewer, who was with the team then, were just about falling on the floor laughing. And Scotty couldn't figure out what everybody was laughing at. And nobody was about to tell him. Finally, he stormed out and I breathed a sigh of relief. If he'd ever found out I tried to magnetize the plate in his head, he'd have sent me so deep in the minors I'd never have made it back.

Here's another one. You should have been there the night Scotty called me a dog. That's right. He said to me, "Hey, Morrison, you are a dog!" And then he started barking at me, "Ruff, ruff, ruff!" That was another time the guys almost fell off the benches laughing.

Noel Picard was the biggest character we had on the

Blues. One night in Boston, he skated to the wrong bench during a line change. Can you imagine that happening? Had to be an NHL first. Frosty, the trainer for Boston, opened the gate for Picard and the big guy sat down among all the Bruins. Then he took a look around and realized where he was and how he'd screwed up. He musta been squirming in embarrassment. But by then play had begun. He didn't know what to do. So he dashed off the Boston bench and tried to sneak across the ice to the Blues' bench. But Noel was a real big guy and the referee spotted him immediately. Blew the whistle and tagged him with a two-minute penalty for too many men on the ice.

Red Berenson cracked up, laughing so hard that Scotty almost went ballistic. Scotty was so furious he ran out of words bawling Picard out.

When Picard retired, he worked as a broadcaster on Blues games—doing colour with Dan Kelly. The Blues' owner was Sid Salomon III, and Picard, with his French accent, kept referring to him as "Sid Salomon the turd." During one game, Kelly asked Picard to give the out-of-town scores and he said, "Here they are, Dan-ee. The scores are 6–3, 6–1 and 4–0." The viewer had to figure out which teams he was talking about. Another time he appeared on camera, but he got confused and did his entire spiel with his back to the camera. God, it was funny.

I remember we took a long road trip up into Canada, then to Vancouver and on to L.A. I sat on the bench game after game. I got hardly any ice time. Now we're playing the Kings and I'm at the end of the bench. An usher whispers to me, "George, can I have your stick after the game?"

By then I was a little frustrated, bored and hungry, so I told him, "Sneak me a hot dog and a Coke and you can have my stick." Moments later, the usher returned with the hot dog and the drink. I took a little bite when Scotty wasn't looking. Then I heard him roar, "Morrison, get out there and kill that penalty!"

Talk about a jolt of surprise. I jumped up and knocked the drink off the bench. Then I quickly stuffed the hot dog down the cuff of my hockey glove. What else could I do with it? But when I leaped into the play, one of the Kings slammed into me, and the hot dog flew in the air, mustard and relish sailing in all directions. This was right in the goal crease. The whistle blew and the officials cleaned up the mess. All the players were laughing while I tried my best to look innocent. Only after I left the Blues for the WHA did I confess I'd stupidly carried a hot dog into an NHL game.

As for the WHA, there were lots of hot dogs on the ice in that league. I played for the Minnesota Fighting Saints in the WHA for three seasons. Scored forty goals there one year.

George failed to mention he holds the WHA record for the fastest hat trick—three goals in forty-three seconds. And he scored another goal in that same game to reach the forty-goal mark.

Our coach, Glen Sonmor, had a glass eye, and one night his eye fell out and rolled around behind the bench. That was another first I witnessed.

We're playing in Cincinnati one time, and they had a guy by the name of Dale Smedsmo, their resident goon—a real tough customer. In the warm-up, I noticed that Smedsmo was sitting on the bench in full uniform. But he didn't have his skates on. So I figured their coach had just put him there to scare us, to try to intimidate us.

Well, I thought I'd show my mates I wasn't the least bit afraid of Smedsmo. I stood right in front of the visiting team's bench and I called Smedsmo all kinds of names. I felt pretty safe because I figured he wasn't going to play in the game or he'd have his skates on. So I'm saying, "You son of a bitch, if you were going to play tonight, I'd crack you open." He didn't say much in reply, so now I turn back and skate away. The game was about to begin.

I line up with the starters for the playing of the national anthem. I look across from me, and suddenly I feel ill. There stands Smedsmo in full uniform—with his skates on! He is going to play after all, and I almost swooned. He is glaring across at me and it was almost as if someone was trying to restrain him from leaping across the ice and pounding me. Someone told me later that he'd been sitting on the bench with his skates off during the warm-up because they needed a touch-up from the sharpener.

That was the night I came down with a sore back in the opening minutes—it was real sudden—and I told the coach, "Christ, coach, I am in such pain I can't play anymore tonight." The truth was I was scared to death that Smedsmo was going to grab me by the throat and kick the crap out of me.

I really shouldn't have worried. My teammates would have come to my rescue. Like most WHA clubs, Minnesota had four or five goons. These guys couldn't lift the puck, but boy, could they fight!

That was the season we were hoping that Bobby Orr would join our club. Minnesota went after Bobby and offered him something like $6 million. It was a good thing he turned them down. Six months later, the team was sold for $1.

One day, Peter Mahovlich showed and we heard he was going to sign with us for something like $250,000 a year plus a yacht and all kinds of perks. They announced a press conference and a signing for the next day. But Pete got up late or something, decided he didn't feel much like signing, and when they looked around he was catching a plane back to Toronto or Montreal or wherever he came from. He never did sign on.

One good thing about Minnesota was our money was guaranteed. Al Eagleson worked out the deal. In Minnesota, the 3M Company owned the Fighting Saints. If they ever got into financial problems, all you had to do was go to the bank and get your dough. It wasn't that way with a lot of clubs.

George died of brain cancer on November 13, 2008. He spent his last days as a volunteer assistant coach in Albany, New York, with the Union College Dutchwomen. He was only fifty-nine.

TO DICK IRVIN

Dear Dick,

Dick, can you believe we'll soon be in our eighties? How can this be possible?

Our careers are now behind us, and it seems like only yesterday we were struggling to get started.

So many of the others are gone: Danny Gallivan, Foster and Bill Hewitt, Dan Kelly, Don Wittman, Ted Darling. And dozens of the players, coaches and managers we met and interviewed over the years—Toe Blake, Punch Imlach, John Ferguson and Sammy Pollock.

Don't you wish we could go back and do it all over again? Most people don't realize we started out before colour television, before instant replays, before we could bring in highlights from out-of-town games. That was back in the mid-'60s. There were just six teams in the NHL when we started—and not all of them employed backup goalies. No names on the jerseys, no helmets, no assistant coaches, no agents, no European players. Well, there was one

European player: a Swedish kid, Ulf Sterner, had a trial with the Rangers and failed to stick. Rookies spent two or three years in the minors "learning the game."

A fellow could call the NHL offices in Montreal and president Clarence Campbell would pick up the phone himself. "Campbell here."

Gary Bettman doesn't do that, does he Dick?

Because teams played each other fourteen times a season, we saw the cream of the crop every week. In Toronto, I would cover a game featuring Detroit's Gordie Howe, Red Kelly, Terry Sawchuk, Alex Delvecchio and Norm Ullman versus George Armstrong, Dave Keon, Frank Mahovlich, Tim Horton, Allan Stanley, Bob Baun and Johnny Bower.

In Montreal, you'd be talking about Maurice and Henri Richard, Jean Béliveau, Dickie Moore, Boom Boom Geoffrion and Jacques Plante as they hosted the Chicago Blackhawks—Bobby and Dennis Hull, Stan Mikita, Pierre Pilote and Glenn Hall.

Even the weaker teams, Boston and New York, had great stars: Andy Bathgate, Dean Prentice, Harry Howell and Gump Worsley. The Bruins had the Uke Line (John Bucyk, Vic Stasiuk and Bronco Horvath) and, in time, the incomparable Bobby Orr and Phil Esposito.

Those were great days, weren't they, Dick?

I recall my first game, in 1965, working with Bill Hewitt from the gondola at Maple Leaf Gardens. My boss stuck his head into the booth just before the puck was dropped. He held up three fingers and said, "McFarlane, I think you should speak three times a period. That'll be a nice balance between you and Bill."

"What if the teams score six goals in the first?" I asked.

"Talk about three of them," was his flippant response.

I broke his edict in the first five minutes of my career.

When I think about it, Dick, you may be the only man I know in Canadian sports broadcasting who started at the top—by which I mean working in a major Canadian market—with no real experience. And you stayed at the top for over forty years.

I'm going to claim some credit for getting you started, Dick. In 1960, I left radio station CFRB in Toronto to become the first sports director of a new TV station in Montreal, CFCF-TV. Shortly after my arrival, I knew I'd made a huge mistake (my salary suddenly turned out to be $2,000 short of what I was promised) and the station manager was reluctant to let me hire additional staff. I realized I would need a full-time assistant.

Several announcers applied, including Don Chevrier, but my bosses said, "No, no, no, we'd have to pay some of those fellows a fortune, maybe ten or $12,000 a year (which was just about what I was earning). And we'd have to pay their moving expenses as well. You want an assistant? Find a Montrealer for the job."

So I found *you*, Dick. You lived just a couple of miles away. I had interviewed you on a program about your famous father and you left a solid impression on me that day.

I asked my bosses if I could hire you—someone with absolutely no experience but loads of potential—and they said, "Yes, but only if he comes cheap. Offer the guy seventy-five bucks a week."

I protested, saying it was a pitiful amount for someone who knew every sports figure in Montreal, had played hockey at McGill, was the official scorer at the Montreal Forum, who could write his own scripts and announce them without stumbling over his words and who showed a keen sense of humour. "What's more," I told them, "the guy is willing to work seven days a week like I do. But $75 a week? Come on. He's willing to leave a job that pays him much more than that."

My bosses shrugged. They were unmoved. "Offer him seventy-five bucks a week."

I said I couldn't do it. They said, "Then send him to us. We'll do it."

I recall you came back from the meeting shaking your head. "Good thing I'm single and living at home," you said. "They offered me seventy-five bucks a week to get into the glamorous world of television."

"Why don't you take it for six months and see how things go?" was my advice to you.

You accepted the job, and when I impulsively left CFCF-TV to return to Toronto a few months later—before I had a nervous breakdown—you replaced me as sports director at the station. I hope they gave you a raise. Soon you had a second job as Danny Gallivan's sidekick on *Hockey Night in Canada*. You were on your way, Dick. I hope you weren't told to speak only three times a period. You and Danny became a famous broadcast duo, as famous as Ron MacLean and Don Cherry, who would come along later and make ten times the money.

You've enjoyed a fabulous career in Canadian broadcasting, and in publishing as well. Nobody in Canada has broadcast more games on radio and TV than you—more than two thousand. Nobody has been in more arenas and interviewed more hockey personalities, from Joe Malone and Cyclone Taylor and Léo Dandurand to Wayne Gretzky and Mario Lemieux.

You've covered twenty-six Stanley Cup finals and you've won many honours. Most rewarding, I'm sure, was your induction into the Hockey Hall of Fame in 1988. And you still show up at every induction ceremony.

Not bad for a kid from Regina who grew up in the shadow of a legendary father, a kid who thought he might be known as Dick Irvin Jr. for as long as he lived. Does anyone call you Junior anymore?

That kid in Regina, skating on a patch of ice behind his house on Sunday mornings, emulated not only his father but also one of his first hockey heroes, Foster Hewitt. You'd call the play-by-play as you skated all alone, "Apps has the puck . . . over to Drillon . . . back to Apps . . . he shoots, he scores!"

Even at that early age you must have been in good voice, because a crabby neighbour would invariably throw open a bedroom window and shout down at you, "Hey, kid, shuddup down there. It's Sunday morning, for crying out loud."

STRANGE BUT TRUE HOCKEY STORIES

Jordan Fenn puts the manuscript down. He sips his coffee. "I didn't know that you and Dick Irvin worked together on a TV station in Montreal," he says. "And I'd forgotten that Boom Boom Geoffrion was Howie Morenz's son-in-law. What a shame the Habs didn't retire his jersey a few weeks earlier."

"I'll say this for the Canadiens," I say. "They've been around for a hundred years and they really know how to honour the great stars from their past."

"Have you got any off-beat material to offer us?" Jordan asks. "Some stories that will really take our readers by surprise?"

"I do," I reply. "Fans are always surprised at Eddie Shore's bizarre behaviour. And I've got some amusing stuff about what happens in the penalty box. Then there's one I call 'A Runner's Nightmare.' That's a scary one. Most surprising, perhaps, is a life-and-death situation involving Wilf Paiement Sr. and his large family. These are true stories and yes, they'll surprise you."

"Sounds good. Let's move along."

KILREA TALKS ABOUT SHORE

Brian Kilrea, the most successful coach in junior hockey, retired after the 2008–09 season. The longtime mentor to the Ottawa 67's left the game with 1,193 victories to his credit (a Canadian junior hockey record) after thirty-two years behind the bench. Nobody's going to break that standard in our lifetime. During the final game of the 2008–09 NHL season, Kilrea was introduced at the Air Canada Centre in Toronto and received a standing ovation. People love the guy.

I met and interviewed Brian in Ottawa years ago, and after our chat I asked him for an Alyn McCauley stick. Everybody said McCauley would become a star in the NHL. It never happened. Kilrea fetched one from the 67's dressing room and I placed it in a hockey museum I owned in Niagara Falls. Nobody seemed to be interested in it.

Kilrea, who is already a member of the Hockey Hall of Fame (2003) on the strength of his coaching career, was less successful as a player. He toiled in the American Hockey League for many seasons in the 1960s. He was given brief trials in the NHL—one game with Detroit and twenty-five more with Los Angeles. He scored the first goal in the Kings' history.

Alas, he was stuck in Springfield for much of his career, under the thumb of the controversial and cantankerous Eddie Shore, owner, manager and coach of the AHL Indians.

I met Shore only once and told him I was writing a book about King Clancy. This was in a hotel corridor in Montreal at the NHL's annual meetings.

"Mr. Shore, would you have a story or two I could use about Clancy?" I asked.

"Son, I can't do that without giving the matter some thought," he replied. "Meet me tomorrow at this same spot and I'll give you some quotes."

We agreed on a time and met the following day. I brought my tape recorder and turned it on.

"Now, Mr. Shore, how about some Clancy stories?"

He paused a moment, then spoke.

"King Clancy was a great hockey player," he said, "one of the best."

There was a long pause.

"Is that it, Mr. Shore?"

"Yes. That's it," he replied, and walked away.

I only recall his response all these years later because I was so shocked by it. He gave me virtually nothing. When I asked Clancy to talk about Shore, he would go on for an hour, spinning yarns about the Boston Hall of Famer. Others would, too. Everybody had a story about Shore.

John "Goose" McCormack told me recently, "Shore owned a team in Fort Worth, Texas, for a season or two, a farm club for his Springfield club. One of his players got slashed on the arm and could not play. Shore handed him one of those old-fashioned sandwich boards advertisers used back then. You throw it over your head and there's a board front and back. The words on the board read HOCKEY TONIGHT AT THE ARENA. GAME TIME 8 P.M. Shore ordered the kid to parade up and down the main street wearing the board. How humiliating is that?"

Milt Schmidt said it best: "Eddie Shore was different."

Now that's an understatement.

Some of Brian Kilrea's stories about the man border on the incredulous. Here are a couple.

During one season I was with Shore—this would be in the '60s—Springfield had to travel to Pittsburgh for a Wednesday game. Shore holds a practice on Tuesday. But somehow he neglects to tell us we're leaving on the bus right after the practice. We show up at the rink for a noon-hour workout, and that's when Eddie tells us that we have to be ready to leave on the bus at 1:30 p.m. Well, most of us didn't bring our travel clothes and when we complain to Eddie he says, "That's just too bad. I don't care. We're leaving at 1:30."

So after practice the guys race home to pack a bag and none of us makes it back to the rink on time. At exactly 1:30 p.m., Eddie says to the bus driver, "Hey, start your engine. Let's go." The bussie says, "But, Eddie, there ain't no players on the bus."

"I don't care," says Shore. "Let's move."

So the bus driver and Eddie take off for Pittsburgh. When the players get to the arena a few moments later, we discover that our bus has gone. It's unbelievable. So we huddle together and decide to drive to Pittsburgh in four or five cars and we get there that night. But this is the start of a road trip—four games in five nights. We're driving our cars all over the eastern U.S.

On that trip we win three games out of four despite the screw-up at the start of it. Now, Eddie, being the generous soul that he is, won't give us any more than $1 per meal—$3 a day—during this trip. Even in those days, you can't find much on any menu for $1. Well, we get back home after living on junk food for a week, but with six big points added to our total. We're dead tired and expect we're going to be rewarded with a bit of a rest. But no—Eddie won't allow that. He schedules an early-morning practice for the very next day.

Well, that was the straw that broke the camel's back. I went to the media and said to them, "You want to know about our road trip? Well, Eddie drives off on the bus without us, we win three out of four, play our hearts out, get squat for food, and now we have to crawl out of bed for an eight o'clock practice. I guess that's Eddie's way of saying thanks. What do you think about the old man now?"

Well, the reporters love it. They all publish stories on what a cheap, demanding guy Shore is. Shore comes into the dressing room the next day and he's fuming. He gets there late because he hates to get up early, but he wasn't too late to read the papers, and he's irate.

He yells at me, "You! Kilrea! Did you have anything to do with this article in this morning's paper?"

And I look all innocent and say, "What article is that, Eddie? I didn't have time to read the paper today."

He says, "Don't give me that crap. It was you, all right. Now get in the corner of the rink and do stops and starts until I tell you to quit."

So I'm on the ice by myself for the next two hours doing stops and starts. Geez, I got snow piled up to my ankles before he calls a halt. And what do I get for all of my hard work? I get demoted to the fourth line that night.

Here's another of my favourite Shore stories. Billy Collins—remember him? Played about seven hundred games in the NHL eventually. Well, Billy gets sent to us from Toronto for some reason. Shore has the club staying in a hotel in Hamilton when Billy arrives. And right in the lobby he has us doing this dance. It's supposed to teach us footwork and balance, I guess. What it really teaches us is how to make total fools of ourselves in public. Anyway, Eddie is there, teaching us this dance, and everyone checking in and out of the hotel is standing around watching and smiling. Of course, they all think we're crazy.

Now Billy Collins comes to check in. It's a warm day and he's wearing shorts. Well, his mouth drops open when he sees these goofy hockey players dancing in the lobby.

He comes over to me and says, "Hey, Killer! What the hell is going on?"

I say, "Hello, Billy, welcome to the club. Did you bring your dancing shoes?"

And he says, "Listen, Killer, I gotta see Shore." Not missing a dance step, I point him in the right direction. So Billy walks over and says hello to Shore.

Shore looks him up and down and says, "Who are you again?"

Collins says, "I'm Billy Collins, you just traded for me." Eddie sees that Billy is wearing shorts.

He bends down to look at his legs and says, "You're awful bowlegged! You'll never be a hockey player. Go back to Toronto." Then Eddie turns and walks away.

Now Billy's in shock. He doesn't know what to make of Shore. So he comes back over to me and he says, "What do I do now, Killer?"

And I tell him, "Billy, the best possible thing for you to do is to go back to Toronto as fast as you can and tell them Shore doesn't want you!" And that's what he did.

And I might add some coaches will tell you that bowlegged guys often make the best kind of hockey players.

MILT SCHMIDT ALSO REMEMBERS SHORE

For more on Shore, we go to Hall of Famer Milt Schmidt, who was never a big fan of the Bruin defenceman. Milt was often a guest analyst on *Hockey Night in Canada*, and I was always thrilled to work with him.

My pal Goose McCormack tells me Schmidt was a peerless performer when he played for the Bruins, as good as any of the best players in the game. Ted Lindsay and others agree.

Early in his career, Schmidt was a teammate of Eddie Shore, who was regarded as the NHL's best blue-liner. I asked him to comment on the eccentric Bruin legend.

Brian, let me tell you about an amazing tribute that man received one night. As long as I live, I'll never forget the ovation the Boston fans gave Eddie Shore after we won the 1939 Stanley Cup.

I don't know why Shore headed straight for the dressing room after the victory, but he did. Shore was funny. Very, very funny. Anyway, he skated off the ice and the crowd wouldn't let NHL president Frank Calder present the Stanley Cup until he came back on the ice. It didn't surprise us because Shore was revered in Boston. He was our Babe Ruth. The crowd howled for Shore, and somebody went to get him and he says, "Eddie, they won't let Calder present the trophy until you go out there."

Now, Shore had his sweater off and one of his skates. The fans were chanting, "We want Shore! We want Shore!" so finally he decided to come out.

He skated out onto that ice surface and the ovation that man received was absolutely incredible. It was ear-shattering. I'm only nineteen years of age at that time and the goose pimples started breaking out all over my body. I couldn't believe it.

The next best salute to that one was in the same arena a few years ago, when they retired Bobby Orr's number 4. When that jersey was lifted up to the rafters, there was an ovation similar to the one the fans had given Shore.

The fans loved Shore, but I'll say this: Shore was not an easy man to play with. He made a bad pass in front of our net one night and bingo, it was in behind our goalie. He gave me a real good tongue-lashing at the end of the period. He comes over and he says, "Joe"—he never called you by your real name, or he might have said, very slowly, "Mister Schmidt— What were you doing over there?"

I said, "Eddie, I was busting out hoping for a pass from you. Why? What's wrong?"

He says, "You shouldn't have been there."

Then I say, "Well, I'm sorry, but I *was* there. Hey, I didn't pass the puck in front of the net—*you* did."

He said, "That may be true, but you made me do it."

I say, "Eddie, come on." Here he is giving me hell for not being where he wanted me to be. Eddie was notorious for passing the puck in front of his own net. He used to do it all the time. As a matter of fact, he made a lot of mistakes back on our blue line, but they were seldom noticed because, well, because he was Eddie Shore. But he gave me hell that day.

And he didn't think much of my skating style. You see, Eddie was a straight-up skater like Gordie Howe, and I was a stooped-over skater. We all learn to skate and develop different styles. Skating bent over, I used a four- or five-lie stick. So I'm buzzing around the ice this day and I hear Shore yell out, "Mr. Schmidt!"

So I go over to him, and it was "Yes, sir" and "No, sir" in those days. I knew enough to keep my eyes and ears open and my mouth shut.

Shore says to me, "Son, let me tell you something. If you do not change your style of skating, you will not last in the NHL." Here I am, a nineteen-year-old rookie, and the great Eddie Shore is telling me what a lousy skater I am. I was scared silly. So he says, "You have got to change your style. Get up on your rear end so that you're balanced instead of being stooped over. You're going to be cut off and you're going to have problems because you won't know where you're going."

His words had me totally confused. For the rest of the workout I skated around straight up. I walked out of that arena and I'm tellin' you, I was sore, really sore. I just couldn't do it Shore's way. Gretzky is a stooped-over skater and I wonder, if Shore were alive today, would he tell Gretzky he'd never last in the NHL? Funny thing is, Gretzky's not a quick skater. I'd sure like to race him—not now, but when I was in my prime.

After Shore tried to change my style, I was a little depressed, so I went to see Art Ross. I said, "Mr. Ross, I just can't seem to change my style of skating. Eddie wants me to work on it but I don't think a fellow can change very much after he reaches his teens."

Mr. Ross says, "Milt, would you just forget that son of a bitch?"

They never got along with one another, you know. Ross and Shore never spoke to one another. In fact, they hated each other. Shore used to hold out every year just to infuriate Ross. So Ross said to me that day, "Forget about Shore, kid. He doesn't know what the hell he's talking about. You stay the way you are. That's good enough for me and that's good enough for the NHL." So I stayed the way I was and I lasted nineteen and a half years.

Shore was so different. He never wore suspenders; he always wore a belt. I asked him about that once and he mumbled something about suspenders hampering his breathing—I don't know how. And he was the only player who hopped on the rubbing table before every game. He insisted on a pre-game massage. On the road he would never room with anybody, he was always alone. He said he had to get his proper sleep.

And then he would take all his hockey sticks, which had to be a certain lie—a seven- or an eight-lie, I believe it was; I know it was almost straight up and down. Nels Stewart was the same way, that's why he was able to score so many goals from in front of the net. He'd be able to hold onto the puck right in around his feet. Shore used to cut off his stick blades. Instead of using a normal-size blade, one about twelve inches long, he'd saw off three or four inches and use a blade only eight or nine inches long. I saw no advantage in that.

Ross finally got so angry at him for doing this, he called Dit Clapper over one day and he said, "Dit, get a saw and cut every one of his damn sticks halfway through so when he goes out there he'll break them. He'll come back and get another one and he'll break that one, too."

Clapper did what he was told and Shore's sticks kept snapping off. But Shore wouldn't dare say anything to Clapper, even if he knew it was Clapper who'd done it. Clapper was tough—my, but he was tough. I know because he looked after me in many of my battles. He was like a father to me.

Anyway, Shore broke three or four sticks that day in a matter of minutes and finally he noticed the nice, clean saw cut and geez, did he ever go crazy. Ross, meanwhile, is up in the stands laughing his guts out. Eventually, Shore found out who cut his sticks, but he wasn't about to tangle with Clapper. So he did nothing.

Before a game, Shore would hold his skate blades up to the light to make sure they were sharp. One day I heard him growl at the trainer, "Mr. Green, these skates have not been sharpened."

Green says, "Oh, yes, they have been, Eddie. Every pair of skates has been sharpened for this game."

Shore says, "I beg your pardon, Mr. Green, but *my* skates have not been sharpened."

So Green shrugs and says to Randall, the clubhouse boy, "Take these skates and get them sharpened."

You won't believe this, but the Bruins didn't have a skate-sharpening machine in the Boston Garden at that time. Randall had to go from the Garden all the way over to the Boston Arena, which was miles away, to have our skates

sharpened. Honest to God. Can you imagine an NHL team
not having a skate-sharpening machine?

So Green says to Randall, "Take Eddie's skates and get
them sharpened. Then hop in a cab and get back here as fast
as you can."

Then he took Randall aside and whispered to him, "Son,
I want you to take Eddie's skates and go for a walk. Have a
cigarette. Bring them back in half an hour." Which he did,
and he hands Eddie the skates.

Shore holds them up to the light, examines the blades and
says, "Ha, that's better. Good work, Randall."

That was Eddie Shore. And that's a true story about the
skate-sharpening machine.

Eventually, the Bruins hired a guy to come around on the
day of every game. He carried a big burlap sack and he'd take
all the skates to Arlington, have them sharpened and bring
them back in time for the game. He stood in behind the bench
in case we needed him to touch up the blade. And we always
needed him—in those days we didn't have a real solid ice
surface in Boston. The Garden was built right over the North
Station and you'd feel the arena vibrate as the trains rolled
in and out beneath you. The cement on the floor had little
heaves in it and you'd be hittin' one of these heaves once in a
while and then you'd see the sparks fly. Oh, God, it was awful.
So the skate sharpener was there with his little stone and he
was kept busy honing off nicks on our blades in every game.

Finally, the guy said to Mr. Adams [Charles Adams, the
Bruins' owner], "I'm going to have to charge you fifty cents
for every pair of skates I have to stone."

Mr. Adams says, "Oh, no you're not."

That did it. The club finally bought their own skate-sharpening machine and the trainer had to learn how to use it.

FROM THE PENALTY BOX

At one of our Oldtimer luncheons I sit next to Sandy Hawley, Canada's most famous jockey and a particular favourite of mine. He is a national treasure, a wonderful ambassador for Canada. It is November 2008 and Sandy is just back from California, where he won a race at Santa Anita called the Living Legends, an event featuring seven other Hall of Fame jockeys long since retired. Sandy is now fifty-nine, gone from the saddle for ten years but still dark-haired and youthful. The oldest jockey in the Living Legends was sixty-five.

It was Sandy's 6,450th victory. He tells me he went on a fitness regimen prior to the race and lost ten pounds—dropping from 120 pounds to 110.

This man has been honoured with an Order of Canada, two Lou Marsh Trophies as Canada's outstanding athlete, an Eclipse Award as North America's top jockey and a host of others. Twice at Woodbine in Toronto, he won seven races on the same day. He was the first man to ride five hundred winners in a season.

He is the Wayne Gretzky or Mario Lemieux of his sport. Like Lemieux, he had a cancer scare a few years ago. Skin cancer threatened his life in 1987, but some radical treatments put the cancer into remission.

Most hockey fans don't know that Sandy has an NHL connection. He was once the penalty timekeeper for the Los Angeles Kings. When he rode in California, he loved attending Kings games and was hired to serve as one of the minor officials.

"It was great fun," he tells me. "I met all the NHL stars that way. And not one who came into my box ever deserved to be penalized. At least that's what they told me.

"I remember Paul Coffey in particular. He was a brilliant defenceman with Edmonton back then. The first time he came into my penalty box he grinned and said, 'You're Sandy Hawley, right?'

"I said, 'That's right.'

"He threw off his glove and shook my hand. 'I'm so pleased to meet you,' he said.

"'And I'm so pleased to meet you, Paul,' I answered.

"'I've heard the roar of the crowd myself and won many big races as a jockey. But one of the best times of my life was sitting in the penalty box at the Los Angeles Forum, kibitzing with the great hockey stars who came by occasionally to visit."

I tell Sandy I know another man who served the game well in a similar capacity: Joe Lamantia.

"Banana" Joe Lamantia was a fixture at Maple Leaf Gardens for decades, the penalty timekeeper for Leaf games. A really nice man who earned his nickname because of his lengthy involvement in the fruit and vegetable business—his daytime vocation. Lamantia has spent more time in the cramped quarters of the penalty box than all the NHL's top sinners combined.

He told me once that some of his "customers" had very poor penalty-box manners. While serving their time they spit and spewed nose droppings all over the floor of the box. "Sometimes I wish I'd brought a slicker and rubber boots to the games," Joe says with a laugh. "Two of the worst offenders were former Leafs Borje Salming and Wilf Paiement. Whenever those two left the box, we had to bring out the mop and clean up the floor.

"It was murder whenever they were penalized at the same time. We were often tempted to break out umbrellas and apply for flood relief.

"Here's a little joke I liked to play on Salming. I guess it's safe to tell it now that he's back in Sweden. Whenever he came in the box, he would bitch and gripe about the heat in the building. Always. So I'd say, 'Too hot for you, Borje?'

"'Yeah, yeah, Joe. Too hot.'

"So I'd grab the phone and pretend I was talking to Dougie Moore, the chief engineer. I'd say, 'Doug, for Chrissake, Borje Salming is sittin' in here and it is too fucking hot for him. So turn the heat down, will you?'

"Then I'd hang up and say, 'Borje, Doug Moore's going to take care of that problem right away.'

"He'd say, 'Thanks, Joe. Thanks a lot.'

"Believe me, no less than thirty seconds later I'd turn to him and ask innocently, 'How is it now, Borje? A little better?'

"And he'd say, 'Yeah, yeah, Joe. It seems to be cooling off. It's okay now.'

"The next time he'd come in he'd start bitching about the organ music. So I'd grab the phone and pretend I was callin' up to Paul Morris, the PA announcer. I'd yell into the mouthpiece, 'Paul, for Chrissake, tell that asshole of an organist to play something we can understand and to tone it down a bit. And do it now! Borje Salming can hardly hear himself think in here.'

"Then I'd hang up and a few seconds later Borje would say, 'Yeah, that's better. It's not too loud now.'

"One time Borje wanted to talk to the organist himself. I had to be quick to say, 'No, no, no, no. I'll have to phone him.'"

Sandy Hawley spoke eloquently at our hockey luncheon. He even told a joke.

The groom was walking by the stable when this horse pokes his head out and says, 'You get me a mare for the night and I'll win that race for you tomorrow.'

"Geez," the groom says, "A talking horse. And he needs a mare for the night."

The groom looks all around the stables and there are no mares available. So he decides to go to a nearby zoo, thinking the zoo may have a mare he can borrow.

The zookeeper says, "Sorry, bud. We don't have any mares. But we do have a zebra. Will that do?"

The groom says, "It's worth a try," and he brings the zebra to the horse. The horse looks the zebra over and says, "Yeah, she'll do."

The groom puts the zebra in the stall but he cautions the horse, "Now don't be up all night. You've got a big race tomorrow."

In the middle of the night, the groom hears the horse neighing and kicking up his heels. He runs to the stable and says, "What's wrong? Why are you acting up?"

And the horse says, "I'm having a devil of a time getting her out of her pajamas."

A RUNNER'S NIGHTMARE

Our telecast crew is in Chicago for a game and a fellow media guy—a handsome devil—tells us what happened to him after we left him in the bar the night before.

It wasn't long after you fellows went up to bed when a couple of lovely flight attendants waltz into the bar. I move right in, manage to buy them a couple of drinks, one thing leads to another and bingo—I get invited back to their apartment building. One is Barbara, the other is Ann. Turns out they both have small apartments on the second floor, directly across the hall from one another.

I'm getting along real well with the lovely Barbara so we say good night to Ann and we go into Barbara's apartment. Oh, this is gonna be good, I say to myself. I've got my rum bottle in my pocket and a great-lookin' girl who's ready for some lovin'. We're on the sofa makin' out when suddenly her buzzer rings, meaning somebody is downstairs and wants to get in. I jump up but she says, "Don't worry about it. It's probably that crazy guy who's been bothering me lately. He's such a jerk. Just ignore it."

Ignore it! How can I ignore it? The buzzer keeps ringing and I'm gettin' more nervous and it's obvious the guy is not going to go away.

"Look, I'll take care of this," says Barbara, jumping up and calling the police. The police are there in a matter of minutes. They poke around outside the apartment but if there was a crazy guy out there, they didn't find him. He must have taken off somewhere.

Well, the cops leave and we relax again. We snuggle up on the sofa and things are gettin' hot when the damn buzzer rings again. "Goddamn him," says Barbara, jumping up. "Come on, we'll go across the hall to Ann's apartment. Then if the jerk does find a way to get in, we won't be here."

As we scurry across the hall, I can hear someone downstairs bellowing and shaking the doors that are keeping him out. I pray the locks are good and strong. We knock on Ann's door, and fortunately she's still up. We tell Ann what's happening and she mutters something like, "Oh, it's that psychopathic creep again," which really unsettles me. A psychopath? I take a couple of swigs from my rum bottle to calm myself. Then Ann tells me the guy downstairs is really strung out on something. "He has the most violent nature of anyone I've ever met," she tells me. Sonofabitch, that calls for more rum. Now my nerves are really on edge.

Just then, we hear a loud crashing noise from the vestibule below and Barbara shrieks, "Oh, my God, he's smashed the security door and he's coming up. He may kill us all." None of us has a clue what to do and I'm certainly in no shape to stand up to some crazed psychopath.

Ann has an idea. She says to me, "Jump into my bed just

in case he should find us here. He'll think you're with me and it's Barb he's after." Then Ann says to Barb, "You run out and intercept him and try to cool him off. Tell him you and I were visiting and we didn't hear him trying to get in."

I tell you, by then I was scared shitless. But I did what Ann told me to do. I slipped out of my clothes and jumped into her bed, where I take another couple of belts from the rum bottle.

Meanwhile, I hear Barbara and this maniac screaming at each other out in the hall. I envision some asshole built like Hulk Hogan is about to stomp me or stab me to death at any moment. I gulp down some more rum and my terror subsides—for all of about a second.

Then Ann dashes into the bedroom. She tells me to get up and run for my life. She says, "Grab your goddamn clothes and get out of here. He's across the hall with Barb and he's threatening to butcher us all."

Christ, I'm so scared I can hardly put my fucking pants on. Anyway, I sneak into the hall and tiptoe down the stairs. But when I reach the landing and grab the door that was forced open, it comes loose in my hand. The guy has broken the fucking hinges. I can't hold it and it crashes to the floor. Shit! Above me I hear a shout. I look up at a huge bugger and he begins screaming obscenities at me, "I'll get you, you little prick. Tryin' to fuck my girl, were you? I'll cut your nuts off for that." He appears to be reaching for a knife or a gun while I'm reaching the end of my rope.

Well, I take off outta there fast. And I'm absolutely petrified. I have no idea where to run. Outside the building there's a huge parking lot. It's almost deserted but it's all lit up. I'm runnin' like Ben Johnson and I look back to see this huge figure filling the doorway. He spots me and takes off after me. Then I hear the roar of a car engine. He's leaped into his car and those tires are burnin' rubber as he wheels across that parking lot at eighty miles an hour. Sonofabitch but I'm scared. I figure if I don't make it into the wooded area across the parking lot I'm a goner. I sprint harder, leap over a metal railing and crash in among the trees. Then I stumble and fall in a ditch. I scramble through bushes and my pulse must be going three hundred beats a minute. Jesus, I'm gonna have cardiac arrest any second, I'm sure of it. Plus, there's not much left in the old rum bottle by now.

Just when my pulse slows a little and I think I've lost the sucker, I hear the roar of that fuckin' engine again. My God, he's circled around and found the old road or riding path I'm standin' on. Oh, fuck, here he comes barrelling down the road. I turn and dive through the woods. I slosh through water up to my knees and my face is whipped by branches I can't see. Finally, I crouch behind a huge tree. While I take another snort of rum, I have visions of some Chicago cops finding my body, slashed to ribbons, sometime in the spring. For the next few minutes, I hear his car moving slowly back and forth. I hear him snarling through the open window, "I know you're in there. I'll get you, you little prick." After ten or fifteen minutes he gives up the search and I hear him drive away. Christ, what a relief!

Or *did* he drive off? I'm not so sure. He's a smart bastard. So I wait another half-hour before I emerge from my hiding place. By now the rum bottle is almost empty. I haven't got a clue where I am. But off in the distance I see the Hotel Hilton sign and I decide to aim for that. I cut across a field and a highway, constantly looking over my shoulder, and when I reach the hotel I'm covered with mud and water. When I stagger up to the desk, the clerk takes one look at me and backs away.

He says, "Hey, wait a minute, man . . ."

I say, "No, no. I'm not here to hold you up. I just need

a cab to get me over to the Marriott. I've had a bit of a problem." He grabs a phone and calls me a cab. He can't wait to get my ass out of his lobby.

The cabbie doesn't want me as a passenger. He keeps looking at me through the mirror, as if to say, "I'd better keep an eye on this dude. He can't be up to anything good." I figure he's driving with one hand and his other is clutching a tire iron.

When we reach the Marriott, I slip a fiver into his palm and run for it. In the hotel, the sickening fear returns. So does my imagination. What if the brute saw me picking up the girls in the hotel bar? What if he's come back and he's waiting for me in there? He could be behind a potted palm, holding a big knife. He could be right outside my room, waiting to gun me down. Shit, I was scared.

I sprint through the lobby, jump into the first elevator I see and punch the button. When I reach my floor, I peek out of the elevator both ways, sprint down the hall and reach the safety of my room. I lock my door, put on the chain; vow never to hustle girls in bars ever, ever again, and I really mean it. I make a vow. Then I take a final shot of rum. I toss the empty bottle aside, take a hot shower, then listen to the radio for an hour, thinking any second I'll hear a bulletin about the murder of two flight attendants. My heart is still pounding too hard for me to sleep, so I stay up the rest of the night, cursing myself for being such a stupid son of a bitch.

When I check out in the morning, the girl at the desk gives me her best smile and says, "We hope you've enjoyed your stay with us, sir."

I give her a sleepy-eyed stare.

"It's been great," I lie.

WALTON GOES DANCING

Mike Walton was a popular player with the Leafs back in the '60s. He came up through the junior Marlboros, where he helped his team win a Memorial Cup in 1964. The following year he was assigned to the Leaf farm club in Tulsa as a nineteen-year-old. He had an outstanding season there, scoring forty goals and winning rookie-of-the-year honours. Stafford Smythe and Harold Ballard were in Tulsa for a few days and Stafford insulted Mike. He told the kid, "You'll never be a Leaf."

"When Smythe said that to me," Mike told me, "I went bonkers. I did a slow burn. I skated around, looking for them in the crowd but I didn't see them. But when they came into the dressing room after the game, one of them tapped me on the bum as if to say 'nice game.' I accosted them. I stood up to Smythe and told him, 'You think I'll never be a Leaf, eh? That's the worst thing you could ever say to me. The worst thing. I'll prove you wrong.'"

And he did, by landing with the big club after winning rookie-of-the-year honours in the American league with Rochester in 1966.

He arrived in Toronto in time to help the Leafs win their last Stanley Cup in 1967. He could score and he could fight and he loved the life of a big leaguer. I recall one stretch where he was named one of the game's three stars on seven straight occasions. None of us could remember that ever happening before.

But he was a rebel and quite a prankster. When Punch Imlach ordered his players to get shorter haircuts, Walton showed up for a game wearing a Beatles wig.

Then he told me one of his favourite stories.

The Leafs were on the road in Los Angeles when Walton joined his mates for dinner in a posh restaurant. Patrons arrived in their limos and Rolls-Royces, and Walton showed up with his date—a blow-up doll he'd purchased down the street.

There were six Leafs in the party, and the wine was ordered.

Then Mike went behind a curtain and blew up this doll. His mates snickered when Mike placed her in a seat at their table.

The players ordered a full-course meal and some more wine. Mike talked constantly to his rubbery companion. "What do you do in L.A., dear? You look like a movie star. I'm so glad you could join us tonight. What kind of wine do you prefer—red or white?"

He snapped his fingers. "Waiter, white wine for the lady, please." He put a glass to her lips. "How does the wine taste, dear? Not too sweet?"

The players began laughing so hard heads began to turn. Waiters smiled nervously. Salads were served and Mike scolded his lady friend: "You're not eating your salad. You don't like it? Is there a problem with the salad? Why didn't you say so? Just eat your friggin' salad. You won't? Don't eat it, then. We'll order you something else."

The guys at the table were laughing like hyenas, and by then the waiters were either laughing hysterically or gritting their teeth.

Mike said to her, "What's that you said? You don't like this place? You talking back to me?" And he gave her a little slap on the head. And her head bobbed back and forth. She almost fell off her chair.

"Now everyone in the place is laughing, caught up in my silly act," Mike told me. "At every other table, conversations ceased. People stood up and stared over at us. Remember, this was in one of the top restaurants in L.A. Now the orchestra arrives and the music begins. So we make up and I give her a little kiss on the cheek. Naturally I asked her to dance with me. She didn't have much choice, did she?

"So we hit the dance floor and she's bobbing up and down in my arms, her rubber legs flopping around, flying in all directions. We're dancing real close—cheek to cheek. And people stood back and started applauding. When the dance was over, I took a little bow, but I couldn't get my partner to bend over. So I threw her under my arm and went back to our table. The other Leafs were practically on the floor.

"What a night! It was the sort of thing you do once in a lifetime, when you are young and foolish and after a little too much wine.

"I think my date had a good time, although she never told me so.

"The players thought it was hilarious. Guys in tuxedos serving us, eh! Her blonde head bobbing up and down. She's rattling around in her chair, a goofy look on her face. They'd never seen anything like that before.

"I can't believe the manager didn't rush over and ask us to pack up and leave. Or he might have grabbed a microphone and apologized to the other patrons, saying something like, 'These fellows are a bunch of crazy hockey players from Canada, folks. They'll be gone as soon as they pay their bill.'"

Walton was traded to Philadelphia and then to Boston, where during the 1972–73 season he almost died on a hotel balcony in St. Louis. Glass doors in a room he shared with Bobby Orr led to the balcony, where some of his teammates were horsing around. One tried to dump water on the others and Walton ducked away, tripped and fell headlong through the doors. He suffered cuts to most of his body, wounds that required two hundred stitches to close. Doctors said he almost bled to death. The incident was hushed up for months.

Like a lot of NHL players, Walton jumped to the World Hockey Association in the 1970s and was the league's leading scorer one season with 117 points.

Mike told me once, "One night, I tangled with Gordie Howe in one of the WHA games. He chased me down the ice and I laughed and yelled at him, 'You can't catch me, old man!' Howe musta been close to fifty then. Well, he did catch me and suddenly I thought for a moment my nose had exploded. It didn't seem to be where it should be on my face."

Hockey doesn't breed characters and colourful flakes like Walton anymore. Too bad.

WILF PAIEMENT

For the past two seasons, as a forward with the Toronto Junior Canadiens of the Ontario Provincial Junior A league, my grandson Kelly Jackson played alongside a kid with a familiar hockey name: Paiement, Eric Paiement. A tall winger with plenty of skill, but not quite enough talent to match his famous father, Wilf Paiement, who played close to a thousand games in the NHL with half a dozen teams.

After watching Eric, I was quite sure he was not going to be a top draft choice like his father was in 1974. Wilf was taken second overall by the Kansas City Scouts just behind Greg Joly, who was selected by Washington.

I saw Wilf at a few of his son's games and often wondered why he didn't attend them more often. What could be keeping him away? He had bulked up from his playing days (don't they all?) and I wished we'd had a chance to talk and reminisce about his days as a Leaf.

Wilf enjoyed an excellent NHL career, totalling 356 goals and 819 points in 946 games. Does that make him Hall of Fame material? Possibly. Why is he seldom mentioned as a candidate?

His career was marred by an ugly stick-swinging incident during the 1978–79 season when he struck Detroit's Dennis Polonich in the face with his stick and was suspended for sixteen games. Polonich, still angry about Paiement's attack when I spoke with him ten years later, sued in civil court and was awarded $850,000 in damages. The money eased some of Dennis's pain, even though Paiement did not have to pay—the insurance company did.

In 1979–80 Paiement was acquired by the Leafs in exchange for one of the most popular players in Leaf history: Lanny McDonald. It was one of several vindictive moves made by an aging and bitter Punch Imlach, and it infuriated Leaf fans.

The Leaf players were so outraged by the deal that they tore the Leaf dressing room apart. And they gave rookie Rocky Saganiuk quite an initiation when he piped up, stating, "Don't worry, boys. I'll take Lanny's place."

Even though he produced good numbers in Toronto, Paiement could never replace McDonald in the hearts of Leaf fans. In 1981–82 Paiement, who wore jersey number 99, was dealt to Quebec for Mirko Frycer. It was not a good deal. Frycer soon found himself feuding with Leaf coach John Brophy. They detested each other.

After stints with the Rangers, Sabres and Penguins, Paiement retired in 1988. There were two or three interesting facts in his bio. He scored the 100,000th goal in NHL history and he was the youngest of sixteen children in the Paiement clan—born in Earlton, Ontario, not far from my own birthplace. As the youngest, Wilf might quip, "I thought my name was 'Get some wood!' until I was twelve. And my brother was 'Get some more wood!'"

His brother Rosaire also played in the NHL and later became somewhat famous for owning a bar in Florida—a hockey hotbed for Canadian snowbirds.

Now we come to the surprising part of the Paiement story. And it's not about Wilf or his son or his brother—it's all about Wilf Paiement Sr.

Let's go back to a game between the Nordiques and Leafs played at Maple Leaf Gardens on February 11, 1983. An hour before game time, I saw Wilf Paiement Sr. sitting next to the visiting team's bench at Maple Leaf Gardens. I often ran into Mr. Paiement when his son played for the Leafs, and he was always an interesting conversationalist. Now he's back to see Wilf in action with Quebec. I flipped my tape recorder on.

"You know, Brian," he says, "I was at the first game played in this building. I remember it was the Chicago Blackhawks who beat Toronto 2–1 and King Clancy was playing that night."

"Yes, and it was Clancy who told me the Gardens looked so big when it was under construction he wondered if they'd ever fill the place," I reply.

I ask Mr. Paiement if he is still arm-wrestling.

"Oh, yeah, I did arm-wrestle in Edmonton a couple of months ago. I was seventy-four when I arm-wrestled there. I'm the only old bugger who arm-wrestles. I was in London, England, this year to arm-wrestle. I was lucky. I won pretty well everything there. I won the arm-wrestling championship in Montreal in 1934. I defeated the man who was for four years the arm-wrestling champion of the world: Wilfred Latour.

"I've been to California a couple of times to arm-wrestle and lots of other places. In Edmonton, between the matches, the referees asked me when I was going to stop arm-wrestling. I said, 'Maybe another fifty years.'

"They laughed and said, 'Why, you'll break your arm, you old fool.'

"And I said, 'I'll not break my arm. I'll bet you $1,000 I'll not break my arm.' I may be seventy-four years old but I'm not stupid. If I'm ever in the breaking position and the referee says to me, 'Do you give up?' I'll say, 'Sure, I give up. You've got the match.'

"One big German guy I arm-wrestled in Edmonton weighed 408 pounds. I got him in the breaking position and when the referee said, 'Do you give up?' he said, 'Oh, no, no, no, no.' So the referee said, 'All right, you are on your own then.'

"So we went on a little more and suddenly his arm broke. Nine of them broke their arms in Edmonton, six men and three women.

"So what's the secret to winning in arm-wrestling? The secret is speed. Lots of men have lots of power. But the speed and the ability not to be nervous is the big thing. You want to be calm. You want to look your opponent right in the eye with a rough, tough look on your face. And squeeze as much as you can. You want to get him going, you want to see him start to sweat. That means you've got him going."

"How long does a match last normally?"

"Oh, I always have long matches. I tell you why. People think I'm laughing at my opponents sometimes. But I'm not. You see, the other guy is no baby, eh. Most the time he's bigger than me. You can't make a move before they say 'Go!' Then you do anything you want according to the rules. Don't try to push him down like that. Pull him like this—right up to your chest. *Bang*, right on your chest. It's pretty hard for him to take his arm out when you've got him like that."

"Have you ever won any big bets, like in bars or places where people want to bet for and against you?"

"No, no. You see, we are insured when we go in those big tournaments, eh. We're not allowed to take part in matches in bars and places like that. I think my arm is insured for $85,000. We're professional."

"Were you a good hockey player?"

"No, I never played hockey in my life. Nobody had any skates when I grew up. We were up north, a bunch of farmers. That was in the early days.

"Now, I'll tell you a story. It was in 1934. I had a big contract in the bush with a lumber company. Labourers were very scarce then, no men. A big wind came along and blew all my timber down. In some places the trees were piled twenty-five feet high. A hell of a job to cut and I couldn't get any men to work. I had to open up my camps by the first of July. Now we're up to the first of August and we only had one man. I had a foreman as well, and a couple of cooks, but I needed workers.

"One day it was nice weather and I was looking through the door of my office and I see a car drive up—a new Plymouth with a Quebec licence. So I walked toward the car and said 'Hello' in French to the occupants. These men didn't know one word of English. They were five brothers from the Gaspé—the Dumont brothers. Altogether there were eleven brothers. They said, 'We're looking for work,' and I said, 'Good. There's lots of work here.'

"So I sent the foreman with them into the bush and they started to work. But they'd never cut trees before, and even though they were big, husky men they weren't much good.

"The next day at noon they came in and said, 'Mr. Paiement, how come you have no other men working here?'

"I said, 'I can't get men to work here.'

"They said, 'You come down to the Gaspé and we'll get you all the men you need. People are starving there.'

"So I go to the bank to pick up some money and I jumped in the car and away we went, all the way to the Gaspé.

"I stayed there with the Dumonts—there were no hotels or nothing. And they were strange farmers—poor country. No horses. They worked the land with bulls and cows.

"I hired 510 men from that area. But the Dumonts were drunkards. They'd drink all night—a strange drink called Saint-Pierre-de-Miquelon. They'd drink it every day and they'd say to me, 'Don't let us drive the car when we're drunk.'

"Now, pretty near every little village there has a taxi—*one* taxi—so I offered these drivers $25 to drive six men in a car, seven with the driver, to get these men all the way to Matachewan, a hundred miles north of where I lived. And they did it. They brought in 510 men.

"The company I was working for was the Murphy Lumber Company from Haileybury. Brian, you lived there. Maybe your dad knew the Murphy brothers. These men worked for thirty-four days and those crazy buggers were nuts. They were wild Indians. And when the Murphy boys came to the camp, the Gaspé workers didn't like them and threatened to kill them. They were going to drown them.

"So I said to them, as calm as could be, 'Listen boys, go back to your bunkhouse. Stay there tonight and come and see me first thing in the morning. If the company agrees to pay you more, we'll talk then. As for me, I'll not pay you half a cent more. If you're not satisfied tomorrow morning, then you'll be paid and you can go home. And you'll pay for the things you bought from the company store before you go. Put that in your thick heads.'

"I was not afraid because I could handle fifty men at a time. No trouble. I'd just touch them and they'd go down. In those days I had terrific power.

"Well, they cursed at me and said, 'You son of a bitch, Paiement. Tomorrow morning you'll go in the bottom of that lake. You and your wife and your kids, too.'

"The next morning they came at five o'clock. All 510 of them. My wife was worried. She was shaking because it looked like we'd all be murdered. I said, 'I'll look after them. Don't worry.'

"I'd already sent the Murphy brothers home because they might have been killed.

"So these Gaspé men crawled into the office in the morning—it was kind of a store as well—and there was a wicket there with a sliding door that closed it off from the rest of the room. And I was in behind the wicket, listening to them talk with their dirty language. I heard them say, 'We're goin' to drown that goddamn Paiement. We'll show that son of a bitch. Where is he? He's such a coward he's run away into town.'

"And when I heard the word 'coward' I was very angry. I took my shirt off and tightened up my belt and I raised that wicket and said, 'Who said that goddamn Paiement is such a coward he ran off to town?' And nobody answered. I said, 'You'd better answer me. Who said that? I'm going to find out.'

"So this guy Dumont stepped toward me and he said, 'I'm the one who said that.'

"I said to Dumont, as I looked him right in the eye, 'You'd better look out, my friend, you're not dealing with a baby.'

"He snarled at me, 'And you're not dealing with a baby, either, Paiement.'

"He pushed his head very close, so I took my big hand and grabbed him by the neck. I smashed fourteen bones in his neck, just with my hand. Then I went right through that wicket, never letting go of his neck. Then I ran him right through a one-inch plank door, knocking guys to the floor as I threw him across the room. Then I lifted him in the air and smashed him into the ceiling two, three times, twirling him around. He died a year and a half later. I was never charged. When the law investigated and found out I was simply defending myself against 510 men, what could they do? They didn't press charges.

"Yes, the other Dumonts and dozens of others tried to gang up on me after that, but I smacked them down. I put fourteen men in the hospital that morning. The rest took off and beat it into the bush. This is not baloney. This is the truth. It was in the *Toronto Star*."

Mr. Paiement finished his story. His words were so believable. I didn't doubt them for a moment.

Years later, I told my friend Ray Bradley (Ray runs a great golf tournament for prostate cancer in London, Ontario, in June each year) the story of Wilf Paiement Sr. and he said, "Everybody up north knows about Wilf. The guy was a legend up there. Owned the hotel in Earlton. He once tackled a bear that was chasing a young kid through a blueberry patch. Wilf ran over and got in between them. When the bear reared up, Wilf barrelled into him and knocked him on his ass. The bear howled and ran away. Wilf saved the kid's life.

"And when Yvon Durelle, the Canadian heavyweight champ, came to Earlton, he challenged Paiement to an arm-wrestling match. Paiement pinned him easily. Durelle left town, ticked off that he'd let an old fellow beat him and embarrass him."

OLD PROS

Jordan Fenn chuckles.

"That was a fascinating yarn about Paiement," he says. "The old boy was quite a character. He was one tough customer. Obviously fearless."

"My dad worked in a lumber camp for a short time back then," I tell Jordan. "He told me the camps were filled with tough customers."

"Was your dad a tough guy?" Jordan asks.

"Heck, no. He was only five foot four and weighed about as much as a jockey. He was the camp dishwasher.

"Kilrea and Schmidt were good, too," I say. "It's hard to believe an NHL club didn't have a skate-sharpening machine. Or that Eddie Shore left on a road trip without his players."

"I see you've got a chapter here called 'Old Pros.' Will our readers recognize the names of the men you write about?"

"Some of them, but not all. One of them, Hobey Baker, wasn't even a pro. But he played like one. He was a huge hockey hero a hundred years ago."

"Is that your next chapter then?"

"That's it. Let me begin with Jim Dorey, a good old Kingston boy. Don Cherry will like this one."

JIM DOREY

Gentleman Jim Dorey, a fourth-round draft choice of the Toronto Maple Leafs in 1964, has no trouble talking about the good times he enjoyed in hockey. And he'll never forget the first impression he left on Leaf fans. We talked on a train one day headed for Montreal.

I think I still hold the Leaf record for penalty minutes in a game, and it happened in my very first game at Maple Leaf Gardens.

It wasn't my fault. Al Smith was in nets and he kept agitating everybody and pointing me out as the guy who was looking for trouble. One fight led to another, and it was wild. I couldn't get off the ice. When I tried to, some guy would step in the way and I'd have to look after him. I took a record forty-eight minutes in penalties that night. It seemed like infinity.

So I get thrown out of the game and I'm sitting in the dressing room nursing sore knuckles. I'm getting my skates off and I'm figuring, "Well, Jim, maybe Imlach will send you so deep in the minors you'll never get back. Or maybe I'm finished with the Leafs and they'll send me home to Kingston." Then in comes King Clancy with Punch Imlach right behind him. I thought it was to deliver my death notice. Clancy grabbed me by the shoulder and said, "That's the kind of hockey we want from you, kid."

Punch gave me a $100 bill and said, "Lookit, get out of town for the weekend because there's gonna be a lot of heat over this." And there was! But I survived that first game and went on to live a life in hockey for another thirteen years.

Travelling by train was a regular routine when I first broke in. On one trip the veterans indicated that this was the time to initiate—shave—the rookies. The rookies at the time were Mike Pelyk, Pat Quinn, Ricky Ley, Terry Clancy, myself and so on. Timmy Horton had been known to take a few drinks once in a while—and this was one of the once-in-a-whiles. Tim Horton was strong as an ox and he said they were going to start with me. So I talked to the other rookies and told them, "If one of us goes down, it is the domino theory: *everybody* goes down." So the rookies sided with me and we went after the vets. We terrorized the car that night. We locked Horton in a room at one end of the car. And we scared the hell out of guys like Murray Oliver, Davey Keon, Bobby Pulford, Johnny Bower, even George Armstrong. They scuttled into their bunks but they found it difficult to lock the curtains. We had a lot of tough rookies and the older guys were pleading with us and trying to buy us off.

Anyways, Horton finally got loose. He ripped open the door down there—and it must have been about four o'clock in the morning—and he wanted revenge. I can remember Pat Quinn and myself and Mike Pelyk being in that small room—that's three rookies against Horton, going toe to toe with him in there for the longest time. Not trying to hurt him, just trying to subdue him. Finally, when it was all over and we got to Toronto, Punch Imlach said, "Geez, I hope you guys got rid of Dorey. Did you throw him off at Kingston?" But he had to put up with me for another couple of years. That was a good rookie story.

In my rookie year with the Leafs, four or five of the guys would have a cab captain to travel with. My cab captains were Johnny Bower and George Armstrong. I had to be in a cab with those guys either going to the hotel or to the rink. Now, Punch used to divvy out seven or eight bucks a trip. That was the cab fare to the nickel, tip included, from the train station to the hotel or from the hotel to the rink and back again. But Johnny Bower, the frugal man that he was at that time, somehow found a way to save a few dimes and nickels from each ride in a cab to buy himself a suit at the end of the year. He'd buy a snappy new suit at Mickey Allen's in Montreal. Imagine that!

It was fun playing road games in the old Chicago Stadium, where Jimmy Dorey was the cock of the walk. I get into a fight with Eric Nesterenko one night, and I've got the dukes up and we're waltzing around and glaring at each other. Nesterenko is a big, tall man and he reaches over my guard quick with two open fingers and dinks me in the eye! That's before I used to turtle on the ice. I didn't know what to do. I had my sweater up over my head and I must have looked like Ichabod Crane, skating from one end of the ice to the other, hoping that he wasn't going to jump me and beat me up. I guess both benches were just rocking with laughter.

This may have been in the same game. I'm on the bench there, I'd just come off a shift and I'm huffing and puffing, and Ronnie Ellis had just let his man—Bobby Hull—get away from him. It was a surprise because Ellis always stuck like glue to Bobby Hull. Now Hull tears off on a breakaway and I'm sitting there with a water bottle. Well, what are you going to do? The obvious! I fired the water bottle and nailed Hull on the shoulder and head. Down he goes, sprawling all over the ice. When I saw the mess I had created, I dove down behind the boards and pretended to be lacing my skates.

Johnny McLellan, our coach, shouted out, "Who's the asshole who did that?" And Ricky Ley didn't quite hear what he said and said something back. Then I popped up and McLellan read between the lines and said, "Dorey, go to the penalty box!" Hull was still fuming, looking like he wanted to kill someone. Now this is going back to 1968 or thereabouts. When I passed by Hull he snarled at me, "You want to fight?" and I said innocently, "Bobby, it wasn't me, it was Ricky Ley!"

It wasn't until 1991 in Kingston that I told Hull the truth. And over all those years, Ricky Ley and Bobby Hull had a lot of feuds. If you check the tapes, you'll find that's the truth.

One time, my dog got me into trouble. My wife thought she heard a burglar in the night. So I leaped out of bed, stark naked, went on the attack, slipped on the floor and ended up in the closet with both my feet up on the wall. It was our dog that woke us up. He had a bad case of diarrhea and shit all over the floor by the bed. And I wound up in the middle of it. There was shit all over everything. When I hit the wall, I broke a toe or two. So, what to do? I had to go down to the rink in real pain. But I slipped on my skates as best I could, skated out and prayed for a shot to come my way. The first one that caromed off my skate, I collapsed in a heap and pretended the shot that hit me on the foot had broken my toes.

I was traded to the Rangers in 1972. Tim Horton wanted me as his defence partner there, but I'd only played one game for them when I hurt my shoulder. Before I recovered, the WHA made me an offer I couldn't refuse. So I jumped to the New England Whalers and made a lot of the Rangers rich by leaving. The Rangers doubled the salaries of guys like Brad Park, Rod Gilbert and Vic Hadfield to make sure they didn't jump, too.

I played in two leagues and in three decades, the '60s, '70s and '80s. My first two years in the NHL I played the role of a gunfighter. Montreal's tough guy, John Ferguson, was at the top of his game and it was my job to challenge him. And you know, I tried to smack him a few times, but Fergie didn't think I was important enough to deal with, so I had to deal with guys like Eddie Shack, and I didn't think that was a fair trade-off.

I wonder if anybody remembers the Evel Knievel story? I was with the Toros in the WHA and Johnny Bassett, the team owner, brought the famous daredevil to Toronto to bring in a crowd. Promised him $10,000 a goal if he could beat Les Binkley, our goalie, in a shootout. We didn't know if Knievel could even skate, but apparently he'd played some junior hockey in some bush league. Butte, Montana, I think it was.

Knievel scored two goals, but that weekend cost Johnny Bassett a lot more than ten grand because I had his credit card. Bassett gave me his gold card and his limousine. He said to Larry Mavety and me, "Lookit, you guys, I want you to take Knievel to the clubs. Keep him out late; let him order whatever he wants. Just make sure he's so hung over that he can't skate tomorrow afternoon."

I said, "What about us? We may be hung over, too."

And Bassett said, "I'm not worried about you two guys playing."

I'll tell you, Larry Mavety and I took Knievel to every gin mill in town that night, until Bassett's credit card was almost worn out. The limo driver was worn out, too. But even with the sun coming up, Evel Knievel was still on his feet. When we brought him back to his hotel at six in the morning, he even invited us up for a nightcap. We knew Bassett and the Toros were in trouble!

The next day, we played Gordie Howe and the Houston Aeros. Our goaltenders were Gilles Gratton and Les Binkley. Johnny Bassett figured he'd go with experience so he put Les Binkley in. Knievel popped in a pair and pocketed twenty grand. Bassett was livid. He came down to the bench and tapped Mavety and me on the shoulder. He chewed us out in front of everybody. He wanted to know what we did last night, and I said, "We did everything!"

But Evel Knievel, I'll tell you one thing about him: he always backed up his wagers with another bet. And he hardly ever lost. I don't think John Bassett knew whom he was dealing with.

I wonder what old Gordie was thinking that day. Knievel made more money on two shots than Gordie did in his first few years with Detroit.

Author's note: Evel Knievel was a much better hockey player than the Toros, or anybody else, imagined. He was once a member of the Charlotte Clippers of the old Eastern Hockey League. He then became the owner, manager, playing-coach and star forward of the Butte Bombers, a semi-pro team that once played the Czech National Team prior to the 1960 Olympic Games at Squaw Valley. When he was ejected from the game, he went missing, along with the gate receipts from the event.

While he was a hero to millions, he had a dark side that became public when author Shelly Saltman wrote a book about his life. Saltman alleged that Knievel abused his wife and kids and did drugs.

Knievel, with both his arms in casts, went to Hollywood and assaulted Saltman. While Knievel's friends held him, Knievel smashed Saltman with a baseball bat. Witnesses heard him shout, "I'm going to kill you," and he almost did. Numerous surgeries were required before Saltman could regain the use of his arm.

On October 14, 1977, Knievel was convicted of assault and sentenced to three months in jail and three years' probation. Ironically, it was later revealed that Knievel's advisors and lawyers had scrutinized Saltman's book and approved every page. Knievel's FBI record runs to almost three hundred pages for crimes of assault, battery and intimidation. Some icon! Some hero!

Knievel, with a world-record thirty-two broken bones in his body, died on November 30, 2007, in Clearwater, Florida at age sixty-nine. Actor Matthew McConaughey delivered the eulogy at his funeral.

Now back to Dorey.

I've gotta mention goalie Gilles Gratton. He was one of
the all-time characters. He wouldn't play if it wasn't in the
stars [he believed in astrology]. He was a streaker. He was a
talented piano player. He'd lived past lives and all that stuff.

One of his disciples had to be Mike Amodeo. [Author's
note: Amodeo is another of our Sunday morning Oldtimers.]
Amodeo played for the Winnipeg Jets and the Toronto Toros.
One time I'm rooming with Amodeo. The normal routine on
game day was to have a pre-game meal, then you'd go to your
room and take a nap or watch the soaps. I was amazed to
see Mike get out a small alarm clock. Then he put a blanket
down. I thought he was into yoga, which was not too bad.

Then Mike said to me, "Jim, I'm just going to be flying
around on this carpet for a while. Think I'll go to Japan for the
afternoon." Then he flopped down on the carpet while I lay
down on the bed, watching him. I know he never moved from
that room. But in his mind, he did some heavy-duty travelling.

About four o'clock, the alarm went off. *Rinngg! Rinngg!* Up
he flew from the carpet. Back to the real world—all the way
from Tokyo. All refreshed and charged up, ready to play that
night. So there you go!

Steve Durbano was another one. Steve and I were in New
York together and the last thing I remember about Stevie
was him having a fight with his wife—they were always
scrapping. He was so upset. He had his skates in the room, I
don't know why. But he took the skates and he threw them
over the bed and they stuck in the wall! That was the last I
saw of Stevie for ten years. I called him when he was doing
time in Joyceville [prison] in Kingston. They caught him
smuggling drugs over the border.

I don't know if this is true, but Parker McDonald says
that he was there when Steve played his last pro game.
Apparently, Steve got a penalty he didn't think he deserved,

so he took off his skates in the box and tossed them across
the ice. After that, he ran across the ice and threw up into the
visiting team's bench. Then he threw up on the ice and again
in his team's room. That was his last game as a pro.

Durbano and his father, Nick, from Welland, Ontario, were wild
men. Nick owned a couple of junior teams and it's alleged he once
tried to run over a referee in a parking lot. Son Steve played junior
for the Marlies, and in a playoff game versus the London Knights he
speared three of the Knights' best players—including Darryl Sittler—
on his first shift. Three of them were laid out, Durbano was smirking
and the London crowd wanted to lynch him.

The New York Rangers, who passed on future stars like Terry
O'Reilly and Larry Robinson in order to get him, drafted him in 1971.
But Durbano was uncontrollable. He frightened his own teammates.
He was as wild as a mountain lion, and just as fearless. He was a
menace for half a dozen years in two leagues. His wife was almost as
hot-tempered and foul-mouthed. She called his hotel room one
night long after curfew and when his roomie—I believe it was Frank
Mahovlich—said he wasn't in, she replied, "Tell him I'm going to
strangle his dog."

He made bigger headlines after he retired. In 1983, he was convicted of drug trafficking and sentenced to seven years in prison. In
1988, when I met him at a hockey event in Welland, he was friendly
and personable. Then I discovered he was facing charges of procure-
ment, attempting to entice a female undercover policeman into a
prostitution ring. He served more time. From jail, he threatened to
kill a reporter who wrote about his cocaine abuse and alcoholism.
Eventually he gravitated to Yellowknife, where he died of liver fail-
ure at age fifty.

Jim has a few more stories about the WHA.

Some other good names from my era were Goldie Goldthorpe and the Hanson brothers. This incident comes from a time when Bobby Baun was a rookie coach with the Toros. The team got rid of Rick Foley and some real tough guys. That left me as the only real scrapper, and I had been in the league for seven or eight years and I needed some help out there. Anyway, we're playing against Minnesota—Shakey Walton's team—with either Harry Neale or Glen Sonmor behind the bench. Their starting forward line—first game of the year—was Curt Brackenbury, Paul Holmgren and the famous Steve Carlson (the big Carlson). I'm thinking there's about two thousand minutes in penalties against little old Jimmy Dorey. They dropped the puck and they threw it in my corner. I watched it go in and went after it. Then I just left my skates and got swept into a whirlwind in there, three of them and one of me. And then our guys—Ricky Cunningham and "Leaping" Lou Nistico, all 150 pounds of him—pile in to help. So Bobby Baun got an introduction to the World Hockey—I mean the World Wrestling Federation. There were no rules in the league.

We played in Denver one night and we beat them 11–8. But Baun didn't like the way we played so he slapped a curfew on us. He came up to me at the airport the next morning and told me he was going to slap me with a $200 fine and a suspension. I said "What for, Bob?" And he said, "Because you weren't in your room for curfew." I said, "That's fine. You do that and I'm going to charge you with break-and-enter, because only a guy who broke into my room would know that I wasn't there last night." So that was settled there and then.

When I was with the New England Whalers in the WHA, every team had a goon or a real character—a Hanson or Gilles Gratton. And the Whalers said, "OK here's what we're

gonna do. We're gonna get a guy by the name of Nick Fotiu."
Remember Nicky Fotiu? He was a New York City boxing
champ. Nicky could skate like the wind but don't put a stick
in his hands. He'd skate around, breezing by everybody,
but—what was this stick used for? We grabbed another
fighter in Jimmy Troy. And he couldn't skate all that well. I
remember we were playing Indianapolis and they had that
Kim Clackson. Remember Kim the clocker? Another legend
in his own mind.

Anyway, fights are breaking out all over and our coach,
Jack Kelley, sends Troy over the boards to get a piece of
somebody. Jimmy starts yelling, "Bring him over here! Bring
him over here!" Troy could fight but he couldn't skate. He
wanted somebody to drag a rival slugger over to the boards so
he could beat the shit out of him.

They were the kind of characters that were around,
and Glen Sather, I remember, was there in Edmonton. He
hired a guy who did time for murder to come out and play
a couple of games—only home games! Sather was a player
and Bep Guidolin was the coach and GM of the Oilers. But
Bep Guidolin just couldn't seem to handle the job and his
off-ice escapades forced him to resign. That's when Sather
kick-started his career. At one time he was a player, a coach
and general manager, and later he named himself president.
How's that for self-promotion?

There was a goalie in Calgary named Smokey McLeod. He
set some sort of crazy record by stopping three penalty shots
in one game—without ever playing in the game. Every time
there was a penalty shot, they replaced the starting goalie
with Smokey. He came in and stopped the first penalty shot.
Later, he was called in to stop a second shot and then a third.
After each shot, he went back to the bench. He played for Joe
the Crow [Joe Crozier] in Calgary. I ended up with Smokey

McLeod in Quebec City. Smokey named his dog "C.C."—for Canadian Club. Old Smokey could do a bottle a day.

Gordie Howe happened to catch my act in my first year in the NHL. He thought I was a pretty wild guy. I had some run-ins with Gordie. He thought I was a little bit out of touch with the way hockey was supposed to be played. I turned around and ended up playing with Gordie, then against him and his sons when he played for Houston. I'll tell you, I can't imagine playing against him when he was at his peak. I just can't at all.

I finished my career in the WHA in Quebec. I'm playing for the Nordiques against the Birmingham Bulls and it has been announced that the league is about to fold. At Quebec we've got a very good hockey team. We've got the likes of Marc Tardif, Rollie Cloutier, Serge Bernier, Richard Brodeur, Wally Weir, Curt Brackenbury and J.C. Tremblay. So we are playing against the Birmingham Bulls and they have some pretty good guys down there, too. They've got guys like Kenny Linseman down there, Gordie Gallant, Ricky Vaive, Rob Ramage, you could go on and on—a good club.

The season is ending and Gordie Gallant nails Baxter of our team good. Legally or illegally doesn't matter because there were no rules. But anyways, they call a penalty on Gallant and Baxter is stretched out on the ice. I'm on the bench and I get a little message in my head, "Dorey, you better do something about this." They carry Baxter off and I get another message: "Get your ass out there!" But how am I going to get at Gallant? He's got a ten-minute misconduct, a five-minute major and two minors. And this is going to be the last time we'll ever see Birmingham. So, mental giant that I am, I'm thinking, "How can I drill this guy?" I can't attack him in the box because they've got a policeman in there and everything. So I lead a rush—a four-man rush. And when

everybody goes by me, I stop right in front of the penalty
box. I turn and fire a slapshot right at Gallant. But he was
quick. He ducks and the puck nails a photographer in there.
He goes down and the puck is rattling around and people
are screaming at me. Anyways, I scramble off the ice and get
out of town fast. But I wound up paying a fine of $9,999.99
in small claims court. There was a $10,000 limit on the fine,
small enough so they could chase me around the United
States trying to collect. It was no big deal in Quebec but in
the southern papers it caused a big stir. Dorey was a "wanted
man" in the state of Alabama.

Gallant was with Minnesota when Harry Neale coached there. After
a game one night, Harry stripped down in his hotel room and was
ready for bed. The phone rang. Gallant's roommate called Harry
with a warning: "Gallant is really pissed off at you and he's on his
way up." Before Neale could react, the door burst open and Gallant
attacked his coach. The battle flowed into the hotel corridor and
Harry, bare-ass naked, tried to defend himself while doors popped
open and astonished hotel guests watched the punch-up. Some team
members arrived to break up the fight, and that marked the end of
Gallant's career as a Fighting Saint.

With Quebec, I hit a skinny kid named Gretzky with a
bodycheck one night. They had to help Gretzky off the
ice and Glen Sather, his coach, was irate. I knew who was
coming at me next: Dave Semenko. As a matter of fact, when
Gretzky was going off the ice I yelled at Sather, "Hurry up
and get Semenko out here before I catch a cold!" The battle
didn't last too long because there was no way I was going
to have a rookie put me down. I had lots of experience, and
even though Semenko was a great fighter, the trick was to get
in close, get two or three quick punches in and then get off.

Because he was a big guy just starting out, and I was winding down my career, I didn't want to get laid out. I remember that well. Gretzky? I didn't know then that he was going to be the superstar he became.

Here's another true hockey story. I forget the year, but you could look it up. It was the year the WHA East–West All-Star Game was played in St. Paul, Minnesota. I was a member of the East team and we were standing in this pitch-dark arena waiting to be introduced. We were lined up on the blue line next to a big flaming hoop. First the West team is introduced, and guys like Keon and Walton are leaping through the hoop and getting a big ovation. Now it's John "Pie" MacKenzie's turn—a guy you either loved or hated. He comes flying through the hoop, the spotlight on him. But he disappears into the dark area at mid-ice and never shows up at the other blue line. Somewhere between the hoop and leaving the spotlight, a couple of guys on the East team left their lineup and decided to lay a beating on this guy. Nobody ever admitted who it was, but I can tell you in the East lineup there were a lot of guys who had been chasing him for years. And they finally got him without Hodge or Cashman around to save his skin.

There was a story every day in the WHA. Somebody nailed the Cincinnati mascot in the warm-up one night—flattened the poor guy dressed up in the bee costume. He was buzzing around when a visiting player, I think it was Kim Clackson, knocked him cold with a bodycheck.

We were in Cincinnati when they held a turkey day at Thanksgiving. I remember Floyd Smith was the coach. Instead of holding a lucky draw for dead turkeys, they had all these live turkeys out on the ice and some guy was busy drawing lucky numbers. The winners started spilling out on the ice and they began chasing these squawking turkeys. You should have seen it. The fans were smashing into the boards,

falling on their asses, falling into each other. There was
turkey shit all over the ice and, oh, it was a sight.

Jim Dorey retired to his home city of Kingston, Ontario, where he
spent several years in the insurance business. He also coached the
Kingston Canadians of the Ontario Hockey League in the 1980s. He
holds a golf tournament each summer, and Jim, I'm really ticked off
that I've never been invited. Too late now, pal. My vision is fading
and I can't see the ball when—and if—I hit it.

DEREK SANDERSON

I often wish I'd gone with Derek Sanderson that night in Manhattan
in 1974. I'm sure it would have been enlightening.

We met in a bar on the East Side after an NBC game in New
York. He was with the Rangers then, having been traded by the
Bruins, and he was living high. Some members of our telecast crew
entered the bar and Derek hailed me from across the room. I'd interviewed him on NBC earlier in the day. He was surrounded by Ranger
fans, some of whom can be the creepiest leeches you've ever seen.
He insisted on buying me a drink.

A few minutes later, he stood up and grabbed me by the elbow.

"Let's get out of here," he said. "I'll take you to a couple of bars
that make this one look like a McDonald's."

"Hey, Derek, I've got an early flight."

"Don't worry, you'll be home by three, four o'clock."

I was tempted. It would be a revelation to see Derek Sanderson,
hockey idol, making the rounds.

Even when he stood up, fans began paying their tabs. It was
obvious they were going to follow him to the next drinking hole.

I demurred. "Catch you next time," I said.

"You bet," he answered. Then he disappeared out the door.

"Jesus, Brian," one of my NBC pals said. "How often does a guy get to see Sanderson at his best—when it's two or three in the morning? You blew it, buddy."

Yeah, maybe I did.

Let me tell you about Derek Sanderson. He grew up in Niagara Falls and led the Niagara Falls Flyers to a Memorial Cup win in 1965. He joined the Bruins a couple of years later, a solid two-way centre-man who could fight. He won the Calder Trophy as rookie of the year in 1968 and played on two Stanley Cup winners in Boston. He was the guy who assisted on Bobby Orr's spectacular goal that cemented the Stanley Cup for the Bruins of 1970. Along the way, he became a rebel, a playboy, and hockey's answer to high-living quarterback Joe Namath. He was voted one of North America's ten sexiest men. He appeared on *The Tonight Show* with Johnny Carson and on *60 Minutes*.

But he couldn't afford to keep pace with his celebrity pals. The Bruins, the NHL's most niggardly team, paid him a paltry salary.

The WHA was born in 1972, and one of the first NHLers to jump to the new league was Sanderson. Over coffee at the old Montreal Forum one night, Derek told me how it happened.

I had no plans to join the new league until Pie McKenzie, my Boston teammate, told me he was signing with the Philadelphia Blazers. He urged me to join him. I was earning $75,000 with the Bruins and asking for $80,000. The girls all loved me in Boston and I told McKenzie I had no intention of leaving.

But I did agree to meet with the owner of the Blazers. I was hung over when we met in my agent's office one morning, and [the owner] started off by offering me a couple of million dollars for five years. I tell you, that got my attention. Nobody made that kind of money back then—in any sport. Still, I had some conditions I wanted him to meet.

I told him, "If I go to Philadelphia, you'll probably wind up selling the team."

"I won't sell if you don't agree to the sale," he fired back.

"You'll trade all my pals on the team," I countered.

"We won't trade anybody without your approval," he said.

"You know I don't like to fly."

"Derek, you can play in all the home games. Forget the road trips."

Holy cow, I thought, is this guy for real?

When he saw me hesitating, he upped the offer to $2.65 million.

I even had him write the offer down, and it looked like a long-distance telephone number.

"You gonna sign with us?" he asked me.

"Maybe. But first I'm going to talk to the Bruins."

The next day, I went to see Mr. [Weston] Adams, the Bruins' owner—a nice man. I met with him because I didn't care for Mr. [Charles] Mulcahy, who was signing players at the time.

Mr. Adams was amazed at the deal Philadelphia was offering, but he counselled me to re-sign with the Bruins. He said, "Derek, I'll make sure you get the $80,000 you've been asking for." Sounded good to me.

"If you don't like Mulcahy," Mr. Adams added, "then sign with my son Westy. His office is just down the hall."

I was in Westy's office, about to sign the $80,000 contract, when Mr. Mulcahy stuck his head in the door and snarled, "Sanderson, I still don't think you're worth eighty grand a season."

That did it. I snatched up the Philadelphia contract and told my agent, Bob Wolff, "Get the Blazers on the phone. I'm gonna sign with them."

But things didn't turn out very well for me in Philly. Can

you believe the team owner, a big man in trucking, came to the rink one day at noon and asked the coach, "Where are all the players?" He was told, "Practice is over. They've gone home." He was amazed. He thought hockey players showed up at nine and left at five—like his truckers.

Anyway, he was happy on opening night because the game was a sellout. The parking lot outside the building was crammed with cars parked every which way. Fans who arrived early were handed souvenir pucks with the Blazers logo on it. But in the warm-up, the strangest thing happened. The Zamboni fell through the ice up to its axles. Unbelievable! Referee Bill Friday, a no-nonsense guy, was there. Friday threw up his arms and said, "That's it. The game is cancelled. Sanderson, you better take a microphone out on the ice and tell the crowd to go home." When I announced the cancellation, the fans hurled hundreds of souvenir pucks at me. But before I fled for my life I gave them a parting shot: "Folks, if you think this is bad, wait until you try to get your cars out of the parking lot." Then I ran for cover.

Soon after he joined the Blazers, Sanderson was injured and played in only eight games, scoring three goals. The Blazers' love affair with him quickly soured. The owner couldn't afford his huge salary and bought him out for $1 million. On an NBC telecast one day, I asked him what happened to that million. He laughed and said, "Gee, I dunno. I don't know what happened to it." Sanderson drifted back to the Bruins, then was traded to the Rangers and went on to play with the Blues, Canucks and Penguins.

When Ted Lindsay was general manager in Detroit, he gave Sanderson a chance at a comeback. He sent Derek over to Windsor to get in shape with the junior team there. Lindsay treated him fairly, and that gave Derek renewed confidence. But within a few weeks, Sanderson was offered a $75,000 contract by the Pittsburgh

Penguins. "I couldn't resist the instant gratification it gave me," he told me later. "So I bolted and let Ted Lindsay down. It was a dumb move on my part. After part of one season, Pittsburgh gave up on me. I saw Teddy months later and apologized and he said, 'Why me, Derek? Why me?'"

By 1978, Sanderson was finished.

Throughout his career, Sanderson battled problems with alcohol and drugs and was found one morning sleeping on a park bench in Central Park. Or so the story goes.

"Do you know who I am?" he asked the rummy sleeping on the next bench. "I was once the highest-paid athlete in the world."

"Yeah, sure you were, pal. I know what you are now. You're a bum—just like me."

Sanderson's lifestyle was often a distraction to his teammates. Phil Esposito says, "He wasn't the perfect guy to room with. He had a bad habit of clearing his throat and spitting on the hotel room floor. When I'd complain and bitch about having to walk through that slime to get to the bathroom, he'd hawk one against the wall. He'd say, 'You don't walk on the fucking walls, do you, Phil?'"

What happened to Derek Sanderson after hockey? In 1980, he decided to re-evaluate his life—concluding that, if he didn't do so, he'd die. He swore off drugs and alcohol and regained his health. And he did it on his own, without outside assistance. He became a commentator on Bruins telecasts, working with my first broadcast partner, Fred Cusick.

He had hip replacement surgery. He began counselling kids in school about the dangers of drugs.

Ironically, he now advises athletes on the need to make wise financial investments. This from a guy who used to light $100 bills with a match to impress the ladies. This from a guy who once owned a Rolls-Royce, dated actress Joey Heatherton and blew millions.

And he no longer spits on hotel room floors. Or the walls.

JIM McKENNY

Jim McKenny was a popular Leaf defenceman in the '70s. In his junior days he was occasionally compared to Bobby Orr. Well, he was no Orr, but he was fun to be around. While most players fretted about their game and their stats and worried about their futures, McKenny was the coolest guy on ice. If you asked him, "Do you ever take the game home with you?" he'd reply, "No, I always leave it in some bar along the way."

It's true that Jim was a drinking man back then. But he's been sober for many years now.

McKenny tells of a stint he had in the minor leagues, after playing eight full seasons for the Leafs.

I guess you don't remember Pierre Giroux, a kid who was playing for the Dallas Black Hawks. I was sent down to Dallas when I was thirty-three. Somebody with the Leafs figured I needed a little more seasoning. One night in Dallas, they held a Bobby Orr Night at the fairgrounds. Bobby's appearance meant a few more fans in the seats, and we were playing against the Fort Worth Texans. Pierre Giroux was on the bubble. It was his last chance to show what he could do. If he didn't play well that night, he was going to be sent even farther down in the minors. A bad game for Pierre and he was facing a twelve-hour drive to Muskegon.

Pierre goes out on his first shift and promptly gives the puck away in our end. He comes to the bench and Gerry McNamara, our coach, is all over his ass. The second time he goes out, he does all right—not a bad shift. But on his third shift—uh-oh—he makes another giveaway, this time in the offensive zone. It didn't look too bad, but Mac still gave him a lot more aggravation.

Suddenly, the kid just freaked out. He turned on Mac,

cursed him out, yelled at him, "You want to go?" and dropped
his gloves. I'd never seen anything like this before. Mac, of
course, just loved to fight, so he was right in his glory. You
could see the smile on his face when the kid turned and
challenged him. And the fists began flying. They just whaled
away at each other. The fans loved it. They were screaming,
cheering—not for anything in the game but for the fight on
our bench.

Then finally our guys got a hold of Pierre and threw him
onto the ice, and we got a penalty for too many men on the
ice. And the kid got his gloves and his stick and he threw
them up into the crowd and he disappeared—never to be
seen again. Next stop, Muskegon.

I was on the end of the bench and I made eye contact with
Bobby, who was up in the press box, and I was just shaking
my head, laughing at all this nonsense. Orr had a big grin
on his face. That was a rare encounter, one I had never seen
before—and I had been playing for something like fifteen
years. That was fabulous.

I liked McNamara. I know a lot of the guys didn't like him.
He got a lot of bad press when he managed the Leafs later on.
Harold Ballard threw him into a bad situation at a bad time.
Harold needed a general manager and put Mac in there too
soon. Mac would probably be a good general manager if he'd
been given another five or six years in the business, sooner
if he'd had someone to learn from, or if he was in a good
organization. Jim Gregory helped him out as best he could.
But with Harold ranting and raving over him and with the
mediocre talent that he had, he was immensely frustrated.
I mean, Mac's first reaction to anything is to, "Go! Go! Let's
go! Let's go at it." But that doesn't work with today's players,
so you know, a lot of guys didn't like him for that, but he is a
beautiful man. You see his family, and his kids are great. His

wife is great and he is doing real well for himself.

You know my nickname was always "Howie" McKenny, and that's because of Howie Young, who played a few years in the league, mostly with Detroit. People said we looked alike. Well, Howie was invited to Toronto for the Charlie Conacher Dinner one year and we palled around for a few days. We went back to where he grew up, in Highland Creek. It was a real treat for me because I hadn't seen Howie for about fifteen or twenty years. When he came back to Toronto, it was like he had died and gone to heaven. They were going to pay him $200,000 to fly in with his girlfriend. He could get to do something that he'd never, ever thought that he would get to do in his whole life. He came here and just had the week of his life. The people from the *Toronto Star* who put on the Conacher Dinner, he just couldn't thank them enough.

Then we went out to his old place and went out for a skate on the pond at Highland Creek. Of course, they had put a drainage ditch in since he skated there as a kid. There was no more pond, there was just sort of like a big puddle that was frozen over. But he had to put the skates on and skate there anyways. I was just witnessing the joy that was coming out of him for that day and a half that I got to spend with him.

We went to a hockey game at the Gardens. We stayed at the game for about a period and a half, and then Howie was so overwhelmed he had to leave the building. We went to the Golden Griddle across the street and sat there until about three o'clock in the morning shooting the shit. You know, it was wonderful.

He talked about playing pro for over twenty years and with all these teams in all these leagues. His last seasons were spent with the Flint Spirits and the New York Slapshots when he was forty-eight years old.

He told me an incredible story—this was in the mid-'60s, when he was with the Los Angeles team in the Western league. It was about his acting career and how he had a good thing going with Frank Sinatra. And how he got into the sauce on a little cruise one day off the coast of Hawaii. He actually threw Frank Sinatra overboard off Frank's yacht just after they filmed the movie *None but the Brave*. Howie had a small role in the movie and he'd had a couple of cocktails—he does admit to that—and the booze always made him a bit impulsive and unpredictable.

He went up to Sinatra and said, "Frank, you're not so tough." And for some reason, he picked Sinatra up and threw him overboard. The rug came off, the guy was about to drown—the whole deal. People were screaming.

Oh, they were way out there on the ocean, a long way from shore. Frank's goons jumped in and rescued Sinatra, and then they came after Howie with a vengeance. They grabbed him and beat the crap out of him. They headed for shore, put a couple of hundred bucks in Howie's pocket and threw him out on the nearest beach.

When Howie woke up the next morning, he thought he had died and gone to heaven. He woke up and there were palm trees swaying and hot sun and a nice breeze. He looks in his pocket and he's got a couple of hundred bucks. He thought, "Wow! This is Paradise." He stayed in Hawaii for about another two weeks and finally they deported him.

He tried to make a comeback after he'd been out of hockey for years. He was in his mid-forties by then. And he'd stopped drinking. He went to Muskegon or somewhere. He said that was mainly out of desperation. But he has done real well. He's been clean now for twenty-seven years, sober, and has helped a lot of other people get sober. He has lived an amazing life and things are starting to turn around for him.

He used to drive around Los Angeles with a monkey on his shoulder, with the cowboy hat, and he had a great big black Cadillac ragtop—of course, the top was worn so there were just the bars. When it rained he'd put the bars up, but it would still be a convertible, and he'd drive around, getting soaked. On the side of the Caddy, he had in spray paint, "*None but the Brave*, starring Howie Young."

He was the toast of Los Angeles there for a while. He still had the Beatle wig. He skated around the rink in Calgary with the Beatle wig on. Then, when the game started, they made him take it off and he had a Mohawk underneath. Everybody laughed at that. He was on about an eighty-eight-dayer at that time. He put a nice drinking streak together back then.

A few years ago, we heard he was driving a school bus in some small place in New Mexico—an Indian settlement. Howie was trying to raise money for a hockey rink so he could teach these Navajo kids how to skate. He'd married again—his third wife—and suddenly he was gone. Dead of a heart attack at sixty-two.

Let me tell you about another Leaf wannabe: "Bam Bam" Bélanger. Alain Bélanger was probably one of the toughest guys in hockey during my time in the game. He'd pick up 200, 300 minutes in penalties every year, but he couldn't really play the game that well. But he scared people. He was in Dallas and they wanted to cut him from the team, but nobody in the organization had the balls to tell him face to face, for fear he'd beat the crap out of them. So he just stayed there for an extra four months and got paid. Then they told him by letter, or telegram, in the off-season that his services were no longer required. They were very pleased that he didn't show up at training camp. If he had, he might have beaten up a few people and enjoyed another ten years in hockey.

In 1977–78, they brought Bam Bam up to Toronto for two weeks. Right off the bat, they wanted him to learn how to cut in on the goal. They told him that as soon as he carried the puck to the blue line, to cut in sharply. But they didn't tell him to get around the defenceman first and *then* cut in. So Bam Bam would take the puck down to the blue line, then plow right into the defenceman. You could hear the bodies smack together up in the rafters.

He did it about fifteen times in a row. No one could figure out what the fuck was going on. He'd say to himself, "Make the cut, make the cut, hit the blue line, make the cut, and cut for the net!" Then he'd slam right into a defenceman and knock him senseless. Oh, God! It was priceless. He played nine games for the Leafs and never scored a goal. But he did earn one assist. Never played in the NHL again.

PETE STEMKOWSKI

At some long-ago hockey event I run into a familiar face: Pete Stemkowski. I greet him warmly because I like this man. "Hello Stemmer, It's good to see you. You were a solid member of the Leafs years ago. You played a huge role in the Leafs' winning their last Stanley Cup in 1967. Tell me about your career."

Yeah, 1967. That was a fun year, wasn't it? Beating Montreal out for the Cup in Canada's Centennial year. I was just a kid, but I picked up twelve playoff points. Then expansion came along and the team was picked apart. I remember when I first joined the Leafs and played for Punch Imlach. Punch was unique. With Punch, when you went to practice you didn't know whether you would be home for lunch, dinner or breakfast the next day, because practices could be two hours, three hours or longer. And if you weren't skating in practice, he would just blow the whistle and you'd start skating some more. I believe his philosophy was, "Hate me and take it out on the other team."

When I joined his team, I was very young. I don't think that three-quarters of the older guys talked to me for the first year. It was as if they were tellin' me, "Prove that you belong and then we will accept you." I can't remember Dave Keon, Bob Pulford or Frank Mahovlich talking to me. If I got a hello out of those guys, I figured I was on the team. Then there was Bob Pulford. Pullie is still very serious. When I see him now, I want to say, "Smile, for God's sake. The world is not that bad."

I was one of the single guys on the team, and we went out to Los Angeles the first year and I met a girl in the bar. A great-looking babe! I said to myself, "I don't know when I'll ever see a girl like this again." And she's hot—really hot. Hot to go. We had already discussed her coming to my room—no problem. But Imlach was very staunch on curfews. He would get a chair and sit by the elevator and check your name off his list as you came in. So I said to the girl, "Listen, I'm going up to my room, here is my room number. Wait about five minutes, then you come up." So I waltz by Punch, he checks me off. Five minutes later, this gorgeous babe walks by and gets on the elevator. What a knockout! Skimpy little skirt, big hooters. Punch must have been pop-eyed. So he checks the elevator and sees the arrow stop on our floor. He's no dummy. He knows there is a broad up there. I remember he came knocking on all the doors to make sure everybody was in. He opened my door and saw that I was in bed. The girl was hiding behind the curtains and he never came in.

The next day, he ripped the hell out of all of us. He says, "One of you guys had a babe up there last night. I know you did. I know she got off on your floor. One of you guys had a babe in his room." I tried to keep from smirking.

One of the older guys told me Punch checked a room one night and went into the bathroom. He pulled the shower curtain back and there was a naked girl standing in the stall. The player whose room it was said, "Honest, coach, I've never seen her before in my life!"

One thing about Punch: boy, he was tough, and the guys would hate him openly. But they would fight for him. I think that's because we had such a veteran team he felt he had to keep the guys that were very devoted to him.

He went bonkers back in the 1960s when he heard they were forming the players' association. He was adamant about that. He said to us, "There's nothing that Eagleson can do for you that I can't do for you. Anybody who joins that association will be gone. I mean it." He scared me, all right. I didn't know what to do. I wasn't one to stand up in the locker room and say anything. I knew that wasn't my place. But I know the guys forming the association got to Frank Mahovlich. They told him certain teams and players were climbing aboard. They said, "Frank, you're a star. Others are joining and you've got to jump on, too. It's not the right thing, not joining."

I know Frank ended up in the hospital with a nervous breakdown, and Punch went crazy. He thought that we had been responsible for Frank's breakdown, and he was bitter and surly for a long while. He skated our butts off for a couple of weeks. He blamed us for putting the Big M in the hospital. But Frank would probably tell you it was Imlach who caused him to break. Would you believe, a year later, after the association did get off the ground, Punch trades Frank to Detroit. One of the guys coming to the Leafs was Norm Ullman, who was president of the players' association. So try and figure that one out.

We had Red Kelly at centre back then. A great player. But I mean, Red wouldn't say ten words all day. And he served as a member of Parliament at the same time he was playing. What a workload! Red would practise, jump on a plane, go to Ottawa, do whatever he had to do, his government duties, come back for a game or practice the next day and people would say, "Boy, is this guy ever gonna be a great coach." And I'm saying to myself, "But the guy doesn't talk, doesn't even swear!" And he turned out to be a pretty good coach.

He went to L.A., he went to Pittsburgh, then to Toronto. Never uttered a cuss word. He would say "goldern" or some such word, and when the word came out and it was a surprise it became humorous. Now I said he didn't talk, but when we played in Montreal and caught the midnight train back to Toronto, we'd get to the station and have about forty-five minutes to grab a sandwich and a beer. Red wasn't a drinker, but he would come with the boys and have a couple of beers. Once he popped a couple of beers, he'd start talking. You couldn't shut him up. So he would go from one extreme to the other. We'd board the train at midnight and in an hour or two the guys have had their sandwich. The game is all but forgotten and Red is still talking away. The guys in their bunks are yelling, "Red, shut up already. Let's get some rest." That was Red Kelly.

Punch got rid of me in March of '68. I was traded to Detroit, along with Frank Mahovlich, and I enjoyed a couple of good seasons there. And Frank did, too. We both seemed to thrive once we got away from Imlach. I remember Frank was on a sports phone-in show shortly after he became a Red Wing. He took a call and the caller said, "Frank, it's great to have you in Detroit. But I have a question. How come you can't skate backwards?"

Frank bristled a little bit and said, "What do you mean I can't skate backwards?"

And the guy said, "Hey, Frank. I've seen you play. You can't skate backwards. How come?"

Now Frank is pissed, and he says to the caller, "You come down to the Olympia tomorrow morning and I'll show you if I can skate backwards or not. Let's take another call."

The next morning at practice, I slide over to Frank and I say, "Well, are you going to show me how you can skate backwards?"

His eyes go wide and he says, "It was you?"

My career as a Red Wing ended after coach Ned Harkness caught me mocking him one day.

He was a college coach. Had some great years at RPI and then Cornell. But his rah-rah college ways didn't go over in Detroit. He ordered us to wear blue blazers and grey slacks. And to get haircuts and give up cigars. Geez, Howe and Delvecchio didn't like that. Fats [Delvecchio] had a cigar in his face since the day he was born.

You can bet there were a few snide comments about the new coach—behind his back, of course. One day, Ned was late for a morning practice, so I got up and played the role of a college cheerleader. "Come on, guys!" I hollered. "Gimme a C! Gimme an O! Gimme an R!" And I was spelling out Cornell. The guys were all laughing, but suddenly the room goes quiet. I look around and who's standing right behind me but Harkness. Geez, talk about mocking someone and he catches you red-handed.

If that little incident didn't finish me in Detroit, there was another one that surely did. We played an exhibition game in Port Huron one night and I played pretty well. But I was more interested in what might happen after the game. I was single at the time and I invited a good-looking girl I knew to come to the game. After the game, we take a walk on the beach and we roll around in the sand for a few minutes. But

Crooner Bing Crosby was a hockey fan and the first Hollywood celebrity I interviewed.
(*Author's collection*)

With Chico Resch, Howie Meeker and Ed Westfall on NBC. Someone said, "We buy our suits from Brooks Brothers, Chico buys his from Ringling Brothers." (*NBC photo*)

After one of our Oldtimer games, former NHLer Howie Menard relaxes in his personal penalty box. (*Author's collection*)

Here I play Santa before a Leaf game in the '60s. Toronto general manager Punch Imlach refused to sign Santa to a contract because "he wears a red and white uniform. The old guy should play for Detroit." (*Author's collection*)

In the studio with coach Jacques Martin. Martin, like Mike Keenan, Ray Shero and Bill Torrey is a St. Lawrence University grad. (*Author's collection*)

Current NHL stars often scrawl a signature. Oldtimers like Cherry, Lindsay, Hull and Howe take pride in their penmanship and fans (and friends) are grateful for it.

(*Author's collection*)

With Chris Haney, co-inventor of Trivial Pursuit, the world's most successful board game with close to 100 million in sales. Chris is a majority owner of Devil's Pulpit Golf Course northwest of Toronto. (*Author's collection*)

King Clancy was kind enough to let me write his life story— my first of more than sixty books. He got me hooked on hockey's fascinating history.

(*Author's collection*)

It was a huge honour and thrill to play for two decades with the NHL Oldtimers—the only amateur on the team. My teammates included John "Goose" McCormack, Murray Henderson, Ivan Irvin, coach Art Smith and Danny Lewicki. The Oldtimers seldom lost a game and many became lifelong friends. (*Author's collection*)

Hall of Famer Eddie Shore, a brilliant defenseman but a bizarre owner and coach. His treatment of AHL players in Springfield led to a strike and the beginnings of the current NHLPA. (*Author's collection*)

Sandy Hawley, Canada's most famous jockey, met dozens of NHL stars during a stint as penalty timekeeper for L.A. Kings' games. (*Ontario Jockey Club photo*)

Four fabulous Red Wings: Marty Pavelich, Gordie Howe, Ted Lindsay and Red Kelly. Kelly is the only non–Montreal Canadien to play on eight Stanley Cup teams. (*Author's collection*)

Walter and Wayne Gretzky pictured in New Jersey, January 1984.

(*Paul Bereswill/Hockey Hall of Fame*)

Former NHL player and coach Bob Murdoch joins me in Fort Myers, Florida, where the Snowbirds play three mornings a week. (*Author's collection*)

The opening of the Total Hockey Museum in Clarington, Ontario. The prime minister's young son, Ben, shares the moment with Kevin Shea, museum curator. (*Courtesy of Marko Shark*)

it's cold and not very comfortable, so I say, "Let's go back to my room."

She says, "What about your roommate?"

I say, "Bobby Baun? He'll be asleep by now. And nothing wakes him up."

So we make our way back to the hotel and I notice I've missed curfew by a few minutes. "We'd better sneak up the back stairs," I suggest. "We don't want to run into Harkness. I'll go up first; you follow in about five minutes. Knock on my door." I gave her my room number.

So I get up to my floor and who the hell is standing in the hall but Harkness. His room was a couple of doors down from mine.

"You've missed curfew," he says.

"Did I?" I act surprised and look at my watch. "Geez, my watch must have stopped."

"Come in my room for a minute," he says.

"Okay."

In his room, he tells me I'd played really well and he was counting on me for a big season. Then he stops and says, "You've got sand on your clothes."

I say, "Do I? Now how the hell did that happen?" I brush myself off. Sand spills out of my cuffs. I say, "Well, I better go."

But just then there's a knock on the door. Ned opens it and there's my date, standing there looking confused.

"Can I come in now, Pete?" she asks.

Ned looks at me in disgust.

"You better get your act together," he threatens.

I knew right then I would not be a Red Wing for long. And sure enough, within a short time I was traded to the Rangers. Best thing that ever happened to me. I had six good years in New York. I loved the fans there and they loved me back.

In retirement, Pete became a hockey broadcaster. He played on a Memorial Cup team with the Marlies in 1964 and a Stanley Cup team in 1967. A Winnipeg native, he's a member of the Manitoba Hockey Hall of Fame.

JOHNNY BOWER AND GEORGE ARMSTRONG

Three or four years ago, Nancy Bower invited me to emcee Johnny Bower's eightieth birthday party in the west end of Toronto. Well, she *said* it was his eightieth. It was a surprise party for a guy who's older than artificial ice, a chap who was Lord Stanley's favourite netminder. And it was a real surprise when former Leaf captain George Armstrong showed up at the party—Army doesn't attend many functions of any kind. But Bower was his roommate for years, and they are very close.

I enjoy Armstrong, and always have. A very funny guy. At Harry Watson's wake, I asked him to tell me a story from his younger days. "When I was a kid, my parents sent me to a summer camp. And you know what the cooks did at summer camps in those days? They put saltpetre in our food. You know what saltpetre does to you, eh? Well it didn't affect *me*—until last year."

At Bower's party, I notice George talking to several of the players' wives. They burst out laughing, and I'm curious. On the drive home, I asked my wife what he said to them.

"George is so funny," she told me. "He was telling us that he doesn't like social events, he doesn't like signing autographs. He talked about one guy who came up to him and asked him to sign his cap. He grunted, 'Oh, all right.' And he signed. The guy then asked him to sign his shirt. George scrawled his name on his shirt. The guy asked George to sign a book. George stared at him for a moment and said, 'I'll bet you'd like me to sign your ass.'

"The guy grinned and said, 'Would you?'

"George said, 'Drop your drawers and turn around.'

"The man obliged.

"George took a big black magic marker and wrote across the guy's bum, 'Johnny Bower.'"

I recall interviewing George many years ago during Christmas week, when society wasn't as politically correct as it is today. He was half-Ojibwa and was named Big Chief Shoot-the-Puck by the Stoney tribe. He wore a huge feathered headdress when they made him an honorary Indian chief. On *Hockey Night in Canada*, I asked him what he bought his wife for Christmas.

"I bought the squaw a new pair of moccasins," he replied.

"But your wife has Scottish roots," I mentioned.

"That's right. I'm Indian and she's a Scot. No wonder our kids are wild and tight."

Bower told me he enjoyed watching Western movies on TV when he roomed with Army on road trips. "But sometimes George would get up and shut off the TV in the middle of a movie. You know those scenes where the wagon train would be surrounded by Indians circling on horseback, and the white settlers would be picking them off one by one with rifle fire? Well, George would jump up and say, 'That's enough. I'm not going to see my people take another beating from the white man.' And click! Off would go the TV."

On *Hockey Night in Canada* one night, I called Armstrong by his nickname, Chief. Everyone called him Chief, and I was amazed when a viewer wrote a stream of letters to my boss condemning me as a racist and demanding that I be fired. To his credit, *Hockey Night in Canada* executive Frank Selke Jr. tried to placate the fan with several explanatory letters, but the man refused to see any viewpoint but his own. When I told Army about the exchange of mail, he just laughed. "I want people to call me Chief," he said. "I'm Chief Shoot-the-Puck."

Without Armstrong and Bower, the Leafs would not have won four Stanley Cups in the '60s. Army was the leader, the captain, and

Bower provided sensational goaltending. At one point, Punch Imlach called Bower "the most amazing athlete in the world."

When he started out, he certainly didn't look like a future four-time Stanley Cup winner and a Hockey Hall of Famer.

The only boy in a family of nine, he had no hand-me-down skates. A family friend gave him his first pair. His dad cut bent branches from trees to whittle them into hockey sticks. And his first goal pads were cut from discarded mattresses.

But he progressed through minor and junior hockey, only to take a detour and enlist in the Canadian Army as a teenager. Records indicate he was only fifteen. Future teammates simply didn't believe he was old enough to have served in World War II. After his army stint, he joined the Cleveland Barons of the American Hockey League, where he set an abundance of records.

No NHL team seemed to notice or care, although the Rangers brought him up for a season. But they had young Gump Worsley on the roster and showered him with a lot of publicity. I guess they figured he'd be a better long-term bet than Bower.

Back to the minors—Vancouver, Providence and Cleveland again—went Bower, where he excelled for several more seasons, until the Leafs finally woke up and brought him aboard.

He was well into his thirties by then, and even Bower didn't think he'd be much help to a last-place team. And Punch Imlach didn't want to pay him much—around $12,000 per season.

But he filled a big hole, and blossoming stars like Dave Keon and Frank Mahovlich filled others. Punch Imlach, a whip-snapper of a coach, drove the Leafs, and in the '60s they won four Stanley Cups.

After one Cup win, Bower was so elated he tossed his goal stick high in the air. While his teammates rushed to embrace him, the stick came tumbling down, struck him on the head and cut him for eight stitches.

Rocket Richard of the Canadiens gave him the most trouble. "That bugger scored more goals on me than any other player. And he would rub it in. He scored a goal on me one night and said to me, 'Hey, Johnny, look out for number two.' I wondered what he meant when suddenly he whipped another one in.

"'Hey, Johnny, that's number two. Be careful of number t'ree.' And by golly, a few minutes later he fired a third goal past me—number t'ree.

"He laughed as he skated past my net. I was so happy when the Rocket retired. I figure it gave me another few years in the NHL."

Jean Béliveau was not as lucky as the Rocket. "Johnny Bower gave me the most trouble of all the netminders I faced. I had a long reach and I liked to fake the goalies, to deke them. But he would never fall for my fakes and he had a great poke check."

Hockey Night in Canada's Howie Meeker said, "Bower was the best stand-up goalie I ever saw."

BOB GAINEY

Bob Gainey, the Hall of Fame forward who spent sixteen years in the NHL and helped Montreal to five Stanley Cups, a four-time winner of the Frank J. Selke Trophy as the NHL's top defensive forward and a Conn Smythe Trophy winner in 1978–79, is one of the most impressive hockey men I have ever met. He handles every situation with dignity and class.

Dick Irvin tells me, "When Bob was a young player he was shy and sensitive, not the best player to interview. Then, almost overnight, he became more forthcoming and very articulate. He became one of my all-time favourite players to interview."

I agree, Dick. And Gainey was thoughtful in the extreme. At a hockey banquet in New York one year, Bob was a head-table guest. I tried some new material on my audience and I didn't think it went over too well. I was a little depressed. Then someone handed me a note from farther down the head table. It was from Gainey. "Your new material was great," he wrote. It was a little touch that meant so much. Easily forgotten but never forgotten.

The hockey world knows that Bob has seen more than his share of tragedy in his lifetime. The loss of his beloved wife Cathy to cancer at age thirty-nine, followed eleven years later by the loss of a vivacious, talented daughter. On December 8, 2006, Bob's daughter, twenty-five-year-old Laura Gainey, was swept off the deck of a 55-metre tall ship, the *Picton Castle*, almost five hundred miles off the shore of Cape Cod. A rogue wave washed her overboard. She was not wearing a life jacket and a four-day search failed to find any trace of her. The Gainey family and others feel there was a cover-up following the incident. If proper safety measures had been followed, Laura might still be alive. The owners of the *Picton Castle* stated it was a "tragic accident" and claimed that Laura was an "unlucky victim." Bob told the CBC, "I am sickened and angry. Something happened and the result was changed."

His fans in Peterborough, Ontario, where he starred in junior hockey for the hometown Petes, held a roast for Bob Gainey one night many years ago. Gainey had finished a stellar career with the Montreal Canadiens and would soon go on to successful management jobs in the NHL with Minnesota and Dallas before returning to Montreal to manage the team he once captained.

In Peterborough we all had our turn roasting Bob, with Roger Neilson getting in the best shots. Then Ken Dryden, the soft-spoken, articulate former Habs goaltender, was handed the microphone.

> It's not often that thirteen-goal scorers get honoured or roasted. So I'm pleased that Bob Gainey is our guest of honour tonight.
>
> When I look around the room and I see NHL players like Doug Jarvis and Jimmy Roberts here, I realize that I may be the only player in the room who scored fewer goals than Bob Gainey [laughter and applause].

The first time I heard of Bob Gainey was during the 1973 draft. I was listening to the radio when I heard someone mention that the Canadiens had drafted Bob Something-or-other. I didn't catch the last name. It wasn't until the next day that I learned the Canadiens had not drafted Bob Neely, but Bob Gainey. A few months later, I left the Canadiens to article with a law firm in Toronto, and some time after that I was in Fredericton for a sports banquet and the TV was on in the reception room after the banquet. I couldn't hear the sound, but on the screen I saw an image I didn't recognize. I couldn't tell who the player was, but I was impressed by how well he could skate. I said to myself, "That fellow can really fly. Someday he's going to be a big star in the NHL." [He pauses.]

A few months later, I realized I was wrong [laughter].

A few months later, I was back in Montreal with the Canadiens and I realized I was wrong again. He was going to be a big star.

I played with Bob for the next four years, and in that time we won four Stanley Cups and each year he played a larger role on the team until he became the driving force on the team. He was a goalie's best friend.

I haven't played for several years now and I don't get to see many games. I don't get to see Bob play very often. But when I close my eyes and think of him, I have a very vivid image of his style. The image begins with me in goal and with the puck in the Montreal zone. Now one of our defencemen—Savard or Robinson—is moving the puck smoothly and carefully up centre ice. At the blue line, suddenly there's a quick pass to Gainey, who's coming out of our defensive zone—the last forward to do so and he's coming from behind the play. I see him moving fast, bent over, charging along like a train through an open field. Now an opposing defenceman comes into the picture, back-pedalling with Gainey in his sights, and he begins to realize how fast Bob is going. The defenceman begins to turn and scramble after Bob and they bump into each other. They're now at the top of the circle and they strain against each other, one big man against another. Now it becomes a contest—*their* contest. I straighten up from my crouch and I watch this battle for, oh, one or two seconds. I'm sure the other players are watching, too. Then, slowly, Bob wins the struggle and powers by. He speeds toward the goal and—well, unfortunately, you know the rest of the story [much laughter, much applause].

It was on that night that Dryden favoured us with an excerpt from the book he was completing, an excerpt that revealed his feelings about Gainey.

One time someone mentioned that Bob Gainey scored very few goals and my wife Linda turned to me, a little surprised. She said, "Do you know, while I've watched him play for nearly five years, I never realized that." Then she shrugged and went on to something else, as if in Gainey's case it really didn't matter.

While a team needs all kinds of players with all kinds of skills to win, it needs prototypes, strong, dependable prototypes, as examples of what you want your team to be. If you want a team to be cool and unflappable, you need at least one [Serge] Savard to reassure you, to let you know that the time you need to do what you want to do is still there.

And if you want a team to succeed, where the goal is to win game after game, you need a player with an emotional and a practical stake in the team game, a player to remind you of that game, to bring you back to it whenever you forget, to be playing conscience of the game—then you need a man like Bob Gainey [thunderous applause].

Bob Gainey may not have scored with the frequency of a Lafleur or a Shutt, but he was a bona fide hero to Habs fans. The Soviets once called him the "greatest hockey player in the world." He went on to coach and manage in the NHL, and in 1999 his Dallas Stars won the Stanley Cup. In May, 2003, Gainey returned to Montreal as General Manager of the Canadiens, pro hockey's most successful franchise.

On February 23, 2008, the Canadiens retired his famous number 23 jersey.

HOBEY BAKER: FIRST AMERICAN HOCKEY HERO

Almost sixty years ago, in the early 1950s, as a college player with St. Lawrence University, I had the opportunity to play against teams from Princeton University. At Princeton, I recall being curious about the name I saw over the arena entrance—Hobey Baker Memorial Arena—and wondering about the man to whom the rink was dedicated. I soon learned that Baker was revered as one of Princeton's greatest athletes and one of the world's greatest hockey players. How could that be, I wondered? The man was never a professional. And he certainly wasn't a Canadian. But further research convinced me that Hobey Baker was indeed a superb all-around athlete and one of the greatest hockey players in North America a hundred years ago.

Here's the story of Hobey Baker.

More than a century ago, long before the New York Rangers and Americans made their splashy debuts in the NHL, hockey was well established not far from Broadway. The last century was a little more than a decade old when a handsome collegian captured the headlines with his prowess on ice.

Outside St. Nicholas Arena in New York, its marquee emblazoned with a huge banner proclaiming "Hobey Baker Plays Tonight," a line of limos would stretch from Columbus Avenue to Central Park West on 66th Street. It was like a night at the opera or the opening of a Broadway show. Inside the arena, fans dressed in their Sunday best filled every seat, lured by the appearance of Hobart Baker, an American kid, a hockey phenom possessed with extraordinary athletic ability.

"Here he comes!" the fans would shriek, leaping to their feet and cheering as the handsome blond rover for St. Nick's circled his goal and began an electrifying dash down the ice. One veteran sportswriter, after seeing Baker perform, said, "I have never heard such spontaneous cheering for a player and I never expect to again. Such an ovation greeted Baker, the former Princeton star, a dozen times a night. Spectators went hysterical when he flashed across the ice, cradling the puck on his stick, swooping and swerving in a most graceful manner. He was an athletic marvel, a phenomenon on metal blades."

This was not a hardened professional or even a semi-pro he was writing about. Baker and his St. Nick's mates were true amateurs. After games, they found no crinkled bills stuffed in their shoes, a common practice in Canada at the time. The St. Nick's boys paid for their ice time at the arena. They were bankers and brokers and men of substance and influence. Incredibly, several players had their personal valets accompany them to games. After the matches, the valets would assist the players into evening attire—tails and white gloves— and off they would go in the waiting limos with their ladies to a posh restaurant or nightclub. Tables would be reserved for them. The band would play their favourite music and they would dance the rest of the night away.

The St. Nicholas ice surface had long been a winter playground to Hobart Amory Hare Baker. He first played under its lights at age sixteen, when he was regarded as the best player ever to perform for St. Paul's School in New Hampshire. It was Christmas 1908 and the St. Paul's preppies came to New York to play a pair of schoolboy games at St. Nicholas against Lawrenceville, a traditional rival. Why St. Nick's? Because several alumni of St. Paul's had purchased a nondescript ice-house and converted it into an arena, complete with artificial ice.

Artificial ice had been around for a long time. The Glacarium, an arena in the Chelsea area of London that opened its doors to skaters in 1876, was the first artificial ice rink. By the turn of the century, similar rinks had opened to skaters in Paris, New York, Melbourne and Johannesburg.

On the eve of the Christmas competition on the artificial ice of St. Nicholas, illness struck the Lawrenceville seven and a team called St. Nick's, composed of older, tougher, ex-collegians, was recruited to stand in. St. Paul's stunned the former college stars with a surprising display of hockey technique, most of it flowing from the strong arms and legs and handsome head of a blond teenager—Hobart "Hobey" Baker.

Who was this lad with the blazing speed, the deadly shot and the stamina of a Canadian pro? It was revealed that he'd been born in Bala Cynwyd on Philadelphia's Main Line in 1892, son of a former Princeton football star, Thornton "Bobby" Baker. In 1903, eleven-year-old Hobey was packed off to St. Paul's School in Concord, New Hampshire.

At St. Paul's, which he attended for seven years, Hobey—more so than his older brother Thornton—discovered the joys of athletic pursuits. He excelled in gymnastics, football, baseball and swimming. He could master almost any sport with little or no training. He donned roller skates for the first time, and in a few minutes was doing stunts on them, often on one foot. By his fifteenth birthday he was regarded as the best athlete on campus, perhaps the best in St. Paul's history.

Hockey was big at St. Paul's, and Baker quickly showed an uncanny ability to play the game. By age fourteen he was a regular on the school team and skating, even then, as well or better than most professionals. He wore then, and would throughout his career, a minimum of padding and never donned a helmet in any of the sports he played—even college football.

After graduating from St. Paul's, he attended Princeton University, where he became the wonder player of college hockey—and football. He captained both teams and became a marked man on the gridiron and on the ice. The light hockey padding he wore made him vulnerable to sticks and fists, and he suffered some brutal beatings in games. He never lost his temper, never retaliated. In his entire college career he received two penalties. His movie-star looks and shock of blond hair made him the idol of the crowds.

On-campus arenas were unknown in Hobey's day. College games were played in big-city rinks like St. Nicholas, and huge crowds began to show up for Princeton games to see the greatest American-born amateur player of them all.

John Davies, Baker's biographer, writes about his acute modesty. "He was always polite and obliging, except when talk got around to his athletic exploits. Then he could be curt and even difficult. His exquisite coordination he regarded as some kind of freak power he had been born with and he took no special pride in it. He was deeply humiliated by the sign 'Hobey Baker Plays Tonight' and sometimes refused to play until it was taken down."

When he joined St. Nick's after graduation, he played against players on various teams who were paid to play hockey. Many were imports from Canada who didn't share Baker's views that hockey was a "gentleman's" game. They tried to bully him into submission, using knees and elbows and every conceivable dirty trick to force him to the sidelines. When he'd had enough, he'd turn his game up a notch, score a brace of goals, then offer a smile and a handshake to the vanquished opponent.

Lester Patrick, who enjoyed a brilliant career as coach and general manager of the NHL's New York Rangers, once said, "Hobey Baker is the only amateur player I've ever seen who could have played professional hockey and been a star in his very first game."

By 1916, Hobey Baker found a fresh outlet for his boundless energy and enthusiasm. He took up flying and, to no one's surprise, mastered it quickly. He was among the first to join a group of American pilots who volunteered for service in France.

He became a commanding officer of the 141st Squadron at Toul in France and downed at least three, and possibly as many as fourteen enemy planes. But the war ended too quickly for Baker, who longed for more combat. With the armistice he was ordered back to Paris, but decided to take one final flight in his Spad, a two-wing fighter plane painted in Princeton colours: orange and black. But a mechanic suggested he take another plane up instead, one ready for a flight test. Baker agreed and took off through the mist. At 600 feet the engine sputtered and quit. Baker threw the craft into a steep dive, obviously hoping to gain enough speed to pull the plane up at the last second and glide to the landing field. But he ran out of altitude. The little Spad hurled itself into the ground and Baker was killed instantly. He was buried with military honours at the nearby American cemetery at Toul. A national day of mourning marked his passing. Eventually, family members made arrangements for his body to be returned to Bala Cynwyd and reburial in West Laurel Hill Cemetery. An anonymous poet penned the following for his headstone:

> You seemed winged, even as a lad,
> With that swift look of those who knew the sky,
> It was no blundering fate that stooped and bade
> You break your wings and fall to earth and die,
> I think that someday you may have flown too high,
> So that immortals saw you and were glad,
> Watching the beauty of your spirits flame,
> Until they loved and called you, and you came.

In 1945, Hobey Baker was enshrined in the Hockey Hall of Fame, a rare honour for an American-born amateur.

U.S. college hockey's most prized award is the Hobey Baker Memorial Award, which goes to the top player in collegiate hockey each year. Recent winners include forward Paul Kariya and goalie Ryan Miller. Kariya was a huge star at the University of Maine, while Miller, who played his minor hockey in California, set an NCAA record for career shutouts at Michigan State with 26. He is one of ten members of the Miller family (grandfather, father, three brothers and five cousins) to play for State. He was drafted 138th by Buffalo in 1999 and recently signed a five-year extension to his contract worth $31.25 million.

A HULL OF A LOT OF LAUGHS: DENNIS AND BOBBY HULL

I have a place in the country, and one of my neighbours is hockey's funniest man, Dennis Hull. His brother Gary lives just down the road. And Bobby, hockey's most married NHLer, comes by from time to time. For young readers, an explanation may be in order. Dennis Hull is Bobby Hull's brother and Brett Hull's uncle. Gary might have been as famous as the rest of the Hulls if he'd focused on the game the way Bobby and Dennis did. By the way, if you don't recognize those names, perhaps you should skip the next few pages. But if you do move ahead, you'll miss out on a couple of laughs—I guarantee it.

Dennis reminisces about his days as a Chicago Blackhawk:

It was 1972, the year the WHA came along. Bobby was gone to Winnipeg for a million dollars and Ralph Backstrom and Pat Stapleton from our team had jumped leagues, too. They became part-owners of the Chicago Cougars. So the main guys left on the Blackhawks were Jim Pappin, Pit Martin and myself. [Author's note: Pit Martin was a good friend of Dennis's. He died in a snowmobile accident in late 2008.]

I finally made the Blackhawks in my third season as a pro. But it was touch and go. I played in a few games in 1966;

in the pre-season I played in the first six games. If I played in any more than six games the Hawks would have to keep me—I couldn't be sent down. Coach Billy Reay confided to my brother Bobby, "I think Dennis may need another year in the minors."

That got Bobby thinking. We're driving to the game that night and he tells me that I won't be playing, that Reay plans to keep me on the bench. He won't play me because if he does, he'll be stuck with me for the rest of the season.

Bobby says to me, "Here's what we're going to do. You know how I start the game and usually stay out for a long shift. Tonight I'll take a short shift. You watch for me. When I skate near the Chicago bench, I'll jump off and you jump on, okay?"

I say, "Okay."

So Bobby whips past the bench in the first few seconds, gives me a nod and leaps over the boards. I begin to jump on, but by then Billy Reay has figured out what's going on and moves fast. He reaches out and grabs me by the back of the jersey just as my skates hit the ice. By then it was too late. I was already legally in the game. And it turned out well because I scored 25 goals that season.

I had a lot of fun playing with the Blackhawks.

One day there was some kind of a meeting and J.P. Bordeleau, one of our Rhodes Scholars on the Hawks, was asked to attend. Don't ask me why. So I told him, "J.P., be sure and keep the minutes of the meeting." He said, "Ho-kay, Dennis."

Now he comes out of the meeting and he sees me standing nearby. He calls over, "Hey, Dennis, twelve minutes."

One year, Billy Reay said he was sick and tired of all the silly questions the sportswriters ask after hockey games. So he decided he wasn't going to allow his players to speak to the media from then on, especially the New York reporters.

He hated those New York guys. But there was a league rule that said the team had to make players available to the press. So Billy introduced Chicago's "designated speaker." Impishly, he selected J.P. Bordeleau to do the talking. At the time, J.P. really struggled with the English language, so you can imagine what kind of answers he gave. That really ticked off the media, but everyone on the team thought it was hilarious—except J.P., of course.

We hated to see Bobby jump leagues and join the WHA. But Bobby had said, "If someone offers me a million dollars, I'll go to the WHA." And a couple of days later, Winnipeg came up with the dough—although the other clubs had to chip in.

Naturally, we all wanted him to stay. Jim Pappin even started a little movement among the Blackhawks. If money was the only problem, we were all willing to take a little less on our contracts just to keep Bobby in Chicago. That's something you never encounter in pro sports.

We had some great times in Montreal, playing at the old Forum. After Maurice Richard retired, we would come off the ice at the Forum and the Rocket would be sitting close by, right above the exit. The Rocket would sit there nursing a beer and he'd shout at us—"Hey Mikita, you little DP, if I was out there I'd keel you. You touch my brudder Henri once more, you son huv a bitch I come out there and keel you."

So we're coming off the ice and Mikita says to me, "Watch this." When the Rocket gave him an earful he reached up and hit Richard's beer container with his stick, dumping beer all over the Rocket's pants.

Oh, the Rocket was mad.

In '67 I was playing against the Canadiens' big line centred by Béliveau. Now Béliveau breaks away from us and he goes in one on one against Pierre Pilote and Pilote falls down. So I rush over and I give him a dandy two-hander right across the arm. Now this is Béliveau, my hero growing up. I even had a big picture of him in my bedroom. Well, he shook off my check and with one hand threw the puck into the Chicago net behind Glenn Hall. Then he turned to me and said, "Dennis, I did not expect that from you."

Well, I could have crawled under the Habs' logo at centre ice. I said, "Geez, I'm sorry, Jean. I'll never do that again."

So Billy Reay, when I go to the bench, said, "What are you doing talking to that guy? What's going on out there?"

I said, "I wanted to apologize to Jean."

He said, "Apologize? Are you nuts? You never apologize to those guys."

You know how coaches often say, "We're all the same on this team." Billy Reay used to tell us, "We're not all the same on this team. Bobby and Stan are a lot better than the rest of you guys. Understand?" We all understood. We accepted it.

Billy had a great sense of humour. A wonderful man, Billy Reay.

Dale Tallon was another guy with a good sense of humour. Dale has done real well in hockey. We never dreamed he'd someday be running the Hawks as general manager. But he is—and he's doing a great job. [Author's note: Tallon was replaced by Scotty Bowman's son Stan on July 14, 2009.]

My first year in Chicago, I finally got a place in the dressing room. And my seat was right next to our goalie, Glenn Hall. Before our first game, Glenn rushed into the bathroom and threw up. I didn't know he was renowned for this. So when he came back I said, "Glenn, do you get sick before every game?" And he growled back, "No, just since you joined the team."

My old man never figured any of his sons would make it in hockey. Or if he did, he never told us. We'd come and visit him

in the summer after we'd been in the NHL for a few years and
Bobby had established himself as one of the greatest players
in history. Dad would just snort if someone mentioned our
accomplishments and bellow out a line we'd heard so often: "I
always said that neither one of you was any damn good."

In 2007, thirty-five years after the eight-game series was decided by
Paul Henderson's winning goal in the final minute of the final game,
I talked with Dennis about Team Canada's trip to Moscow in 1972.

When Henderson scored, I looked up to where Soviet
Premier Brezhnev was sitting. Boy, did he look sour.

Three or four of the Team Canada players quit early and
went home. Richard Martin and Gilbert Perreault were two
I remember who left—and the Rangers' Vic Hadfield. I was
actually thinking of going home with Hadfield. If you weren't
going to play, it seemed hopeless.

But for some reason, I stayed. I was glad I stayed because
I got to play with one of the greatest guys I've ever met: Jean
Ratelle. He reminded me of Jean Béliveau—classy.

I thought [Valeri] Kharlamov and [Alexander] Yakushev
played great hockey for the Soviets. Yakushev was just
fabulous. A big left winger, he was right in my face all the time.
And he could fly—almost as fast as Kharlamov. A great player!

He could shoot the puck a hundred miles an hour, but
when he positioned himself twenty feet out from our net,
he'd pass it! Don't ask me why.

On the plane to Moscow, Frank Mahovlich had allergy
problems and his eyes were swollen shut. I said, "Frank, what
happened?" He said, "The Russians caught me after the game
in Vancouver and beat me up."

I guess everybody remembers an incident in the final
game in Moscow when Jean-Paul Parisé got thrown out of the

game for threatening to hit the referee with his stick. Well, a funny thing happened on the way to Prague after the series was over. We were stopping there for an exhibition game with the Czechs. The referee Parisé went after was on our flight, and he was really afraid. You could see him shaking. And Jean-Paul came down the aisle just as a meal was being served. Jean-Paul walked by and flipped the ref's tray up, dumping food all over him. I guess he figured the ref couldn't throw him out of an airplane. We thought it was hilarious.

When Stan Mikita played in Czechoslovakia—this was in a game after the Summit Series—I had tears in my eyes. Stan was born there. His birth name was Stanislav Gvoth. Well, they loved him. He received a ten-minute standing ovation and it was very emotional.

Pat Stapleton and Bill White played superbly in Moscow. I remember Stapleton for his wicked sense of humour.

Hockey players aren't brain surgeons, right? Well, in Moscow, Patty not only convinced the players there was a great Chinese restaurant in town, but he had fifteen players sign up for a trip to the Moscow Golf and Country Club.

Most of the guys were saying, "Gee, I didn't know they played golf in Russia. And they have Chinese food over here?"

See? No brain surgeons in that group.

Marcel Dionne was an NHL rookie then—just a kid. Patty took him aside and said, "Marcel, you're going to be my roommate when we get to Moscow, but there's a problem. There's such a shortage of beds in Moscow that when the wives and girlfriends come over, we're going to have to sleep four people in one bed. But I'm married, so you can't sleep next to my wife, Jackie. So here's how it's going to work: Jackie will sleep on the outside and I'll be next to her. But I don't want to sleep next to you, so it'll be your girlfriend next to me and then you."

Marcel said, "But I don't want you sleeping next to my girlfriend." Marcel was so upset he went to Harry Sinden and lodged a complaint about four in a bed.

On the flight home, Bobby Clarke and I decided we'd try to find out how many times we could get Harry Sinden to shake hands. So we'd mill around him. "Great series, Harry," we'd say. And we'd shake his hand. A minute later, "Great coaching, Harry." And we'd shake his hand. This happened fifteen times before he shouted, "What the hell is going on with you two?"

Then, in Montreal, Bobby Clarke and I flanked Canadian Prime Minister Trudeau on a fire truck in the big parade. Someone had given us stickers with our jersey numbers on them—to stick to our baggage. We had a couple of extra stickers in our pockets, so I took mine and slapped Trudeau on the back, leaving my number 10 on his suit. Then Bobby did the same thing. So the prime minister's walking around with our team numbers decorating his suit.

Guy Lapointe was a big part of that team. A great guy, a funny man. We played a reunion game against the Russians in Ottawa a few years ago and Guy kept giving us words of encouragement. After the first period, he said, "You're playin' good, guys. But don' get a swelled head." After the second period he said it again—"You're playin' good, guys, but don' get a swelled head." Then he went into the can for a smoke. So I took a screwdriver from the trainer and made Guy's helmet a lot smaller. Well, he came out of the john and said, "Let's go, guys, but don' get a swelled head." Then he jammed his helmet on and he couldn't get it over his ears. Geez, the guys howled at that little scene. Guy knew I'd done it because he pointed at me and said, "You, Dennis, you're a funny son of a bitch, eh."

A guy came up to me once and said, "Dennis, if only your brother Bobby had played for Team Canada, the series wouldn't have been so close—or so memorable." And I said,

"That's right. The Russians would have won eight straight games." The guy didn't think it was funny.

The more I saw Phil Esposito play in 1972, the more I thought how stupid Chicago was to trade him away. He wouldn't let anybody quit. He became a great team leader and showed the same qualities Bobby Clarke showed in leading the Flyers to the Stanley Cup a couple of years later. Phil was fabulous.

Early in his career, with Chicago, he was a little weak on faceoffs. I remember a faceoff next to our goalie Glenn Hall, and coach Billy Reay called Phil to the bench. He said, "Phil, after you lose the draw, stay with your man."

I've been very busy since I retired from the NHL. I bought a farm east of Toronto and I enjoy country living. My brother Gary lives nearby and comes around to help me out. I was athletic director of a small college outside Chicago for a time. And I was involved in a car dealership in the Niagara area. But I'm known more for my speechmaking than anything else, having been booked at hundreds of events over the past 20 years. I followed a famous opera singer on stage one night. She was a very large lady but she had a beautiful voice and got a long ovation. Then it was my turn. I don't think she liked it when I began by saying, "Folks, I bet you thought the show was over because the fat lady sang."

Except for her, people seem to enjoy my humour, especially my stories (some of them even true) about my brother Bobby. People say I laugh harder at my own jokes than anyone else. I tell them, "That's because I never heard most of them before." Oh yes, I also put a lot of these stories in a book titled *The Third Best Hull*.

Every June, Brian and I attend the Canadian Association of New York hockey banquet at the Waldorf-Astoria. All the hockey greats have been honoured there over the years. One year, Rocket Richard was the honoured guest. Bobby was there and Gordie Howe and many others.

I told the audience a story about my father. "My dad took me to the Montreal Forum one night to see the Rocket play. And my father told Bobby, 'I want to see you just before the game.' I thought, 'Wow! I'm going to be in on something really important here. My dad is going to tell Bobby something great.' So he took Bobby aside and he said, 'Listen closely, Bobby. When the Rocket scores tonight and the fans throw all those toe rubbers on the ice, I want you to pick me out a good pair—size ten.'

"Bobby got him the toe rubbers. Unfortunately, they were both lefts."

Not long ago, Dennis Hull was on The Fan 590, a sports radio station in Toronto. I heard him promoting a new DVD package of the famous 1972 series between Canada and Russia. He drew three laughs within thirty seconds.

"I can't stand to watch the series myself," he said. "I'm always afraid we are going to lose." Then he added, "We were out promoting the DVD at Walmart—Tony Esposito, Peter Mahovlich and myself. Someone came up and said, 'It's so nice to meet you fellows. It would be even nicer if we could meet your brothers.'"

The host of the program closed by suggesting that Dennis could now go back to his farm near Burnley, Ontario, and milk his cows.

"Hey," Dennis retorted, "I brought my cows with me. They've never been to Toronto."

When he was finished, I told Dennis a couple of Hull jokes he might consider using somewhere down the line.

Dennis and Gary went into town one day to get a trailer full of manure for the garden. On the way back, there was a bad accident. The trailer was smashed and there was manure all over the road.

The Hulls stood around, wondering what to do, when an old

fellow came along on a tractor. "Fellows," he said, "looks to me like the trailer can be repaired, but there ain't a hell of a lot left of your cow."

When Dennis was a little kid he skated all alone on the frozen pond deep in the woods. A stranger came by one day, headed for his winter cabin, and saw Dennis fall through the ice. He leaped out of his truck, pulled Dennis from the icy water and sent him home.

An hour later, there was a knock on the cabin door. When he opened it, Mrs. Hull was standing there. "Are you the chap who pulled little Dennis out of the pond?" she asked.

"Yes, ma'am, I am."

"Tell me, you didn't happen to see his mittens, did you?"

In Pointe Anne, where the Hulls grew up, there were two sisters who lived together for years and years and were scared to death of men. Never dated, never wanted to. And they had an old female cat as a pet. They taught that cat to be afraid of males, too.

By some quirk of fate, one of the sisters finally got married and went off on her honeymoon. A few days later, the sister who stayed behind got a post card. All it said was, "Let the cat out!"

Dennis says his brother Bobby is so stubborn and contrary, he told him, "If you ever fell in the river and drowned, they'd look for your body upstream."

Dennis heard someone bragging about his ancestors, who came across on the *Mayflower*. Dennis said, "None of my ancestors came across on the *Mayflower*, but my sister Maxine came across in a canoe."

BOBBY HULL

It was early June 1988, and Joan and I were in New York City for the annual Canadian Association Hockey Dinner. This year, the Canadian

Society was honouring Bobby Hull, and he had invited his three brothers and their wives, plus Jim Pappin and his wife, Keith Magnuson and spouse—all expenses paid. (In December 2003, Magnuson was killed in an auto accident while returning from a funeral for Keith McCreary, a longtime member of the NHL Oldtimers.) Bobby's younger brother Gary and his wife, Lois, have been good friends and country neighbours to the McFarlanes for many years.

Joan and I always fly in a day early, check into the Waldorf and then, with a number of head-table guests, attend a cocktail party at the posh apartment of Canada's consul general.

After the reception, Paul Levesque, a Manhattan stockbroker and one-time member of Canada's 1962 Olympic bobsled team, invited a few select guests to dinner and a nightcap. This time it was at Jacqueline's, a fine French restaurant.

Bobby Hull and his wife, Deborah, were there, along with Jean Béliveau and his wife, Élise, Red Fisher of the *Montreal Gazette* and his wife, Paul Levesque and his date, Connie Hill, a New York correspondent for the *Globe and Mail*, and of course, Joan and me.

The wine flowed as smoothly as the conversation, which was mostly about hockey. Then Guy Lafleur's name came up. Suddenly, Bobby was pointing across the table at me. "You media guys screwed Guy Lafleur," he said accusingly. "All that crap you wrote and said about him. Always jumping all over him."

I was stunned. I hadn't said anything negative about Guy Lafleur that I could recall. Not publicly, anyway.

Before I could answer, Jean Béliveau said quietly, "Wait a minute, Bobby. Guy Lafleur at times had reasons to be criticized."

I jumped in, "Jean is right, Bobby. Guy was probably his own worst enemy. Driving at high speeds and nearly killing himself. Chain-smoking cigarettes. Putting hockey ahead of everything including his family. Frankly, I'm not sure I admired his lifestyle."

"Oh, yeah?" growled Bobby. "Then I suppose you don't admire mine."

"Not particularly," I shot back. I don't know why I said it, but I did. It just popped out.

My wife nudged me with her knee. "We'd better be going soon," she said sweetly.

The next morning, Bobby was all smiles and full of apologies.

"I'm sorry about last night," he said, gripping my hand.

"So am I," I said, and I meant it. "Let's forget it."

We were back in New York a year later to honour Red Kelly, and once again I offended Bobby. Believe me, I didn't intend to. This time, we were wined and dined by Paul at an Italian eatery—Il Vagabondo—where the wine bottles were lined up on the table like tenpins.

I said to Bobby, "You know, I feel badly I never saw you play on that big line with Winnipeg in the WHA—Hull, Hedberg and Nilsson."

He swung around and glared at me. "Hell, you had plenty of chances to see us play." He turned to the people across the table and said to the Devils' Ken Daneyko, "I don't want anything to do with those two," pointing a thumb at us. He was really angry.

Joan protested as Bobby turned his broad back on her, almost knocking her off her chair. "Bobby, why include me in this? I didn't say anything." But he ignored her—and me—for the rest of the evening.

The thing is, I don't recollect that I did have many chances to see the Jets play in the WHA. I was travelling extensively in those days, covering NHL games, and seldom saw the WHA brand of hockey. I heard Bobby tell Ken Daneyko he'd "lost all respect for that guy over there," nodding in my direction.

His comments really astonished me. In fact, all the wine bottles seemed to gravitate toward Bobby and it wasn't long until they were empty. I was tempted to remind him of the hundreds of flattering words I'd said about him over the years, to a TV audience of millions, praising his ability on the ice, his sportsmanship, his willingness to sign countless autographs for the fans. Not many hockey commentators did more to mould Bobby Hull's image than I did.

I thought hard about my relationship with Bobby, which dates back to his rookie season with Chicago, 1957–58. I interviewed him on CFRB radio in mid-December and we chatted about hockey players having to spend Christmas Day playing hockey. He showed great poise and charm and I suggested he consider a career in radio and TV someday. "Why wait?" he said, flashing a broad grin.

On the strength of those two words, I approached the station manager with a proposal. "Why don't we hire Bobby as a disc jockey?" I said. "We'll give him a tape recorder and he can carry it with him. He can introduce his favourite records on tape and talk about hockey matters in between the records. I can help put the show together. How about an hour on Saturday afternoon, before the game on *Hockey Night in Canada*?"

The manager frowned. "I don't think so," he said. "All of our disc jockeys do their shows live. They come to the studio. Can you get Hull to come in and do a live show?"

"Of course not," I shot back, annoyed at his response. "He's going to be the greatest hockey player on the planet, the most charismatic. He's in a different city every week. He says he'll do the show and it won't cost you much. But it has to be done on tape."

"Let me think about it," the manager said. He may have thought about it, but he never did anything about it.

A year or two later I met Bobby at the Ford plant in Oakville. He was there for some long-forgotten promotion. We talked about his salary demands, which had been in the news. He was looking for a big raise from the Blackhawks, perhaps as much as a hundred thousand a season.

"Brian, I'm only doing what the Rocket and Gordie should have done years ago. They took what was offered them—a pittance compared to pro athletes in other sports—and it kept everybody back. If they'd demanded big bucks, we'd all be better off."

I picture Bobby signing autographs for kids, hundreds of kids, thousands of kids. Signing, grinning, kibitzing. At rinkside, outside the dressing room, in the corridor, on the street. One day, I convinced my *Hockey Night in Canada* bosses to let me film Bobby after a game at Maple Leaf Gardens. The cameraman followed him from the moment he stepped out of the dressing room, where he was greeted by his father, and kept pace with him as he moved slowly through a swarm of autograph seekers toward the front doors of the building. No sneaking out the back way for Bobby. No glance of disapproval when a kid stepped on his foot or clutched at his sleeve. Always the grin—the big, happy grin. On the street, he and his dad turned right and headed for the subway entrance. No fancy limo, no taxi for the Hulls. The subway, for a token, would take them back to the Royal York Hotel. The mass of humanity, mostly young people, trotted along, pleading with Bobby to sign scraps of paper and hockey programs. "One more, Bobby," they shouted. "One more." He couldn't possibly sign them all, but he tried. He signed hundreds. It took him ten minutes, perhaps fifteen, to reach the steps leading down into the bowels of the subway. He turned and waved, grinning. The camera followed father and son as they disappeared into the darkness. I still remember that shot. They were similar in stature. They were wearing trench coats, similar in colour. Their broad backs filled the narrow entrance. Then they were gone. When the feature appeared on our next telecast, it drew rave reviews. Simple in concept, it showed Hull to be the ultimate hockey celebrity, the most accessible, the most popular athlete in Canada.

That was before all his problems began—marital problems, injury problems, and contract problems. That was when he was truly the Golden Jet.

On the day following the banquet at the Waldorf, dinner chairman Paul Levesque invited a number of us to lunch at Mickey Mantle's famous restaurant. Bobby and Deborah Hull were already there, so we sat next to them. Finally, Paul arrived with some other people. We had a long lunch at Mantle's, and midway through, the Hall of Fame slugger came over to say hello. He was showing his years, and limped quite noticeably, because of the knee injuries he'd suffered during his long career with the Yankees. I thought it was a rare moment—baseball's greatest slugger and hockey's greatest scorer—meeting for the first time, grinning at each other, shaking hands, making small talk. And nobody there with a camera.

Moose Skowron, another former Yankee star, joined us. To me, he looked like some guy who'd been plucked from an old-timers' hockey team in Kirkland Lake or somewhere—grey crewcut, grizzled, weather-beaten features with rows of deep wrinkles and lines. But a pleasant enough fellow. We were in pretty good athletic company, with Hull sitting at our table and Mantle and Skowron at a table just a few feet away.

Somebody pointed out a former Giants football player who was sitting at the next table. Lunch over, Bobby's wife reached down for her purse—and it was gone. "Shit!" said Bobby. "Somebody's stolen the damn thing and we had all our money, our credit cards, car keys, everything in it." We searched everywhere, but to no avail.

I said, "Bobby, I have a couple of hundred dollars with me. You can have half of that." Before I could get my wallet out, the football player was at our side. "Bobby, let me give you a thousand to help you out. You can pay me back when you get home." Did I feel like a piker—I'm offering Bobby a hundred and a complete stranger steps up and plunks a thousand in front of him!

You can't say people don't love Bobby Hull. They go out of their way to be kind to him, to do him favours. They remember him as the Golden Jet, the most electrifying player of his era. That's the way we should all remember him. He lit up arenas wherever he played. And he lit up a million kids' faces.

After lunch and the vain attempt to find Deborah's purse, Joan and I went for a walk. We were tired when we got back to the hotel and flopped on the bed. Just then, the phone rang. It was Bobby, calling from the lobby. "Get your asses down here," he demanded.

"We're going to the theatre. Meet you in the lobby in ten minutes."

We scrambled into some clothes and dashed for the lobby. Bobby escorted us through the revolving door and into a rainy night. But we didn't need our umbrellas. Waiting for us was a uniformed chauffeur who assisted us into a vintage Rolls-Royce—complete with a rose in the bud vase—that was idling at the curb.

"What's all this?" I asked.

"Oh, I met some billionaire last night in the bar. He's a fan of mine and loaned us his Rolls," Bobby explained. "And he gave us four tickets for *Me and My Girl*." (It was merely the hottest show on Broadway, with a three-month wait for tickets.) "And he told us to have dinner afterwards," said Bobby. "His treat."

As we entered the theatre, a young man came up behind me and said, "Mr. McFarlane, may I have your autograph?"

I was surprised to be recognized—honestly. This seldom happens to me. While I was signing, I said, "You know, Bobby Hull is just ahead of us. You better hurry if you want to get his autograph."

He said, "No rush. I've seen him a lot. But I've never met you before. I see you on *Hockey Night in Canada*. I'm a big fan of yours."

Did that kid make my day or what?

It was a fine evening. But I must learn to hold my tongue when Bobby's around. Keeping on his good side has its advantages.

Bobby showed up at the Canadian Society dinner that year wearing his tuxedo. Everyone else was in business attire. One of the guys was laughing. He said, "We went to a function somewhere, a big event, and everybody was in tuxedos and Bobby showed up in a two-piece suit. Tonight, everybody shows up in a two-piece suit and he shows up in a tuxedo. Did you notice he has a big safety pin in the shirt because his shirt is falling apart?" We all laughed about that, even Bobby.

Bobby told me about the night he hit Harold Ballard in the face with one of his slapshots during a warmup at Maple Leaf Gardens. Did you ever hear that story? He drove a shot at the net, but the puck hit the crossbar and flew up into the crowd. Ballard and Clancy were standing up in their private box and didn't see the deflected missile coming.

Bobby said, "As soon as that puck hit the crossbar I knew it was headed right for Ballard. Sure enough it caught the Leaf owner right between the eyes. I felt terrible."

Harold was rushed to the medical room for treatment.

Bobby said, "When I came out of the Hawk dressing room to go back on the ice for the start of the game, Harold grabbed me by the arm and yanked me into the room next door. By then his eyes were starting to turn black. I said, 'Gee, Harold, I'm sorry. I didn't mean to do that.' And he said, 'Don't worry about it, Bobby. I just want to get a photo of the two of us together.' He had a photographer standing by.

"Just then my coach, Billy Reay, yanked me out of the room by the back of my shirt. He said to me, 'You're not getting your picture taken with that son of a bitch.' Reay had been fired by the Leafs years earlier and he was still hot about it."

"What a shame," I told him. "That would have been a great shot, Harold with his black eyes, standing next to you."

"You're right, but Billy Reay wouldn't let it happen."

I'm at a banquet in Belleville—part of the Rick Meagher Celebrity Golf Tournament—and Bobby is in the audience, puffing on a big cigar as kids surround him for autographs. I say to Bobby, "You don't mind if I poke a little fun at you tonight, do you?" He says, "Brian, say anything you want. My brother Dennis does. He never lets up."

So I tell the audience I saw a Bobby Hull bumper sticker in the parking lot: "Honk If You've Been Married to the Golden Jet." And I add, "When Bobby divorced his first wife, the judge said, 'Bobby, I'm going to give your ex-wife $3,000 a month.' Bobby says, 'That's great, Your Honour. And I'll try to chip in a few bucks myself.'"

At another tournament, I told a joke on myself and Bobby ad-libbed a line that got the biggest laugh of the night.

I said, "Folks, my wife went to her new doctor the other day—
Dr. Astaphan. And when she came home she said, 'Dr. Astaphan said
a woman in my age bracket should be making love fifteen times a
month.'

"I said to her, 'That's great, dear. Put me down for three.'"

People laughed, but they truly roared when Bobby waved his
arm and yelled out from the back of the room, "Put me down for the
other twelve, Brian."

I've often wondered if Bobby was kidding or not. My wife is a
very attractive woman.

Later, Dennis Hull would quip, "I didn't think Bobby could do
the math."

The late Jim Proudfoot, a columnist for the *Toronto Star*, recalled
an incident in Helsinki when a WHA version of Team Canada played
there in 1974.

"We were standing around with Bobby when Joanne, Bobby's
first wife, came over. Yak, yak, yak.

"So Bobby pulls out some money and says, 'Why don't you go
shopping?'

"She says, 'Yeah, I think I will.'

"When she leaves, Bobby says, 'See that woman? She made me
a millionaire. The thing is, I had four million when I met her.'"

(It's a joke both Bobby and Dennis have told at banquets numerous times.)

Proudfoot added: "Later, on the same trip but in Moscow, Benny
Hatskin, a noted lobby-sitter, saw Bobby and Joanne enter their
hotel. They're yak-yak-yakking at each other and Bobby is saying,
'Oh, shut up,' and Benny says to me, 'Imagine the poor KGB agent
who has to listen to the tapes from their room.'

"You know," he concluded, "Joanne may be open to criticism
but I'll say this: guys like Brett and Bobby Junior show evidence of
being well brought up."

Someone asked: "Wasn't it Brett who offered that great answer at the press conference when he signed with Calgary? Someone asked him what his father contributed to his career and he said, 'Genetics.'"

"That's correct," Proudfoot confirmed. "And what I like about Brett [is that], when he became a star, a major star, a couple of years ago, he might very well have told Bobby to fuck off. But he admitted him into his world and allowed the media to take photos of them together.

"And then Bobby, who hadn't been in touch with Brett in six or seven years, suddenly talks about becoming his agent and telling reporters what he'd advise Brett to do when it comes to contracts and that sort of thing."

By now, some of my readers are surely thinking, "What is this— a chapter in a book or a gossip column?"

Recently, I heard that Bobby had given up the red wine and was a changed man. Good for Bobby. His life has been turbulent. Let's hope his relationship with Brett is running smoothly. They remain, after all, the only father-son tandem to win the Hart Trophy as the NHL's most valuable player. Bobby won it twice, in 1965 and '66, Brett in 1991.

They are the only father-son combo to each top 1,000 points. Brett retired with 1,391, Bobby with 1,170 (plus 638 more in the WHA). Both played on Stanley Cup winners, Bobby with Chicago in 1961, Brett with Dallas—he scored a controversial Cup-winning goal against Buffalo—in 1999. Brett emerged a winner again with Detroit in 2002. Brett outscored his *père* with 741 career goals to Bobby's 610 in the NHL (and 303 in the WHA). Bobby was only the third NHL player to grace the cover of *Time* magazine and was the first NHL player to score 50 goals in a season more than once. Brett was the only player to score at least 50 goals in a season at three levels of hockey—in the NCAA at Minnesota-Duluth, with Moncton in the American Hockey League and for five straight seasons in the NHL. Bobby and Brett form the only father-son combo in any pro sport to have their respective jerseys retired.

Brett, who retired in 2006, will have joined his father in the Hockey Hall of Fame by the time Jordan has this book in print.

Just for fun, let me pick the most unlikely Hall of Famer I can think of: forward Shorty Green, who played with the old Hamilton Tigers and the New York Americans. Let's compare his stats to Brett Hull's. Green played in a mere 103 NHL games, amassing 33 goals and 20 assists for 53 points. Green, a friend of my father's, a man who once took me for a ride around Haileybury in his new convertible, was inducted in 1962. Brett Hull amassed 741 goals and 650 assists for 1,391 points. Some difference, wouldn't you say? As much as I appreciated the ride in the convertible, I can't believe dad's pal Shorty deserved Hall of Fame recognition. He even led a strike of his Tigers against his team owner and the NHL in 1925.

As for the Golden Jet, let's hope Bobby will excel in his new role as an ambassador for the Chicago Blackhawks. I know one thing. Bobby will never turn down a kid's request for an autograph, even though he can get big bucks at a card show for a single signature.

WOMEN IN THE GAME

I nudge Jordan. He had dozed off while reading my manuscript.

"Jordan," I say, "try to stay awake for this next chapter. It's about some of the famous women in the game. Did you know that the Hockey Hall of Fame is finally going to welcome women members? Albertine Lapensee might have been considered as an inductee but for one little problem. Albertine was the biggest name in women's hockey during World War One."

Jordan yawns. "No kidding," he says. "Never heard of her. But I know about Hayley Wickenheiser. What was Albertine's little problem?"

"Jordan, I know you like surprise endings," I say. "There's a real surprise at the end of my tale about Albertine."

HOCKEY'S MIRACLE MAID

Several years ago, while doing research into my book on the history of women's hockey, I stumbled on the story of Albertine Lapensee, hailed as Canada's greatest female player in 1916.

Miss Lapensee, from Cornwall, Ontario, was billed as "The Miracle

Maid of Hockey" for her on-ice exploits. Crowds came in droves—from three to five thousand—to see her perform. She was a brilliant skater and stickhandler and scored about 80 per cent of her team's goals. But suddenly, the newspaper articles about her stopped. Her name disappeared from the headlines, and I wondered why. Perhaps she had been in an accident. Perhaps she had married and retired from hockey. Perhaps she had moved away from Cornwall. I was determined to find out why this remarkable female athlete vanished.

In time, I tracked down a nephew, Connie Lapensee, who lived in Cornwall. I called him, made an appointment, and drove from Toronto to see him.

Connie greeted me warmly and invited me inside his modest home. He was in his late sixties, maybe even his early seventies. He offered me a beer although it was still morning. He showed me a nice collection of his hockey memorabilia.

But I was eager to get to the point. I turned on my tape recorder.

"Have you got a photo of your aunt Albertine?" I asked him. I was curious to know what Cornwall's "Miracle Maid" looked like.

"No, no photos," he smiled. "I don't know if any exist."

"Too bad," I replied. I was surprised. How could a young woman dazzle everyone in hockey and not have her photo taken?

"Look, Connie, I brought a newspaper clipping along, one that points out her incredible skills with a hockey stick and puck. It's an account from 1917, when the Cornwall women's team went undefeated. Let me read it to you."

Cornwall manager Runyons predicts that the Cornwall team will continue to excel. They have not been defeated this season. They intend to seek games in Detroit, Boston, New York, Pittsburgh and Cleveland. It would be a great tribute to them if they could be billed as the "undefeated champions of Canada."

For the first time, women will be wearing numbers on their sweaters.

When asked about his star player, Miss Lapensee, her mentor fairly beamed.

"'Miracle Maid' is right," said manager Runyons, discussing the wonderful play of Miss Lapensee. "She is playing 100 per cent better than last season. In the most recent games she did remarkable work. None of the NHA [National Hockey Association] male stars can teach this little lady anything about the fine points of stickhandling."

"And here's another item about Miss Lapensee," I said, "from January 20, 1917."

Ladies hockey, with all its frills and glamour, was ushered back into the spotlight last night when teams representing the Ottawa Alerts and the Cornwall Club came together at the Laurier Avenue rink. A crowd of about 2,000 hysterically enthusiastic spectators turned out to take in the excitement of the match.

After an exhibition, which provided several unexpected thrills, resulting in a win for the Cornwall girls by a score of 6 goals to 3. However, the Alerts gave the visitors one of the liveliest games they have ever had, holding them down surprisingly well.

Miss Albertine Lapensee, the Miracle Maid in ladies hockey, was, of course, one of the girls who excelled on the ice. In fact, it was to see Miss Lapensee, one of the most advertised girls in the Dominion, that a majority of people braved the cold weather to see her perform. She scored five of the six goals for Cornwall and gave a whirlwind display of stickhandling, skating, shooting and checking that was sufficient to make the average male pro blush with envy. Last year, Miss Lapensee was pronounced a sensation wherever she played. She skates and handles herself like a seasoned professional. Time and time again last night, despite the close checking, she dodged from end to end and wound up with a cannonball shot at Ottawa goalie Miss Labarge. Occasionally, as if determined to emphasize her superiority over everyone else, she deftly dashed toward the net, skillfully handling her stick with one hand. She brought rounds of applause from all parts of the rink and especially from a number of Cornwall enthusiasts who had come up for the occasion. Special trains are often chartered so that fans can follow her to games away from home. They cheered themselves hoarse as the fair little miss shot up and down the ice. Miss Lapensee proved to be the individual star of the game.

"And here's one more, Connie."

Late in the season, Miss Lapensee scored all three goals as Cornwall defeated the Montreal Westerns 3–0 before a huge crowd in Montreal. It was said to be the largest crowd ever to see a ladies hockey game in Canada.

"Your aunt was a sensation, a true pioneer of women's hockey," I reminded Connie. "But after 1917, there's a total blank. She disappeared. How come I couldn't find a trace of her in any of the newspapers of that era?"

Connie chuckled, then sipped from his glass. He put it down and said, "Brian, that's an easy question to answer. My aunt left the country after that season. That's why nothing more was written about her. She went to New York and stayed there for months."

"New York? She quit hockey and went to New York? Whatever for?"

"Well, if you must know, she went there to have a sex change."

I almost fell from my chair. "A sex change? That's incredible. Did she have an operation? That seems too early for such a procedure."

But then, what did I know about sex-change operations? I'd always had suspicions about my uncle Max—but that's another story.

"I really don't know," Connie said. "All I know is she came back to Cornwall as a man. She called herself—well, *himself*—Albert Smyth. Smyth with a *y*. And a few months later, she—or he—got married. I'll call him 'he' from now on. He—Albert—and his wife opened a gas station not far from here, on the border of Quebec. That's about all I can tell you about my aunt Albertine."

"That's it? Albertine Lapensee became Albert Smyth. With a *y*. And she/he never played hockey again?"

"Not that I know of. The Smyths kept a low profile. We went to visit them once or twice. They seemed like a nice couple, a normal couple. Nobody knew the man who filled their tank and cleaned their windshield was once the Miracle Maid of Cornwall—the greatest female hockey player in the world."

On my drive back to Toronto, I keep thinking of the strange story of Albertine Lapensee. I could picture the famous American commentator, Paul Harvey, who passed away at age ninety while I was putting this book together, relating her story. His famous tag line would be perfect: "And now you know . . . the rest of the story."

MICKEY WALKER, THE OLDEST FEMALE HOCKEY PLAYER

Many years ago, through hockey, I met with Mickey Walker, the oldest female hockey player in the world. We became good friends and called each other frequently.

On March 13, 2008, I sat at my computer and wrote an article about Mickey. It was for this book, to be published in 2009. I wanted to write about many of the fascinating men and women I have encountered in hockey, and Mickey was one of the best—a real gem.

I completed the article and made up my mind to call Mickey in the next day or two to tell her of my plans. But when I read my email minutes later, Kevin Shea, another writer, informed me that Mickey had passed away that very day—at age ninety.

Mickey Walker was possibly the most famous resident of Bala, Ontario. She played a weekly game of hockey well into her eighties. When I talked to her years ago about her amazing career on ice, she was then in her seventies. We met at a women's hockey tournament in Brampton and I was invited to play right wing on Mickey's line in an exhibition game. I wasn't going to pass up a chance like that. What a thrill it was to play on a line with such a compelling, gutsy woman. Someone took a photo of us standing together after the game (Mickey had butted her cigarette), and it appears in my memoir, *Brian McFarlane's World of Hockey*.

"I get a lot of attention for being the oldest registered female player in the world," she told me. "But really, I'm only doing what comes naturally. In Bala, a group of us gather every Monday night for a game in the local rink. The ages range from twelve to my age— seventy-four. We have such a good time. Occasionally we play games against the male old-timers. And again, that is so much fun.

"Even though I may be the oldest player on the ice, I don't expect to be treated differently than anybody else. Of course, there's no bodychecking, so there's not much chance of getting hurt.

"Some time ago, my daughter bought me an Oilers hockey jersey with number 99 on the back. So I wear that proudly. Wayne Gretzky is my hero. I think he's the best in the world.

"I must say I'm no fan of Don Cherry. Oh, Brian, I know he's your friend, but the way that man talks about violence and fighting—he glorifies fighting, which I abhor.

"I've always played centre—ever since I was sixteen, the year we competed for the Canadian championship. That was back in 1934–35.

"I guess I come by my interest in sports honestly. My mom and dad were excellent athletes and sportsmen. And my brothers were good hockey players. I learned a lot about hockey by playing with my brothers out on the frozen lake. We lived right next to Lake Muskoka. My brothers taught me how to stickhandle. I'm the youngest of eight children and I followed right along, doing what my brothers did.

"I can still remember one of my first hockey games. I'd be about twelve and it was at a rink in Stayner—in an old Quonset hut–type building. I recall wondering if the roof was going to fall in on us. That sort of thing often happened in those days.

"I try to encourage the young people in Bala to stay involved in sports. I tell them they're not old just because they've reached the age of thirty or even forty. Sometimes they come up to me and say, 'Mickey, if you can do it, we can do it.' And I tell them, 'Yes, you can.' And quite often people my own age tell me, 'Mickey, I think it's great what you're doing.'

"I was wearing my old tube skates until last spring. Had them about thirty-five years, I guess. One day I said to myself, 'Mickey, you need new skates.' So I went to a store in Gravenhurst and picked out a new pair of CCM skates. And when I asked the price, the man said, '$180.' I almost fell over. I remember when skates cost $4 or $5. I told him, 'I can't afford $180.'

"My first pair of really good skates cost me nothing. Somebody told the coach of the women's team in Bracebridge that I was a good teenage hockey player. He asked me to come and try out for his team. Well, you can imagine how skates get passed down in a family of eight, so the skates I had were pretty worn. So I showed up in Bracebridge and the entire toe in one boot was gone—worn right out. And my toes were sticking out. I guess the other girls may have been snickering, but I was happy as could be with what I had.

"Well, Kim Ecclestone was there and she was about twenty-two. She said to me, 'Mickey, you can't play hockey in those old skates.' I said, 'Oh, they're fine.' And she said, 'Come on, we'll go down to my dad's hardware store.' And her father brought out a brand new pair of skates and he gave them to me. He insisted I take them. They were a gift. I couldn't believe how kind the Ecclestones were to me.

"It wasn't long after that that we played the famous Preston Rivulettes for the Canadian championship. They went almost undefeated for about ten years back in the '30s—a marvellous team. It was a one-game challenge, and I know I didn't play up to my potential in that game. The arena was packed with fans, and I think at age sixteen I was a little bit stagestruck. Player for player, I think we were every bit as good as the Rivulettes, but they had more experience and beat us 3–1.

"The next season, I played for a Gravenhurst team and in the spring we journeyed back to Preston to take on the Rivulettes. My hair was naturally curly and we wore no helmets. And suddenly I hear people shouting, 'Get Curly! Get Curly!' I don't know why they wanted to get me. And my brother was there—probably our only fan.

"I looked up and one of the Rivulette stars—her name was Marg Schmuck, and she was big—and she was coming at me. And I heard my brother shout, 'Step into her, Mickey!' So I stepped into her and she went down hard. And as she went down, her stick flew up and caught me right on the nose—and oh, that hurt. Later, I had two black eyes and I realized that it wasn't an accident. At least, I never thought it was. Yes, she came after me. And there was a woman next to the boards—with an umbrella! And when I'd skate by she'd reach out and try to slap me with the umbrella. I wasn't used to that kind of hockey.

"I had to play nearly the entire sixty minutes that night. I played centre, then went back on defence and back to centre again.

"Unfortunately, I never was with a team that won the Canadian championship, but what's more important are the friendships I made from hockey. And I spend a lot of my time encouraging young people to stay involved in sport—yes, I do. I believe that's awfully important."

A few days after Mickey's passing, the fifth annual Mickey Walker Trophy for sportsmanship was awarded at the conclusion of the women's national hockey championships in Charlottetown.

Fran Rider recalls the 1990 women's world hockey championships in Ottawa and how Mickey showed up with her face painted red and white and dressed completely in Canadian hockey gear.

I recall acting as emcee for the opening ceremonies of that first-ever World Series of women's hockey for another reason. A young teenager came up to me and said, "Mr. McFarlane, I'll be singing the national anthem for the title game. I believe you'll be introducing me."

"Indeed I will, miss. And what is your name?"

"It's Alanis Morissette."

It was the first time I'd heard that name. It would not be the last.

HURRICANE HAZEL STILL SKATING

I cannot write about women in the game without mentioning the incredible story of "Hurricane" Hazel McCallion, the longtime mayor of Mississauga, the third-largest city in Ontario.

Hazel is eighty-eight years old and still going strong in the political realm and the hockey world. Can you believe she's been the mayor for thirty-one years? She has won eleven consecutive elections and runs a debt-free city—debt-free, folks! With $700 million in reserves!

And she loves hockey. She told me once, "Brian, when I moved from the Maritimes to Montreal in the '40s, I played for money—$5 per game. That was big money for women in those days."

There's an open ice rink near her office. She carries her skates in the trunk of her car. She can still stickhandle and shoot the puck. She's an absolute marvel.

She is fiercely supportive of women's hockey and is a personal friend to hundreds of the best distaff players in the nation. She helped me immensely with my book on women's hockey.

She proudly wears a pink hockey jersey with a huge letter M adorning the front. She has been invited to "drop the puck" at dozens—no, make that hundreds—of tournament games.

"That's why I keep my skates in the car," she told the CBC's Rick Mercer recently.

"But other politicians drop the puck," Rick told her. "They don't wear skates."

"Maybe they're too old," she quipped.

Hazel keeps more active than most teenagers. She can bowl and dance and ride the stationary bike. She never slows down, not even when hit by a truck. "A truck bowled me over a couple of years ago," she told Mercer. "I was all right, but someone took the truck in for repairs."

Can you believe it? Hazel has a 92 per cent approval rating. Make that a hundred per cent in the world of hockey.

LORD STANLEY'S DAUGHTER WAS A PIONEER

In researching a history of women's hockey in Canada, I discovered that women have been part of the hockey establishment for well over a hundred years.

I was surprised to discover that Lady Isobel Stanley, the daughter of Canada's governor general, Lord Stanley of Preston, an English nobleman who donated the Stanley Cup to hockey, was a player in Ottawa in 1890. Lady Isobel, her friend Lulu Lemoine and other young women took part in games played on the outdoor rink next to Rideau Hall, the Governor General's official residence.

KNOCKING GLADYS FOR A LOOP

One innovative miss became an instant star back in 1894. She scored three goals in a game between women's teams at McGill University using a technique that had never been seen before. This young student wore skates with an added accessory: a strap across each blade to prevent the puck from slipping through the opening.

Several times during the action, she charged at the puck and trapped it between her skates. Then she used her stick, pushing it into the ice like some Venetian gondolier to keep her speed up. In this manner, she propelled herself toward the opposing goal.

When she got close to her destination, she released the puck and swatted it with her stick at the rival goaltender. She scored three times in this manner.

Midway through her next foray up the ice, with the puck wedged firmly between her blades, a frustrated opponent came up with a simple, if unladylike, solution to the problem. She delivered a two-hander with her stick to the puck carrier's feet—with predictable results. The scorer of the hat trick collapsed to the ice, howling in pain, and the puck squirted free. The stick-wielding opponent was banished from the game and suspended for the rest of the season.

BEND DOWN, BERTHA AND BLOCK THAT SHOT

Early in the last century, pioneer women players, wearing ankle-length dresses, often crouched down in front of their goaltender in games. Their dresses would spread out along the ice and opposing players found it difficult to shoot the puck through the mass of material. It was a defensive play that male players could never adopt—it would take a brave man to show up at the rink wearing a long skirt.

ABBY BROKE THE BARRIER

Half a century ago, it was unheard of for teams in minor hockey to include female players on their rosters. When one of them did, unwittingly, it created a sensation.

In 1955, eight-year-old Abigail Hoffman, posing as Ab Hoffman, played a full season in an all-boys' league. She arrived for the games dressed in full hockey uniform, and with her bobbed hair, no one questioned her gender. Late in the season, officials checked her birth certificate after she had been selected for the all-star team—and discovered she was a girl. When her secret was revealed, Abigail was interviewed on TV and radio; her story was featured in newspapers and magazines. She went on to become a two-time Olympic athlete—not in hockey, but in track and field.

PRESTON ALMOST PERFECT

Between 1930 and 1940, the Preston (Ontario) Rivulettes reigned as Canadian women's hockey champions for ten straight years, winning all but two of 350 games played.

U.S. TEAM WINS FIRST OLYMPIC GOLD

In 1998, the U.S. women's hockey team upset Canada to win the first gold medal in women's hockey at the Winter Olympic Games played in Nagano, Japan.

MANON MAKES HISTORY

On November 26, 1991, a teenaged girl named Manon Rhéaume became the first female to play in a major junior hockey game when she skated on in relief of Trois-Rivières netminder Jocelyn Thibault midway through a game with Granby. She played for seventeen minutes until a high slapshot gashed her head.

Both goalies, Thibault and Rhéaume, later appeared in the NHL. Thibault had a 587-game career with Quebec, Colorado, Montreal, Chicago, Pittsburgh and Buffalo. And in 1992, Rhéaume became the first woman to play for an NHL team when she played the first period of a pre-season game between the Lightning and the St. Louis Blues. She faced nine shots, allowed two goals, and drew a standing ovation from the fans. She signed a professional contract with Tampa Bay and was assigned to the Atlanta Knights of the International Hockey League. On December 13, 1993, she became the first woman to play in a regular-season professional game when she played for almost six minutes in a game versus Salt Lake City. Her team lost 4–1.

The following season, she played in the East Coast Hockey League and for Canada's national women's team. She has earned more money from hockey than any other female player—a reported $500,000 per year during her prime, most of it from endorsements and personal appearances.

THE HOCKEY GIRL

With the rising number of female hockey players worldwide in mind, I recently penned the words to a hockey song. You might call it a follow-up to a song I wrote forty years ago—"Clear the Track, Here Comes Shack." That one spent nine weeks on the CHUM radio hit parade in Toronto, topping the chart for two weeks. Now I need someone to write the music and handle the vocals for "The Hockey Girl." Where are you when I need you, Alanis?

The Hockey Girl
Threw on my pads, laced up my skates
Grabbed my stick, rushed through the gates
Buzzed around the ice, so cold and slick
Nothin' like a grip on a hockey stick . . . 'cause

I'm a hockey girl
I'm a hockey girl
Love the game that's fast and rough
Love the game, never get enough

Took a pass, knocked a girl down
Grabbed that puck and went to town
Split the defence, was on a roll
Took my best shot and scored a goal

I'm a hockey girl
A hockey girl
Love the game that's fast and rough
Love the game, never get enough

A man said, "Hockey girl, come play with me"
He gave me the elbow, gave me the knee
"This is a man's game, doll," is what he said,
"Give it up, darlin'"—and I saw red . . . 'cause

I'm a hockey girl
A hockey girl
Love the game that's fast and rough
Love the game, never get enough

That man sneered as he rushed my way
I stopped him cold, stole the puck away
Dropped him like a stone with a solid hip check
Didn't look back when he hit the deck . . . 'cause

I'm a hockey girl
A hockey girl
Love the game that's fast and rough
Love the game, never get enough

Mastered the slapshot, know how to deke
Scored my first hat trick just last week
Heard the crowd roar, helped win the game
Since I found hockey, life is not the same . . . 'cause

I'm a hockey girl
A hockey girl
Love the game that's fast and rough
Love the game, never get enough

Making the Olympics is my dream
And winning gold with that awesome team
Playing for my country would be so grand
I'd be the happiest player in the land . . . 'cause

I'm a hockey girl
A hockey girl
Love the game that's fast and rough
Love the game, never get enough!

MEDIA GUYS AND MARTIN KRUZE

I say to Jordan, "I don't know whether there's a place in this book for my thoughts on the huge sex scandal that rocked Maple Leaf Gardens a few years ago."

"I remember it well," Jordan says. "A young man jumped off a bridge because of it."

"That's right—Martin Kruze. A real tragedy. He was only thirty-four. I was around the Gardens a lot when it was happening, but I didn't have a clue it was going on. I don't know anybody who did."

"And you want to write about it?"

"Sure."

Jordan says, "Go for it."

Most of my career in the broadcast booth was spent high above the ice at Maple Leaf Gardens, where I shared space with play-by-play legends Foster and Bill Hewitt, Bob Cole and colour commentators and analysts like Bob Goldham, Gary Dornhoefer, Mickey Redmond, Bobby Orr, Wren Blair and many others, including my "Gee Whillikers" friend Howie Meeker.

Directly across from our perch was the press box, inhabited by many of the most respected writers and beat reporters in Canada, there to follow the Leaf fortunes and, more commonly, misfortunes. The Toronto writers and columnists of that era were the best in the business.

The media guys worked "upstairs," away from the action below. And, as we would all discover years later, there was action going on below that was unrelated to hockey. It involved sordid acts by child molesters, sexual abuse perpetrated by Gardens employees away from the glare of the arena lights. These acts, these crimes, would come to repel us and shock us—but not until enormous damage had been done, not until a staggering number of young lives had been consumed by feelings of shame and guilt.

These were the Ballard years—the late 1960s, '70s and '80s, when Stanley Cups were promised but never delivered, when controversy was an everyday occurrence, when a fraud conviction sent the owner to jail, and, most shocking and shameful—and incredibly hard to believe—when sexual abuse of children and teenagers was secretly rampant all around us. Few of us noticed or suspected, few of us were aware until charges of indecent assault and gross indecency against two Gardens employees rocked the House That Smythe Built.

I say that few of us caught on. But members of the media are not dummies. They have sharp eyes and ears. There may have been one or two who were aware and chose not to write or speak about it, much less report it to authorities.

One of the abused victims, thirty-four-year-old Martin Kruze, haunted by his past, unable to contain the guilt and the shame, exposed the pedophiles in 1997, naming Gordon Stuckless, 47, and John Paul Roby, 54, as his molesters. George Hannah, equipment manager for the junior Marlboros, was named as a third perpetrator. Hannah had died in 1984.

The molestations went on for twenty years or more.

Stuckless, was convicted of multiple counts of indecent assault and sexual assault and sentenced—to two years less a day in Toronto's Don Jail.

Three days later, Kruze, tormented by the light sentence to his predator, committed suicide by jumping off the Prince Edward Viaduct that spans the Don River. A prison guard overheard Stuckless say of the Kruze death, "Too bad that worthless piece of shit didn't do it sooner. If he had, I wouldn't be in here."

A court of appeal later extended the Stuckless sentence to six years, less twelve months for time already served. He was released in February 2001. A spokesman for the Corrections Board of Canada stated, "Stuckless is unlikely to re-offend."

Hah! That's the closest thing to a punchline you'll find on this page.

Roby received what amounted to a lifetime sentence but died in prison of a heart attack a year into his incarceration. His family may have mourned his passing. Nobody else did.

I knew George Hannah—I'd see him in the Gardens coffee shop from time to time—and never suspected he was a pedophile. I'd wave hello to John Paul Roby when I entered the Gardens on game nights. He was an usher. He looked and acted a little strange, not the kind of guy you'd stop to talk with—but a pedophile? Who would know? I must have encountered Stuckless as well, but I can't place him.

It's inconceivable that others didn't observe the crimes, were unaware of the depth of the depravity. Kruze said that many knew and chose to remain silent. Even the owner, Harold Ballard, may have known.

Doug Moore, my best friend and chief engineer at the Gardens, would not have known, nor would Shanty McKenzie, the building superintendent. I'm sure of it. They would not have kept silent.

It's a big building, and there are many places to hide, many nooks and crannies where molestations could take place. But over two decades, with dozens of young kids flitting around the Gardens, one or two at a time, at all hours and for no valid reasons, someone must have known. Someone must have known instinctively that all was not right, that aberrant behaviour was possible and probable and that dirty little secrets were being kept.

Did Harold Ballard know? Did he turn a blind eye? Is it possible he condoned the crimes being committed on the premises?

I'm reminded of an old nursery rhyme we recited as kids:

I'm the king of the castle
And you're the dirty rascal
I'm the king of the castle
Get down, you dirty rascal

Ballard lived in an apartment in the Gardens. He lived there alone—until Yolanda came along. He was the king of his castle. An insomniac, he roamed the building at all hours of the night. One of the abused men testified that Ballard walked by on occasion when naked young men emerged from the sauna. So he may have seen the dirty rascals. Did he tell them to get down or get out?

Over the years, I have been one of Ballard's strongest critics. I worked in public relations for the man for several months. As a broadcaster, I often annoyed him. The man wanted me tossed out of the broadcast booth from time to time. I understand why. I am not being malicious now or seeking revenge for long-ago bruises to my ego. That's all history.

My fingers pause over the keyboard of my computer. It is not difficult to accuse Ballard of many wrongdoings. I did that when he was alive. But it is difficult to accuse, or even suggest, that he was complicit in a sex-abuse scandal involving his employees. Even wondering about his awareness of the scandalous acts—did he know or not know?—and raising doubts may be unfair to a man who can't speak out in his own defence.

But then, is raising doubt so outrageous?

Let's look deeper into the Ballard file. There are disturbing facts on the Internet. On April 9, 2002, a King City woman identified only as R.M. alleged that Ballard had sexually abused her when she was a child and did so continually until she became an adult—and his driver. (I don't remember him having a woman driver.) Long after Ballard's death, she sued Maple Leaf Sports and Entertainment, current owners of the franchise, for well over $1 million. At about the same time, there was another suit alleging the Leaf owner had abused a young male. Both suits were settled quietly and out of court.

Was there truth in the allegations, or did they stem from parties hoping to make a financial score? We may never know. But Ballard's reputation, never pristine to begin with, was tarnished with the same brush that tarnished his beloved building.

The Gardens has been closed for a decade, its future still uncertain. But the blemish remains. There were dozens of abuse victims. One young woman says, "I shudder whenever I pass that building."

Conn Smythe, who died in 1980, would have been sickened had he known about the taint that permeated his great landmark in its final years. Smythe would have been appalled at the sick practices of the pedophiles and predators who brazenly used the dressing rooms, the offices and quite possibly the sauna and even the *Hockey Night in Canada* studio to prey on young bodies in return for tickets to games, ice time and hockey sticks.

Smythe would have known. He made it his business to know everything about the Gardens. He would have been horrified and irate to discover any late-night shenanigans. He would not have hired men off the street, ex-cons and others with shady reputations, for menial jobs—and without performing background checks—as Ballard did.

Nor would he have countenanced the leasing of an apartment in a building across the street for late-night trysts and daytime dalliances.

Smythe was principled, ethical. He ran a tight ship. And he insisted his ice palace be kept spotlessly clean.

But in Ballard's era, it was a working environment that kept everyone on edge. Surely the same turbulent atmosphere, the strained relations between management, the owner and the media, were not common in other NHL cities.

During my career with *Hockey Night in Canada*, the Gardens and the Forum in Montreal were the finest arenas in the world. They were Meccas for the game, sacred shrines housing cherished teams. The difference? Montreal iced winning teams, championship teams. Young and old tingled with excitement whenever they were fortunate to witness games from those cramped seats in those special, splendid buildings.

Wayne Gretzky, on seeing his first game at Maple Leaf Gardens, sat in the back row, as far from ice level as it was possible to be. It didn't matter. He was thrilled to be there, sitting next to his grandmother. He was so captivated by the Gardens' atmosphere he refused to leave his seat at the end of the game.

Later, as the NHL's brightest star, he would say of plans to replace the Gardens with a spanking new venue, "We'll never replace the atmosphere we felt in that old building."

I stood next to Wayne one night at the Zamboni entrance in the Gardens. The Oilers were in town and it was two hours before game time. The building was eerily quiet. No one passed by as we stood there, staring out at the ice. It was not the time for me to ask Wayne foolish questions, not the time to interrupt his pre-game thoughts. This was his private time.

One minute passed, then two, three, possibly four.

No words were exchanged. I'm sure we were thinking similar thoughts. Isn't this a marvellous place? How still it is in here, how serene. How fortunate I am to be part of a great team game; to know I'll be playing a role in a televised spectacle in the hours ahead with millions watching; to be at the Gardens, where the best on ice have sweated and strained, given their best, since 1931.

Finally, Wayne turned away. He flashed me a shy grin.

"Well, I'd better go."

"Have a good one tonight," I said.

"I'll try."

As he walked toward the Oilers' dressing room, I thought, I *know* he'll try. He always does. Many of the most spectacular outings of his magical career have taken place on Gardens ice.

While the Oilers were soaring in the '80s, Ballard's beauties were constantly struggling. In 1979 Imlach came back as the team's general manager and they went into a tailspin, missing the playoffs six times in the next dozen years. In 1984–85 the team finished with a horrible 20–52–8 record.

It seems the media had a new crisis or controversy to deal with every day. Coaches and managers were hired and fired, often at Ballard's whim. Security was laughable. An American acquaintance showed up from time to time and I asked him, "Gary, how do you get tickets for Leaf games?" He laughed and patted a tiny pin stuck in his lapel. "I don't," he said. "I just flash this pin at the gate and tell the guy I'm with NHL offices in New York. He lets me walk in." A broadcasting colleague told me once, "If I bring a friend to a game and hand the guy at the gate a bottle of rum, that usually works. My friend slips in with me."

Some interviews I conducted with media guys during that era will give you some idea of the way it was back then.

On April 16, 1984, I interviewed esteemed journalist Trent Frayne and we chatted about Don Cherry, NHL goaltenders and Harold Ballard. I call this one "Frayne on a Plane."

On a flight from Washington to Toronto I sit next to Trent Frayne, one of Canada's most respected writers. Don Cherry, a relative newcomer to *Hockey Night in Canada*, is getting a lot of attention from the media. I have worked with him several times and think he brings a real spark to our show.

"I find him to be uninhibited and somewhat enjoyable," Frayne says. "He's like Muhammad Ali but not as funny. And I think he prepares some of his stories—the stuff about his dog Blue—but that's all right. He is an outgoing guy and pretty interesting. He could be around for a while."

I point out that when Don coached in Colorado, there was a contest called "The Ugliest Dog in Denver Contest." Someone called Grapes about it and he was outraged. But he was quickly pacified when they mentioned they wanted Don and Blue to be judges of the competition. "There's no bloody way Blue would be entered in the event," Don told me. "She's too beautiful for that."

We chat about NHL goaltenders. "What a temperamental and strange breed they are," Frayne observes. "Or at least they used to be. I'm not so sure they are as crazy today. Maybe it is because they've got masks and don't live as dangerously. They used to be such a breed apart. I remember Jack Adams, when he ran the Red Wings, and how he would sit beside Terry Sawchuk in the Detroit dressing room. Without saying a word he would put his right hand on Terry's left thigh, just to try to calm him down before a game.

"Then there was Chicago's Glenn Hall, who used to upchuck before every game and sometimes between periods. I don't know that he ever played a single game when he didn't throw up. Imagine getting that tense.

"In the Chicago Stadium one night, a playoff night, there was a fight on the ice. Hawks coach Rudy Pilous was watching the fight, and finally they got the bodies untangled. The teams were about ready to play again when Rudy happened to look over at his own team's net and it was empty! Glenn Hall was nowhere to be found. In the old Chicago Stadium, behind each team's goal, there was a flight of stairs leading down to the team dressing rooms. The Hawks had no goalie!

"Before the referee could hand out a delay-of-game penalty, suddenly Hall reappeared, clumping up the stairs and onto the ice. He had taken advantage of the fight to go downstairs and upchuck."

I ask Trent his opinion of Ballard and the Leafs and their woeful 1983–84 record.

"Well, Ballard has really disappointed me. I know Ballard is a man of a hundred faces. Strangely, I always got along with him. I had written a few columns about his failures with the team. When I was at the [*Toronto*] *Sun*, I used to call him 'H' for 'Happy' Ballard or 'H' for 'Horrible' or 'H' for something that would apply to him or one of his faux pas. I used to get a little upset with his personal denigration of his own players. Harold would say of young [Inge] Hammarstrom that he could go into the corners with eggs in his pockets and not break a single one—that sort of thing. But even though I had written, perhaps unkindly, about him, he was always agreeable whenever we would meet. He didn't seem to hold any grudges. He might say, 'Listen, you little son of a bitch, where would you be without me?' But we'd get along.

"But last winter, everything seemed to go sour with the Maple Leafs and their relations with the media, particularly the *Globe and Mail*. It baffled me why this happened. I know the *Globe* wasn't very kind to the Maple Leafs, but let's face it: they were a very bad hockey team. Defensively, they were among the two or three worst in the league for something like five of the last seven years. It baffled me how this team could endlessly have this same problem. Every time they drafted a defenceman, they would brag about his 64 goals and 123 assists in Portland or wherever. I could never understand why they never brought in somebody who could play defensive hockey. Where were the defensive defencemen?

"Now, the role of a newspaper is not to be always on the side of the home team. Thousands of people in Toronto are not from Toronto, and Toronto isn't their favourite team. Somebody must play the adversarial role. You just can't go around endlessly making excuses for Harold's many shortcomings.

"Anyway, I thought he was professional enough to recognize this. But this has been a bitter winter, the winter of 1983–84. It was unbelievable that he banned the *Globe and Mail* reporters from the press box. One night, Stan Obodiac who runs the press box actually showed up with two burly commissionaires in tow and heaved the two *Globe* reporters out of the building. In what other sport has that ever happened?

"I encountered him only once this season. I followed the Oilers on a trip they made to Washington, then to the [Long] Island and Boston. After the game in Boston, Toronto came in to play the Bruins. I stayed over and covered that game. It was one of those games where that young fellow, Allan Bester, played a marvellous game in goal. He [faced] 52 shots and the Leafs won 6–2 or 6–1. So I dashed to the dressing room, even though I knew it was a bad place for *Globe* people to be, because I wanted to talk to Bester. The Leaf coach, Mike Nykoluk, had stopped speaking to me. The general manager, Gerry McNamara, wouldn't speak to me. It's really a very sad situation.

"Anyway, I went into the dressing room, and as I turned away after chatting with Bester, my eyes happened to come directly into contact with Ballard's. We stared at each other for a few seconds. Then he snarled at me, 'You've got a lot of fucking nerve coming into this room.' I stared back at him and then he said, 'You're nothing but a fucking leech.' I thought for a moment he might be kidding, because in the past he often talked that way, but with a twinkle in his eye. But this time I could see he was in deadly earnest, so I just waved my hand at him and started to walk away. He shouted after me, 'Why don't you get your fucking hair cut? You look like a fucking violinist.' I just shook my head, thinking that the man has so little self-control.

"You know, here's a man who is in charge of a highly respected hockey franchise, a great franchise, a team that has the greatest following, and the most unbelievable support. Leaf fans have to be crazy to be so loyal to such a miserable last-place team and its erratic owner. I really lost an enormous amount of respect for Ballard that day. That's really all I have to say about the subject."

"Trent," I reply, "I worked for the guy for a number of months—

in public relations. He didn't give a crap about public relations. One time, a group called me to ask if a number of mentally challenged children could attend a game at the Gardens. There were perhaps five or six of them. I was told they were all well behaved and how much they loved the Leafs. I found a spot where they could sit, next to the press row. And when I asked Harold for permission to bring them to the game, he turned me down. 'I don't want a bunch of idiots falling out on the ice,' he barked and walked away.

"Another time, I was watching TV one night and Stan Obodiac, Harold's biggest fan and most underpaid employee, was debating with a professor from the University of Toronto, John Farina, over the Gardens' policy of banning women from the press box. The professor cut Obodiac to ribbons in the debate.

"I went to Harold the next day and said, 'Harold, if you won't allow women in the press box, at least come up with an explanation. You can say, "If the women are certified members of the Hockey Writers' Association, they're welcome" or "We're finding some new seats for them." But you risk offending women if you allow Obodiac to declare that the ban on women is "a strict Gardens policy" or that "the blue language in the press box will be offensive to women."'

"Harold looked at me like I was a dummy. 'Let's get one thing straight, McFarlane. No fuckin' women in the press box!' He walked away."

"He is totally unpredictable, all right," Frayne says. "Frank Orr wrote something that annoyed him and he didn't speak to the man for three years."

The mention of Frank Orr makes me smile, and reminds me of a story. "I once asked Orr how he and Ballard were getting along. 'Just great,' said Frank. 'He called me a homosexual, which surprised my wife. But whenever we're in Bulgaria at the same time we have lunch together.'"

I tell Frayne another story about Orr. "Orr was a goaltender at one time in his youth. He once talked about a bizarre incident in his puck-stopping career. He said, 'I must be the only goalie in history who was pissed on in the middle of a game. I was playing in Beeton, Ontario, one night and the fans were throwing things at me. An apple bounced off my head—no masks in those days—and somebody poured a soft drink over me. That wasn't so bad, but the final indignity came when I looked up at the railing above my head, and a fan had his joint out, and he was pissing on me.'"

I recall another incident involving Harold and Bobby Hull. I mention it to Trent.

"Bobby joined us for a few games on *Hockey Night in Canada*. He never prepared for the job—didn't do his homework. Was running around getting tickets for people when he should have been in the studio. And Ballard was angry with Hull because he'd threatened to remove his memorabilia from the Hockey Hall of Fame when they started charging admission. Ballard told our bosses, 'Get that SOB Hull out of here, that ungrateful so-and-so.' So Hull said to me, 'Did Ballard really say he wanted me out of the Gardens?' I said, 'Bobby, I don't know exactly what he said. Why don't you go and ask him?' Bobby said, 'By God, I will.' He confronted Ballard and Harold told him, 'No, no, Bobby. I'd never say that about you. You're a great guy. You are welcome around here anytime.' But that was an outright lie. We all knew he'd ordered our people to get rid of Hull.

"Hull was upset and said, 'I don't need this bullshit.' We didn't see much of him after that."

"Ballard could be a vicious guy," Frayne says.

"Yes," I agree, "he could be very vicious."

"I have a theory," Frayne says. "I think maybe Earl McRae had him figured out. He wrote a magazine article about Harold and indicated that everything went sour with him when his wife died. He wrote that after that happened, he just didn't give a damn. There has to be something that accounts for his 'don't-give-a-damnness.' He just doesn't. He lies. Even you have indicated that.

"But I remember when I worked at the *Sun*, Fred Shero hired

Mike Nykoluk as his assistant. It was a time when teams were beginning to have assistant coaches and Shero was one of the first. I remember we phoned Harold—I think John Iaboni phoned him— and asked him if he'd given any thought to the Leafs hiring an assistant coach. He said to Iaboni, 'Have I given any thought to it? You bet your ass I have. I've got a man who is probably going to join our team as an assistant right now.'

"Oh, my goodness. That's interesting. Iaboni has a good story. 'Who is he?' he asks. And Ballard says, 'John Ferguson in Montreal.' Wow! Fergie at that time wasn't into hockey at all. He'd retired as a player. So Iaboni, before he writes the story, phones Fergie in Montreal. Fergie says, 'Are you nuts, John? I've never heard from Ballard. I don't know what you're talking about.'

"Sometimes, I think he just says whatever pops into his head or, maybe there is just something wrong up there—with his head, I mean."

I ask Trent to tell me about his relationship with Leaf manager Gerry McNamara.

"I happened to be standing beside McNamara in the press box at the Boston Garden and I said, 'Hello Gerry.' No answer. I thought that he hadn't heard me so I said again, 'Hello Gerry.' Still no answer. I thought that was so dumb that I bent down, right in front of him, so that I was down—like, at his vest level because he is a tall guy— and I said loudly, 'Gerry, hello.' And he sort of grunted, so I said, 'What's your problem?' He said, 'I've got no use for people from the *Globe and Mail*.' I said, 'Oh, for heaven's sake, what's wrong?' He said, 'You lie—you people lie. I hope there is a court case over this thing because I've got proof—you people lie.' I said, 'Gerry, you're with a professional sports operation. You are dealing with the public all the time. You don't have to be mad at everybody at the *Globe and Mail* just because you are mad at a few things you see in the paper.' Then I said, 'I wrote a piece about you a year ago when I was with the *Sun*, and that's the last time I mentioned your name. So I don't know what you are so hot about.' He said, 'Well, I didn't like anything you wrote in the *Sun* either. What's more, you had me uttering an oath.' I said, 'A what?' He said, 'You heard me—an oath.' I said, 'In the paper?' And he said, 'Yes, in the paper. And we don't use oaths in this organization.' I said, 'Does that include the owner? Harold has never called anyone that he hates a broad-sucker or other choice word?' He didn't answer. I said, 'Well, if it was in the paper, it couldn't have been very severe. It might have been hell or it might have been damn. It couldn't have been anything else.' He insisted, 'I don't utter oaths. You misquoted me!'

"I suddenly thought that maybe this guy is a little nuts. He could throw me right out of this press box. You know, it's a low balcony thing in Boston, and I thought perhaps he is crazy enough, mad enough to just drop me over—so long, liar.

"So I just said, 'Okay, Gerry, let it go.'

"A few days later, I was looking around my home for something and came upon this column about the Leafs and McNamara. Right at the end, I had quoted him, when he was talking about Harold and how great Harold had been to him and had let him run the team: 'Hell, he's been great!' And he had remembered that hell—that oath—for over a year!

"Then there's Mike Nykoluk, the coach. I knew him when he was with Shero at Philadelphia. Again, this Boston day, I was in the hotel lobby of the Sheraton there, and I strolled over to where he was talking with assistant coach Dan Maloney. I was a working person, and wanted to know whether there had been any new developments, trades or injuries. I've got a column to write. So, I strolled over and said, 'Can a person from the *Globe and Mail* talk to you two guys without being thrown out of the lobby?'

"And Maloney laughed. He said, 'Oh, sure, no problem.' But when I looked again, Nykoluk is standing twenty or thirty feet away, holding his cigar, glaring at me. He wasn't going to talk to me.

"So you see, there was that incident, then the next thing is

McNamara in the press box calling me a liar. After that, it's Ballard cursing at me in the dressing room!

"Then they wonder why they are getting bad ink!

"Not to mention that idiotic stunt Obodiac pulled, getting those two commissionaires to throw the *Globe and Mail* reporters out of the press box. He should have been certifiably put away for that. It was outrageous!"

Changing the subject, I ask, "Have you had trouble interviewing athletes lately? Especially those in other sports who earn astronomical salaries?"

"I find that the richer the athletes become, the more difficult they become—which, I suppose, is understandable. They are young guys and certainly not world-wise. They suddenly have a ton of money with independence thrust upon them. Some of them simply can't be bothered. You encounter it in baseball most frequently. Walking into the Yankee dressing room or the California Angels' room is really difficult. Some of those people . . . Reggie Jackson, well, he is a moody guy to begin with, but there are others . . . Fred Lynn, Greg Nettles—oh God, the list is endless. They look right through you; you don't exist. They are surly, disinterested and uncooperative. You don't expect them to fall all over you and say, 'Sure, pal, let's have a conversation,' but they could at least be civil.

"Dave Stieb of the Blue Jays really annoyed me one time last season when I wanted to do a piece on pitching. Tony Kubek had said the designated hitter is really putting a strain on starting pitchers because they don't lift them nearly as often. So I thought that I would go in and ask Stieb about it, since he is their best pitcher. He was kneeling down in front of his locker, getting some stuff out of his duffle bag. You have to be careful with him—he is a highly strung guy. So the way I phrased my question was, 'Dave, would you have a minute?' Meaning now, or in future, or whenever. And he looked up to see who it was, and when he saw it was me, he said, 'I'm not interested, really.' And the 'really,' I remember real well—it came out 'rilly.' 'I'm not interested "rilly."' I was somewhat taken aback, because usually, even if he grunts, he will give you a minute. So I said, 'Well, when would you be interested?' He said, 'I don't think I will be interested, rilly.' And he went right on unpacking his bag.

"Curiously enough, golfers, perhaps because they are more mature—guys like Tom Watson, Jack Nicklaus or Arnold Palmer—are wonderful people to talk to. They seem to be trying to sell their game. They will talk to you endlessly. If you've got an idea, they'll expand on it. Well, not endlessly. After a while they might say, in a very polite way, 'I'm sorry, I'm busy now,' or 'I'm going to the practice tee. I'll see you in half an hour.' That's what I wish the rich young ballplayers would do—just say, 'I'm sorry, I'm busy now, I'll see you later.'"

I ask if he has ever had any difficulty with Bobby Orr or Wayne Gretzky.

"Gretzky is marvellous!" he enthuses. "And Orr—both are great! They are two remarkable young guys. And I can't say enough about the whole Sutter family. On Long Island, I talked to Brent and to Duane. And then I talked to the twins [Ron and Rich] when Philly was in Toronto. They are just wonderful young men—like most hockey guys. I'm sure it has to do with their upbringing."

I mention that I've interviewed the unknown Sutter once. Six Sutter brothers made it to the NHL—a seventh, Gary, didn't.

"Why didn't Gary ever play hockey?" Frayne asks.

"He did play—up to Junior B, or something," I say. "They say he had a lot of skill, and could have made it all the way, but I guess he lost interest, or lacked enough confidence, or something."

"A wonderful family, the Sutters," says Frayne.

"Gary told me how the boys used to play hockey up in their barn when they were kids. And he told me a funny story about his mother going to the hospital, to have the latest baby. All the boys were sitting at home waiting for the news. And how the dishes were piled up in the sink and the boys finally got around to washing them. One of them said, 'Gee, I hope Mom has a girl this time. A girl wouldn't mind doing all these dishes.' Then their father walked in the door with a grin on his face. 'Guess what, fellows,' he said. 'Mom had twin boys.' The other boys all groaned—'Oh, no.'"

"I liked Mrs. Orr, Bobby's mother. She had an unusual first name—I believe it was Arva," Trent recalls. "She was a very warm, pleasant, bright woman, and very much concerned about Bob's welfare. Doug, his father, seemed more of a fan. He seemed to be living almost vicariously in Bobby. He was the proud father and good for him! But the mother, she was sensible and I got the feeling that she raised the boys. Doug was a sports fan and he worked and brought the money home. She was more the rock, the foundation of the Orr family. I really liked her!"

"But you didn't care much for Dave Stieb?"

"No," Frayne laughs, "not 'rilly.'"

Al Strachan was the hockey reporter for the *Globe and Mail* back then—one of the guys banned from the press box at the Gardens. Ballard not only had him kicked off press row, but Strachan was manhandled in the Leaf dressing room one night. It was deplorable. It's a wonder Al didn't have someone charged with assault. Here's how he told it to me.

"The *Globe and Mail* wanted me to do a hatchet job on Mike Nykoluk. I said to my boss, 'I don't want to do a hatchet job on the man; he is a very nice man.' He said, 'Well, say what you can say about him, and if you want to say he is a nice man, then go ahead.' So I wrote that he was a very nice man and perhaps he was sometimes too nice. And that some of the Leafs said that he treated them very fairly and he was not hard on them at all. And there were times when other NHL coaches might be spending their afternoons thinking of ways to make life difficult for their players; Nykoluk would be spending his time at the racetrack. And perhaps he spent too much time at the racetrack.

"When he read that, he did not at all appreciate the fact that I had mentioned this. When I went down to the dressing room that night, he started shouting at me, 'You're no reporter! You've got no business in here.' Then he grabbed me and tried to throw me out of the room. But I guess with years of association with the Maple Leafs he couldn't do anything right, because he missed the door and threw me into the wall instead. One of the ushers came along and eased me out of the room."

I asked what happened next.

"Well, Dan Maloney, the assistant coach, was outside and I got into a shouting match with him, because there was a photographer nearby. Maloney turned and threatened to place his camera where the sun doesn't shine. So I started shouting at Maloney and as a result of all this altercation, the *Globe and Mail* was banned from the entire building for a while. And for a month or so after that, until it was eventually resolved by the league, we had to buy tickets, sit in the stands, make notes while we were sitting there, and then, after the game, we would go back into the dressing room. Because even though they tried to bar us from that hallowed space, the league said they couldn't. So after we finished in there, we had a room rented at the Carlton Inn next door, and we would go there and write our stories."

"Did you ever have a run-in with Ballard himself?"

"I had many run-ins with Ballard over the years. At one time he used to be a friend of mine, but then I guess I started writing stuff about his finances, and that really upset him.

"The one incident I remember the best was when I was travelling around the league. It was a Sunday, early afternoon in Edmonton. The Leafs had played the Oilers the night before and were heading to Vancouver, and so was I. I had made my own travel plans, of course, because the Leafs won't make any travel plans for you. I showed up at the airport. I'm minding my own business. And Ballard and his entourage troop in and he started shouting at me.

"'You're not on our plane, are you, you little bastard?' And I said,

'You're on *my* plane, Harold.' And there was a bunch of little kids standing around, four and five years old, and he started calling me a cocksucker and a son of a bitch and yelling at me. Everybody in the airport was just amazed, shocked at his language. So I just walked away and I ended up just going on the plane by myself."

"I hear he gave it to Dave Hodge one night, too," I said. "I don't know whether you were there. In a restaurant he really laid into him with the same kind of language. He was totally unpredictable in those situations. I know that Hodge and I were invited by Jim Gregory to get on the team bus in Vancouver one day, going to the airport. When Harold got on, he snarled at us, 'What the fuck are you doing on our bus? Get the hell off. Take a cab.' And that was the last time we were ever on the bus."

"Well, I guess the *Globe* guys used to take the team bus and be allowed on," Strachan said, "until Lawrence Martin wrote about the fact that Dave Keon and some woman passenger got into an argument on a flight the Leafs were on. Martin wrote that Keon was drunk, and that's when the trouble began. After that, all the media was banned from the buses and from their planes and everything. It is still in effect to this day. As far as I know, they are the only team in any sport that doesn't let you travel on their buses."

Colourful Dick Beddoes, a third reporter and a fellow broadcaster with me on mid-week Leaf telecasts, was closer to Ballard than all of us media guys.

I was listening to CFRB radio one day and host John Stall was interviewing Beddoes. Dick had written a book about Leaf owner Harold Ballard called *Pal Hal*. I switched on my tape recorder and recorded their chat.

Stall: Dick, I'm wondering if the accounting firm of Peat Marwick should put you on the payroll to figure out the

Ballard estate. I guess there is nobody who knows as much about the situation as you do and what it's going to take to sort this thing out.

Beddoes: John, Don Crump for the last three years has really been running the Gardens. He ran the football team in Hamilton for Harold. He was the guy, not Harold. Harold went to the games, Don Crump took care of the cash box. And, I might add, if Don Crump had been at Maple Leaf Gardens in the late '60s and early '70s, Harold Ballard does not go to jail. Crump would have said, "Harold, you can't forge these chits for a house you are building and say it's a Maple Leaf Gardens expense." Don Crump would not have allowed that to happen. In fact, Crump came along in the early '70s to pick up the awful hash that Harold and his late partner, Stafford Smythe, had made of running the place. He became the comptroller and, until then, the place had been run by a grade-twelve bookkeeper. So when Crump quit in 1990 to become commissioner of the Canadian Football League, it was a major loss.

Stall: But Yolanda stands to make a score. There is no question about that, is there?

Beddoes: Yolanda is already in pretty strongly. Harold has given the lovely Yolanda a condo unit at Jarvis and Carlton streets in midtown Toronto. For listeners outside Toronto, geographically, it is a block from the Gardens. It's probably now worth $500,000.00, given our real estate boom. She wants them to live there, but he won't leave the Gardens. They live in a very awful, gritty apartment.

Stall: What does that place look like?

Beddoes: I first saw it in 1972 or 1973 when he got out of jail. He was in jail for one year. In 1973 he was looking for some friends. He liked me because I had never given it to him when he was in jail like some of my colleagues in the Toronto media had. I thought that, "C'mon, this guy can't fight back now. We don't win in our jobs if we kick the old apple lady. We win if we take on the guy in the top hat!" And when Harold was in jail, and I'm being figurative obviously, he was an old apple lady. And I wasn't going to kick him or knock him around, and he liked me for that reason. He obviously liked Milt Dunnell at the [*Toronto*] *Star*, too. Milt was his closest media friend, I think.

Harold took me aside and he said, "Beddoes, I want to show you where I am gonna live now." I said, "Why are you going to move, Harold? You've got a nice house out in Etobicoke. It's gotta be worth $800,000 to $900,000 at the moment. It's a lovely house."

He said, "Listen, I'm not going to live there anymore. That part of my life's over. I'm going to live here now." He said, "I'm going to show you where I live." He took me into a nice three-room studio apartment. Not very big, but it had a bed with a canopy on it. I bet you have not seen a bed with a canopy on it outside of some old castle in England. I had to laugh. For God's sake, this guy Ballard has got a bed with a canopy on it!

Stall: Does he sleep there with Yolanda?

Beddoes: Sure. They sleep there. It's a rather comfortable queen size, I think. He told me they bought it the first day that she met him. She came along, John, in 1983. We were all saying in the media in Toronto, "Isn't it marvellous, Ballard, the old dinosaur, has made it to the age of eighty." It was July 30. There were pictures and everything! She was looking around. She was bankrupt, you know. She had declared bankruptcy in the area of about 800,000 bucks. So she was looking for a score. She was out of jail, too. She was given a two-year term for fixing a phony will down at Walkerville, near Windsor. She got caught because there was a real will and handwriting experts were able to determine which was the phony. She was involved, so she got a two-year term, served about five months, I think, at the Brampton reformatory for women.

So now, she is on her rear end and is looking now to bail out. She's got debts. She had run a golf course—badly—in Walkerville. She was just . . . well, she stiffed two lawyers. She was in terrible shape! Declared bankruptcy, and now she is looking to bail out, and looking to get back on her feet. She had been turfed out of the Palace Pier, a marvellous condo unit on the lakeshore in Toronto.

So she is looking for a date. She tried to get Steve Roman—the late Steve Roman of Dennison Mines, the second-biggest gold mine, I guess, in the world after something in South Africa. Her maiden name was Babich. She was born in Thunder Bay, 1933. She is now fifty-seven, and came here at twenty. She was always on the make a little bit.

And she got a young lawyer, whose name was MacMillan and who decided when he left the University of Toronto—I guess Osgoode Hall—that he would go home to Windsor and pick up business there which his family was involved in. Well, he didn't have enough clout for Yolanda. She quickly moved up, as it were, and had a lover called Robert Irwin, another lawyer. And between them they contrived to fix a will—a scam involving three million bucks! I've seen the court documents. So now I have it in the book called *Pal Hal*—all the documents.

Stall: She must love you . . .

Beddoes: Never mind that, John. Before the book *Pal Hal*
came out, Ballard called me and said, "Beddoes, what's this
effin' book all about? I'd like to sell it at the Gardens." I said,
"Harold, we would give you a big discount. Macmillan, the
publisher, will supply any number at half-rate and then you
can give any profits to charity or to her." Four days later, when
I went down to seal the deal with him, he said, "I've gotta tell
you, she don't like the book. Doesn't want me to promote it."
And he said, "Remember, I've gotta live with her, not you."

Now, the pad at the Gardens had been a very nice place
in the beginning. Then it came to look like something out
of the Arabian Nights. It had very garish wallpaper. It was
so garish and so . . . awful. It just was trash in some ways.
Frank Sinatra, when he came to sing here last time, had some
time to kill between the afternoon and evening concert and
Harold and Yolanda offered him their pad. He took one look
and said, "I can't stay there." So they fixed him a place in the
Maple Leaf dressing room.

Anyway, she is a bad housekeeper. The place is grungy;
there are cockroaches all over. And when I go in there, Harold
says, "Do you want a drink?" and I say, "Yeah, what have you
got?" And he says, "Royal Cola." I look at it and it's pink! I say,
"For God's sake, Harold, it ain't cola and it ain't even cold!"

Stall: Well, his cottage looks like a mess too. I'm not far from
his cottage and from the outside, I mean, all that white and
blue paint. And the big lion heads he has at the driveway.

Beddoes: John, the lions at the driveway have gotta go. Harold
thought they were tiger-cats. But I'll tell you, that's a nice place.
Well, what it looks like inside, I don't know. But we are talking

now, for the listeners' edification, we're talking Midland, Thunder Beach. And you can look right out at Christian Island where Roger Whittaker and a few guys have written songs about, even Gordon Lightfoot, so that's a good spot.

But he won't spend any time there. He told me last summer when I said, "Why are you always in your car, driving away somewhere? Why don't you spend some time at your lovely cottage and so on? And you've got a pretty nice boat." He said, "Richard, if I can keep moving, I ain't gonna get caught by that guy with the scythe—Death!" He thinks that if he can physically keep moving, he ain't gonna get caught!

Listen, I don't want him to die because I always found him a great bit of fun. But she has fenced him off from everybody—his family, all of us!

The Ballard era was the bleakest period in the history of the Toronto Maple Leafs. The team enjoyed only six winning seasons in Ballard's eighteen years at the helm and never finished above third in their division.

Despite his team's dreadful record, Ballard was inducted into the Hockey Hall of Fame in 1977. Stan Obodiac, his most obedient servant, once recommended Ballard for an Order of Canada. The day after Obodiac died, Ballard sent a flunky to the Obodiac home to pick up his company car.

Ballard died in April of 1990.

Yolanda Ballard (she had her surname legally changed to Ballard, although they never married) was despised by the three Ballard children—Bill, Harold Jr. and Mary Elizabeth Flynn. Bill Ballard struck her one day, was convicted of assault and fined $500.

Yolanda was outraged at the piddling amount Ballard willed her—$50,000 per year for life. Barred from the funeral and the reading of the will, she sued for $192,600, later upped that figure to $381,000, and ultimately was awarded $91,000.

QUICK SHOTS

66 "This book is rapidly filling up," Jordan notes. "I hope you don't have too many more lengthy stories."

"I've got lots of short ones," I tell him. "How about a chapter called 'Quick Shots'? I can lead off with a funny tale told by hockey's winningest coach, Scotty Bowman."

BOWMAN GETS A LAUGH

I'm at a sports banquet in St. Catharines, Ontario, on October 8, 2002, and Scotty Bowman gets up to speak. He tells a good story about his coaching days in St. Louis.

> My team was in a close contest with Detroit and trailed 1–0 after Gordie Howe scored the game's only goal. With five minutes to play, a young woman behind the Blues' bench screamed at me, "Bowman, you dummy. Pull the goalie!"
>
> Of course I ignored her, but with four minutes to play she screamed again, "Hey, you dummy coach! Pull the goalie!"

She issued the same order with three minutes, then two minutes to play.

Finally, with a minute left on the clock, I waved my goaltender to the bench and sent out an extra forward.

Just then, Gordie Howe snared the puck and lofted it over everyone's head and it landed in our empty net. Red Wings 2, Blues 0.

The lady behind our bench blasted me one more time: "You dummy coach. You should have pulled the *other* goalie."

They didn't know a whole lot about hockey in St. Louis in those days.

GRAPES IS HOT

Don Cherry was fuming. "I'm going to be all over coach Bob Johnson's ass this season."

"How come?" I asked.

"Because he told everyone watching on TV during the Canada Cup, 'That Swedish team is as tough as any of those Boston clubs when they were coached by Don Cherry.' Imagine him saying that."

Cherry and I were in his bar in Hamilton in the early autumn of 1991, and some of the players from Team Sweden came in. What a surprise! And they were there to drink, not to picket the place.

Right away, Cherry grabbed Kent Nilsson and took him to a wall where a huge photo of Mats Näslund hung. "Kent, look at that photo," Don said. "How can anyone say I'm prejudiced against the Swedes? There's Mats, big as life, and that's after he scored the overtime goal that put the Bruins out of the playoffs one year."

Nilsson was unimpressed. He asked innocently, "Is that the time you put too many men on the ice?"

HERE'S ANOTHER CHERRY-ISM

Dick Irvin and Grapes are talking about the Habs' Chris Nilan.

Cherry says, "Dick, in the paper, how could Red Fisher call Nilan a cementhead?"

Dick corrects him. "Not cement*head*, Don. He said Nilan has cement *hands*."

"Oh, I knew it was cement something," says Cherry.

ONE MORE ABOUT CHERRY

Hockey Night in Canada's Bob Cole went to Cherry when he first coached the Bruins and asked him for the Bruins' starting lineup. Cherry named a couple of starters and said, "Ricky Middleton will be at centre." Don thought later, "Christ, Middleton doesn't even play centre and I told *Hockey Night in Canada* he'll be starting there."

When the game was about to begin, Cherry said, "Ricky, you take centre ice."

"Grapes, I don't play centre ice," Middleton protested.

"You do tonight," Cherry said. "Get the hell out there." Just to satisfy Bob Cole and *Hockey Night in Canada*, Grapes started Middleton at centre.

PAT MEETS MATS

Red Fisher, Montreal's best-known hockey writer, entered the Canadiens' dressing room with another sportswriter, Pat Hickey, in tow. He was there to introduce Hickey to Canadiens star Mats Näslund.

When they shook hands, Hickey said, "You know, Mats, Red taught me everything I know."

Näslund feigned surprise. "Really?" he quipped. "How the hell do you make a living?"

Chris Chelios, a young Hab defenceman, asked Fisher a question one day. "Tell me, Red, who is that kid on the Kings . . . the good young kid. His name starts with a *B*."

"Well," Red began, "the Kings have two or three good kids. You mean Robitaille?"

And Chris said, "Yeah, that's the guy."

LET'S GO, BOYS

Coach Jacques Demers was giving his Montreal Canadiens a pep talk before a playoff game one night.

"This is the kind of game that separates the men from the boys," he told them. "Now let's go, boys!"

THE OPEN NET

The late Bill Durnan once told me the following goaltending story.

"Many years ago, there was a goaltender named Alex Woods, who played in the American league. One night, Woods did something that all goaltenders probably wanted to do. He was losing a game 8–0 when, in the third period, an opposing player got a breakaway. He skated in on Woods, and when he lined up his shot, Woods stepped aside, waved at the empty net, and said, 'Be my guest.' The player threw the puck into the empty net to make it 9–0 while the crowd roared with laughter."

Durnan, speaking for all goalies, said, "That's something we all would loved to have done sometime in our careers, but none of us had the guts to do it."

THE WATER BOTTLE WIN

Let's go back to February 3, 2000. I'm invited to emcee a charity hockey game in Whitby, Ontario, my old hometown.

There I meet the legendary junior hockey coach Ernie McLean and he tells me a fascinating story about a Memorial Cup his team won back in 1977.

"I was coaching the New Westminster Bruins back then," he tells me, "and we had a good team but not a great team. We squeaked into the WHL [Western Hockey League] playoffs, but we had to win the last four games on our schedule to do it. Then, in the first round, we faced the powerful Portland Winter Hawks, who had won the league championship by thirty points.

"Everybody said there was no way we could topple Portland. But sometimes a coach will do anything to get a win, even if it means bending the rules. And I did something in the first game with Portland that I should regret, but I don't.

"The game was tight and the score was tied 1–1 late in the game when Portland's Blake Wesley got two minutes for high-sticking. That's when I saw an opportunity and seized it. As referee Robbie Shick skated over to the box to announce the penalty, I reached into the Portland bench, which was next to our bench, and grabbed the nearest water bottle. I hurled it at Shick. The water bottle bounced across the ice and Shick was furious. He picked it up, spotted the Portland logo on the bottle and assumed a Portland player had thrown it. He tacked on another bench minor to go with Wesley's penalty. We scored a power-play goal and hung on for dear life to win the hockey game 2–1. That win gave us a huge boost, and we stayed hot to win the series four games to one.

"Then we went on to win the Memorial Cup. I always thought my water bottle trick was the turning point in the playoffs that year."

WAS IT THE WORST TEAM EVER?

"We may not have been the worst team in hockey history, but we were certainly the worst road team," recalls Ron Low, goaltender on the 1974–75 Washington Capitals. "We were an expansion team— small and slow—and got pushed around by all the other teams. We didn't win our first road game until late in March, when the season was almost over."

After thirty-seven road defeats, the Caps stunned the hockey world by defeating California on March 28, and the victory touched off a dressing-room celebration comparable to a Stanley Cup victory party.

Low says forward Garnet "Ace" Bailey, who'd been on a Cup winner with the Boston Bruins in 1972 (and who died on September 11, 2001, when the airliner he was on crashed into one of the World Trade Center towers in New York), grabbed a dressing-room garbage can and held it overhead. It was an imaginary Stanley Cup. Another forward, Tommy Williams, insisted the players sign the garbage can before leading them in a noisy parade around the dressing room. The players may have kissed the rim of the can, but not one of them suggested they drink beer or champagne from its grimy bowels.

"We won only eight games that season and lost sixty-seven," Low recalls. "I was lucky to be in goal for all the wins and a couple of ties. My backup, Michel Belhumeur, lost twenty-four times. But he did manage three ties. John Adams, our third netminder, went 0–7 and didn't earn a point. We allowed ten or more goals on seven occasions."

The sweet win in Oakland was to be the Caps' only road victory. They finished the season 1–39 away from home. The team chewed up three coaches along the way—Jimmy Anderson, Red Sullivan and GM Milt Schmidt.

"It was a terribly frustrating season," says Low. "There wasn't any parity in the NHL, and the WHA was grabbing some of the best players. But none who were there will ever forget that victory celebration in Oakland."

HOCKEY'S PERFECT GENTLEMAN

Each year, the NHL recognizes its most gentlemanly player with the Lady Byng Memorial Trophy. The New York Rangers' Frank Boucher won it seven times in eight years. Wayne Gretzky captured it five times and Red Kelly four. But if the league ever decided to single out the all-time cleanest player in the game, I would nominate an unheralded former Red Wing, forward Val Fonteyne. In my book, he'll forever reign as Mr. Clean.

During one stretch in his thirteen-year NHL career, which began in 1959–60, Fonteyne played in 185 consecutive games without serving any time in the penalty box. Later he compiled a second streak of 157 penalty-free games.

Fonteyne was a swift, lightweight winger, about five feet, nine inches and 155 pounds, who excelled as a penalty killer in his Detroit days. He also played with the Rangers and the Penguins. In the course of his 820 NHL games he spent a grand total of 26 minutes in the box. Compare that to tough guy Randy Holt, who once took 67 penalty minutes in one period! Or Chris Nilan, who once took ten penalties in one game. Or Tiger Williams, who holds the record for most penalty minutes in a career—3,966 of them.

Fonteyne is the only player to complete three consecutive

seasons without taking a single minor penalty, and the only one to record five penalty-free seasons during his career.

How come he never won the Lady Byng, you ask? Because there's a proviso. The trophy goes to a player who is not only a gentleman, but who combines good conduct with a high standard of play. Top scorers always overshadow top penalty killers.

With today's tighter refereeing, the game may never see another perfect gentleman like Val Fonteyne.

OLD KATE BOOSTED THE FLYERS

Late in the 1968–69 NHL season, the Philadelphia Flyers decided to replace the national anthem normally played before Flyer home games with Kate Smith's stirring version of "God Bless America."

Kate Smith had been a popular singer on radio during the 1930s and '40s and had long been retired. The Flyers won the game that night, and management figured it was because Kate had brought them good luck. They played her recording several more times, and each time the Flyers skated off with a win. Some fans protested, arguing that only "The Star-Spangled Banner" should be played at sports events. Before long, the media and fans alike were keeping track of Kate Smith's winning record, and it was impressive. Her mark soon stood at 37–3–1.

Before the start of the 1973–74 season, the Flyers convinced Kate to appear live—to sing "God Bless America" before the home opener. When she stepped out on the red carpet and belted out her song, the roof almost came off the building. Fans adored the old girl, who hadn't appeared in public in years. Goalie Bernie Parent shut out the Leafs that night, 1–0, and Kate, too, came out a winner.

She appeared live again that season, prior to the sixth game of the Stanley Cup final. In 1974, the Flyers, hoping to become the first expansion team to win the Stanley Cup, met the Boston Bruins in the finals. The Bruins were a team with two superstars, Bobby Orr and Phil Esposito. For years they had humiliated the Flyers, winning all but four of their games against Philly in the seven years leading up to 1973–74. But the tenacious Flyers, led by Bobby Clarke, found a way to win three times in the '74 final. What a morale boost Kate Smith gave the Flyers before game six, when she stepped out to centre ice to belt out "God Bless America"! Thunderous applause and cheering drowned out her final words. I scrambled up into the stands to interview her for our NBC telecast. Then the Flyers went to work and shut out the Bruins 1–0 behind Bernie Parent's goaltending. The Flyers had never blanked Boston before. No team had shut them out all season. Some Philadelphians called it a "playoff miracle"; others said, "No, it was all Kate Smith's doing."

And years later, in 2001, following the dreadful calamity in New York City on September 11, when all of North America needed an emotional boost, it was "God Bless America" that was heard and sung most often. This time, from beyond her grave, Kate stirred a whole nation with her voice, not just a hockey team.

WAS THIS THE FIRST FACE MASK?

On January 22, 1899, the *Kingston Times* reported that Edgar Hiscock, the sturdy goalkeeper of the Frontenac hockey team whose nose was broken in a recent match, would be forced to wear a baseball mask in the coming games. "This is a new idea," the *Times* observed. "One which, perhaps, will create some amusement among the spectators at first, but yet there is not the least doubt of it being carried into effect, as something should be worn by goalkeepers to protect the head from the swift shots of some hockey players."

Twenty-eight years later, in 1927, Elizabeth Graham, a lady

goaltender on the Queen's University team in Kingston, wore a fencing mask to protect her pretty features.

Three years after that, in 1930, Clint Benedict of the Montreal Maroons wore the first goal mask in NHL history, to protect a broken nose.

In 1959, Montreal Canadiens goalie Jacques Plante introduced a fibreglass mask that he wore throughout the rest of his career.

Goalies in every league around the world now wear facemasks.

GORDIE HOWE TALKS ABOUT THE ROCKET

Gordie Howe was asked for his opinion of Maurice "Rocket" Richard.

> Rocket Richard was one of the greatest players I ever saw.
> I remember when I thought he was a miserable bugger
> who wore number 9. Then I realized how good he was, so
> I studied the old black-and-white movies of him playing
> for Montreal. I tried to emulate all the good things he
> did, but I couldn't do it. He was the yardstick for the rest
> us—competitive, honest, hardworking, dedicated, all of those
> important things. If there were anything I'd like to do over
> in my career, it would be to be as dedicated to the game as
> the Rocket. They tell me he'd be getting ready for training
> camp and he'd say, "Don't talk to me. I'm getting ready for the
> hockey season." Hell, I couldn't do that. But that's what the
> Rocket was made of, that's what made him so great.
>
> People often say that I wore number 9 because the Rocket
> did. Not true. I got number 9 because the lower berths on the
> train went to players with the low numbers.
>
> But if I had chosen number 9, I couldn't have chosen

a better number, a better man to follow. He soared above all the people in the game of hockey. He was the Gretzky of the '40s and '50s. He set records for the rest of us to try and match. And they were hard to achieve. He was the man who made the game of hockey so popular. Imagine! He'd go grocery shopping in Montreal and get a standing ovation from the customers and the staff.

The respect I have for Rocket Richard grew tremendously over the years. He made hockey what it is today. He made life for me and the Gretzkys and all the young kids coming along very, very good.

MY OLDTIMER FRIENDS

It's always a sad occasion when we lose an old friend. In recent years, I've attended a lot of funerals and wakes for some of our Oldtimers: Bob Goldham, Harry Watson, Sid Smith, Jackie Hamilton, Cal Gardner, Carl Brewer, Ike Hildebrand—to name just a few. Their passing makes us much more conscious of the days remaining for the rest of us. We still enjoy our monthly luncheons and our annual Christmas parties, but some of the familiar faces continue to go missing.

In 2006, I spoke a few words to the players and their spouses at our Christmas get-together. And I relied on the Internet for my inspiration. I found some lovely words by a couple of anonymous writers, which I mixed with my own thoughts of love and friendship and how blessed we all should feel.

When I look around the room today, I can't help but think how fortunate we are to be here, many of us getting on in years, but most of us in reasonably good health, enjoying the company of long-standing friends and acquaintances.

I look at you and I see good, solid Canadians. I see proud Canadians who have come a long way together.

I see people who really respect and admire each other. I see tolerant people. We tolerate those who've mocked us and fooled us—like the Ballards and the Eaglesons—in our world of hockey. We tolerate politicians who distribute millions of our tax dollars to their pals. We tolerate leaders who tell us they'll protect us and defend us with submarines that never submerge and helicopters that are too old to fly. We tolerate those who try to turn us against our friendly neighbours to the south. And we tolerate those who come to our great country to begin a new life but refuse to speak our language or adopt our customs.

The friends we mingle with today should be applauded for their tolerance and their survival skills. We should congratulate ourselves for surviving several decades of the last century and a wee bit of this one. Decades which included a major depression, a world war, a cold war and threats of a nuclear war, as well as 9/11 and a number of other threats and perils to our health and well-being.

It's a wonder we survived so splendidly, because we were born to mothers who smoked and drank while they carried us. They didn't have Dr. Spock or Oprah or Dr. Phil to give them advice and guidance.

When we were babies, we breathed second-hand smoke and the cribs we slept in, with our noses pressed against the bars, that were covered with brightly coloured lead-based paint.

We had no childproof lids on medicine bottles or bottles of bleach and other poisons. Some of these chemicals were carelessly kept under our noses—under the kitchen sink.

When we rode our bikes, we had no helmets and we were allowed to ride anywhere we wanted.

Today, we shudder to think of the risks we took hitch-hiking. Back then, we didn't know the meaning of the word pedophile.

Back then, our parents drove us around in cars—in my case, my father never owned a car—with no seat belts, no air bags, no special seats for babies and often with bald tires. Some dads would let their kids sit on their laps and let them steer the damn car.

My first car was a '31 Chevy with no brakes. I had no licence or insurance and I drove that car all around Pembroke one summer. How stupid was that?

We drank water from a garden hose or a well or a tap and not from a sanitized bottle. We ate snow off the blades of our hockey sticks and sucked on chunks of ice from the ice wagons that roamed our streets.

We shared one soft drink with four friends from one bottle—I remember when a bottle of Kik Cola cost only a few pennies—and no one ever died from this.

We ate cupcakes and doughnuts, white Wonder bread—lots of it, because it was cheap. And we smothered it with real butter. We drank gallons of pop weighted down with sugar, but we never got fat because we were always outside playing. We played until the street-lights came on. Then it was time to head home. We didn't shower. We had no showers. We took a bath once a week.

Sometimes we wrapped dry leaves in cigarette paper so that we could smoke behind the shed or barn. Some of the older guys were more ingenious. They'd pluck tobacco from cigarette butts they found on the sidewalk and then "roll their own."

In winter—colder then and longer then—we played road hockey and shinny on the pond, wearing hand-me-down skates and using toothpick sticks clutched by the same mitts we wore to school. And yes, we wore magazines or the Eaton's catalogue for shin pads.

In summer we played baseball and softball in some deserted field or playground, avoiding rocks and broken glass and cow flops, using balls that sometimes became lopsided and split apart at the seams. Occasionally one of us would smash a ball so hard it would clear the fence and break a neighbour's window and we'd all run like hell.

We'd tear and muddy our clothes playing football. A lucky few had helmets. We played red rover and run-sheep-run and kick the can and prisoner's base. As teenagers we'd sometimes dare to play spin the bottle, which started hormones spinning off in all directions—whatever hormones were.

We'd play all day in the hot sun or lie on the beach and get sunburned, but we never worried about sunstroke or skin cancer.

On Halloween some of the most devilish kids would move an outhouse off its moorings and set it back about six feet from the hole. An old fellow going for a midnight poop without a flashlight might suddenly find himself up to his knees in crap. Surely the miscreants who thought such devilment was hilarious at the time look back today with a small measure of shame and guilt. Then again, perhaps they don't.

We traded comic books and Big Little books and we watched double bills at the Rialto Theatre on Saturday afternoons. There was Tom Mix and Hopalong Cassidy and the thrilling serials that kept us on the edges of our seats. We didn't believe our pal Ed when he told us a girl sitting next to him in the theatre reached out and fondled him one day. Ed was always bragging.

For hockey thrills, we listened to Foster Hewitt on the radio every Saturday night. We pictured him speaking from his famous gondola on *Hockey Night in Canada*. He would greet hockey fans in Canada and the United States—and Newfoundland. Newfoundland then was an island somewhere off to the east, still seeking an identity. In time, it became Canada's newest province.

Perhaps some of you recall the names of the members of the old Hot Stove League that filled the intermissions on *Hockey Night in Canada*: Baldy Cotton, Elmer Ferguson, Syl Apps, Wes McKnight, to mention a few. You may have forgotten host Court Benson. Surely you remember the birth of television in 1952. Families that couldn't afford a TV set would gather in front of the stores that sold them and witness wondrous events through the window on the small black-and-white screen. On hockey night, there was Murray Westgate in his service station uniform and cap, shilling for Imperial Oil. He was so believable that some viewers actually thought he owned a service station. And Syl Apps, my boyhood hero, was a regular. The former Leaf captain signed an autograph for me once.

On most weekends we would leave home early and play all day, so long as were back when the streetlights came on.

No parent was able to reach us all day, nor did they bother to try. We always showed up sooner or later.

We would go tobogganing down steep and treacherous hills, narrowly missing trees and hidden stumps and boulders. Our parents didn't know this. In summer we'd make homemade go-karts out of orange crates and, without knowing how to add brakes, we'd wind up in ditches and bushes at the end of a long run.

In spring we'd go skinny-dipping, almost before the ice was gone from the river or pond. We'd swim and dive into unknown waters and make flimsy rafts in spring to float across a flooded gully or ditch.

There came a time when Little League baseball and minor hockey teams had tryouts and not everybody made the team. No parents came to see us play, but we'd often recruit a reluctant father to be the coach or umpire. No parent ever pulled a player from a team just because he wasn't named captain or didn't get enough ice time or because a coach shouted at him, "Shut up and sit down!"

No parent was asked to pay hundreds or thousands of dollars to have a son join a team. No teams travelled hundreds of miles across two nations, by car, bus, train or plane or to play in tournaments. If you reached the Junior A level, you might get a team jacket. You might even get a few dollars per game.

Growing up, we didn't know much about sex or why dogs sometimes got stuck together, and the mystery of pregnancy eluded us. You'd never dream of asking your parents about such things, and if you did they'd stammer a mumbled response. One thing we knew: it wasn't the stork that brought us. An older boy might fill our heads with misinformation and advice. He'd say, "Listen, kid, if it happens to a girl you've been with, just take her down a rough road on a bicycle. That'll stop it right there." We'd believe him, of course. Or, more likely, wonder what the hell he was talking about.

We knew absolutely nothing about same-sex relationships and

the urges afflicting certain men, or we might not have been so trusting with our coaches and our Boy Scout leaders.

One of my Scout leaders was Mr. Perfect. But he wasn't so perfect. Mr. Perfect asked me to stay after a Scout meeting one night. When we were alone, he said he wanted to show me how the veins and arteries in my body functioned. I got a queasy feeling and told him I had to get home. I had homework to do. I left in a rush and very much confused. A few days later, a father of one of the Scouts, brandishing a shotgun, chased Mr. Perfect out of town. We never saw Mr. Perfect again.

As children, we had no TV, no computer, no PlayStations, no Internet, no surround sound, no movies on tape, no cell phones. In fact, several families shared a telephone. They were called party lines. Do you remember party lines?

But we always had old hand-me-down skates and toothpick sticks. Our footballs even had bladders inside them that you blew up by mouth, and there were always those softballs that split apart at the seams, and bats that were cracked and were heavily taped.

And we always had friends—really good friends, lots of them. And we had games to play—really fun games—and most of us supplemented our twenty-five or fifty-cent allowances with part-time jobs. We had newspapers to deliver and grass to cut and snow to shovel. We were seldom completely broke and never bored.

We had no rock concerts with pot and blaring music with vocals no sane person could understand. None of us dyed our hair a gawdawful colour or pierced our bodies or put rings in our ears or eyebrows.

We tuned in our radios to *Let's Pretend*, the *Lux Radio Theatre*, and *Your Hit Parade* with Frank Sinatra, and we were proud that Guy Lombardo and the Royal Canadians were from London, Ontario. On New Year's Eve, we'd listen to the celebrations from Times Square in New York that seemed to be a million miles away. Our parents would let us stay up for the dramatic countdown to another year while Guy and the Royal Canadians played "Auld Lang Syne"—"the sweetest music this side of Heaven"—from the Taft Ballroom. I stayed there once as an adult. It was a dump. We never imagined in our lifetime we'd visit New York, and a trip to Florida was as unlikely as a trip to the moon.

As we grew up, we fell out of trees, broke some of our bones and maybe fell through thin ice or lost a few teeth in a hockey game. Nobody suggested we wear helmets or visors or mouth guards back then. Somebody should have. What were our parents thinking? We suffered minor concussions and split lips and bent noses and got right back in the game. Nobody ever flew into a rage and filed lawsuits from these accidents.

The idea of a parent suing or bailing us out if we broke the law was never considered. Parents sided with the law.

We ate wormy apples and green apples and corn stolen from a farmer's field. We learned how to poop in the woods and how to wipe our asses with broad leaves. We learned how to throw up without hitting our shoes.

We walked everywhere, and when we came to a friend's house, the door was always open, not triple-locked. We just walked in. A true friend would make us a peanut-butter-and-jam sandwich. We'd pour milk from a bottle with an inch of cream on the top. The milk would be delivered early each morning by a milkman who'd find payment tucked into an empty bottle. When we weren't walking, we were cycling. If a kid wanted a bike, he'd save money or earn money for half the cost; his folks would pay the other half. It seemed like a fair deal.

We were given BB guns and peashooters, made up games with sticks and balls, threw rocks at each other, and although we were warned it would happen, we didn't put out very many eyes.

Occasionally, we would lose a friend or an acquaintance. The boy down the street, showing off, dove from the top of a waterfall and split his head open on the rocks below. The goalie on our hockey team fell from a canoe and drowned when the rubber boots he was wearing filled with water. The boy who sat in front of me in high school was found dead in his room, a gun in his hand. He had a crush on a girl in the same class, and when she refused his invitation to take her to the movies, he shot himself.

To boys, the best gifts were always hockey gifts—a new stick, a puck, or a pair of skates. Even a new pair of laces was treasured. To be taken to see a game at Maple Leaf Gardens was sheer delight, an incredible experience.

Our heroes were the strong young men who made it to the pros: Apps, Drillon and Broda, and later Lindsay, Richard, Howe and Schmidt.

All of us prized our collections of Bee Hive hockey photos. There were enough cans of corn syrup in our homes to last a generation. When we left home for good, our mothers tossed all our hockey cards in the garbage; never suspecting that someday, many would become valuable beyond belief.

And while the hockey pros were idolized, we somehow learned that they too had to be survivors. They survived years of exploitation by heartless, greedy, penny-pinching owners and demanding coaches and managers. As teenagers, they signed C-forms for $100—which handcuffed them to a team for the rest of their lives.

In their world, it was survival of the fittest. Rookies were often shaved bald, above and below the waist. Speak your mind, get married in mid-season, break curfews, ask for a raise, criticize the system and you'd find yourself on a one-way trip to the minors.

Thank God for Ted Lindsay and later, Carl Brewer and others. They fought the establishment.

No thanks to Alan Eagleson. Too often he sided with the establishment. He took advantage. He broke the rules and betrayed the players' trust. He stole. He went to jail.

Looking back, it seems that our generation has produced some of the best risk-takers, entrepreneurs, problem solvers, money managers, mentors, athletes and parents. As parents ourselves—

don't ask me how—we became men and women with character and common sense. We have aged well, have we not?

Today's parents and grandparents are not old and feeble and worn down by life, sitting in rocking chairs, fumbling in a glass for their dentures, drooling and nodding off at the kitchen table. We are not at all like our parents and grandparents, who seemed ancient in their fifties and sixties.

I'm a fair example. At seventy-eight, I still play hockey three times a week—even in Florida. I still write books, make speeches, paint pictures and run a business involving Peter Puck. I'm a diabetic and have arthritis. My hearing and vision are failing, but so what? My wife looks twenty years younger than she is. She works out every morning, is as fit as her grandchildren, rollerblades with them, helps run the business, edits books and does a multitude of other tasks. She is still a beauty.

Today we call such people multitaskers because today's generation insists on a fancy name for everything.

After fifty-three years of marriage—and fifty-seven years of "togetherness"—we are still "thinking young." We are energetic, worldly and (hopefully) wise. We can still keep up. We have fortitude, faith and fun.

I'm also describing you, my friends—all of you, I trust—all of you aging survivors. So give yourselves a round of applause. You've earned it.

Thank you for reading this book.